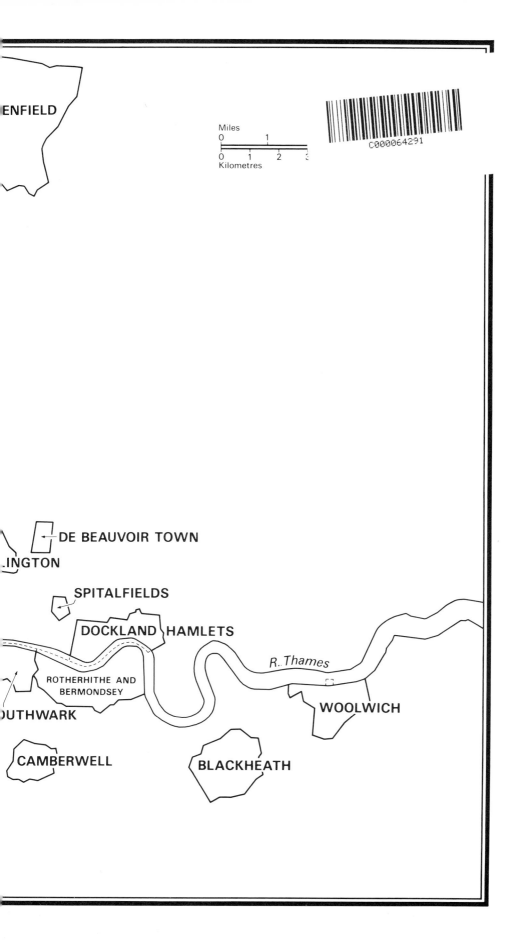

ENFIELD

Miles
0   1

0   1   2   3
Kilometres

C000064291

DE BEAUVOIR TOWN

ISLINGTON

SPITALFIELDS

DOCKLAND HAMLETS

R. Thames

ROTHERHITHE AND
BERMONDSEY

SOUTHWARK

WOOLWICH

CAMBERWELL

BLACKHEATH

The Illustrated London News
Book of London's Villages

By the same author:

BATTLE OF THE ENVIRONMENT

GOODBYE, BRITAIN?

LONDON (IN THE WORLD'S CITIES SERIES)

LANDSCAPE BY DESIGN

CHANGING BRISTOL: ARCHITECTURE
CONSERVATION AND PLANNING, 1960–80

(frontispiece overleaf: see pages 135–6)

The Illustrated London News

Book of London's Villages

by
Tony Aldous

Secker & Warburg
London

This book first published in England 1980 by
Martin Secker & Warburg Limited
54 Poland Street, London W1V 3DF

Copyright © 1980 by The Illustrated London News
and Martin Secker & Warburg Limited

SBN: 436 01150 6

Printed in Great Britain by
Westerham Press Limited, Westerham, Kent

Acknowledgments

All the photographs in this book are the property of *The Illustrated London News*.

The maps in the text were re-drawn by The Kirkham Studios from originals kindly supplied by John Bartholomew & Son Limited, Edinburgh.

To the Villagers of London

Contents

Introduction

"London, thou art the flower of cities all"; "When a man is tired of London he is tired of life"; "mery London, my most kindly nurse" – Dunbar, Johnson, Spenser and many more have written of this place called London. And yet it seems to have fallen to a stranger from overseas, the Dane, Steen Eiler Rasmussen, writing in 1934, to throw into relief a factor that for centuries has made Britain's capital different from the great cities of continental Europe. In his *London: the Unique City* he described it as a "scattered city", and went on to show that historically the tightness of its fortifications, and perhaps the accident of government being centred a couple of miles upstream at Westminster, led to this scattered effect. Settlements spread out from and way beyond the walls; and, unlike such cities as Paris or Cologne, London never seriously contemplated bringing them within any new, more extensive and all-embracing line of fortifications. So London became in effect a city of villages. Rasmussen does not, as far as I can find, call it that; but the qualities of wide-spreading development with two- and three-storey houses with gardens, and decentralized shopping and social focuses, are very much those he praised in *London: the Unique City*, considering it (unlike most commentators) a mercy that Wren's tidily geometric plan for rebuilding after the Great Fire never came to fruition. With the advantage of forty-five years' hindsight, some of Rasmussen's enthusiasms inevitably today appear naïve; and yet his was a remarkably prescient view of the nature of cities. He liked the London of the 1930s because it was haphazard, companionable and organic in growth, responding more or less successfully to economic and social need rather than a cut-and-dried formal plan; and in his final chapter, "A Most Unhappy Ending", he expressed his dismay – in 1934, mark you – that the authorities in London were following the Continental mistake of pushing their poorer citizens into blocks of flats.

London has now learned belatedly that he was right, and in recent years its citizens have left the men at Town Hall and County Hall in no doubt that the bits of London they particularly like are those with distinct personalities of their own: the "villages" of my title. The word is, however, a slippery one; and its use in the way this book uses it needs explaining. By "village" I mean a neighbourhood or district with an identity and character of its own, and some sort of a focus for the community, with shops, pubs and probably churches, but not necessarily civic buildings. Above all, a true London village can be tested by the attitude of its inhabitants – do they look towards the place with affection and concern? Do they feel they belong there? That test I think works with all the twenty-four villages in this book, originally explored and portrayed for a series of articles I wrote for *The Illustrated London News* in 1977 and 1978.

Since the first of those articles appeared, a number of other books and magazines have used the expression "London villages", or "villages of London", as the title for writings which look at different areas of London, often from a very different standpoint from that of the *ILN* series – sometimes, as it seemed to me, with a lively but rather more superficial look at currently fashionable neighbourhoods; sometimes as guides to places of entertainment and gastronomic delight; sometimes looking primarily at the history of places and what the tourist or enthusiast would find charming or quaint. By contrast, in my London Villages series I tried always to look at the present reality, the living community, and not just dusty ghosts from history books; tried to highlight local environmental and social issues; tried to get "under the skin" of each village and find out what makes its "villagers" contented or worried or angry or despondent about their chunk of London; and tried to show my readers less-known and often under-appreciated quarters as well as the better-known villages like Hampstead or Chelsea. But as to the expression "London village", I pretend to no copyright in it; mine is just one of a number of possible approaches to the subject. The name has no great originality. It has happened that when I groped round for a title for the series, "village" was the only word that seemed to fit!

So what kinds of places does it cover? I think I can distinguish five or six distinct categories. First, there are the genuine villages, which began as free-standing rural settlements among the fields, woods and orchards of Middlesex or Surrey, Kent or Essex; and which, though now embedded in suburbia, have retained something of their original form and character. Highgate is recognizably one of these, with its still rural looking high street, former coaching inns and sense of community focus where South Grove and Pond Square run into the High Street; so too, surviving precariously on the edge of a large and ugly council estate, is Charlton, with its church, Bugle Horn pub, Jacobean manor house, and short but harmonious high street all of a piece together. Of both these villages the words of my fellow-journalist, Gerry Isaaman of the *Hampstead and Highgate Express*, spoken of *his* village, hold good: "You could never build that if you designed it from scratch. It would never get planning permission or pass the fire regulations". Yet people are extraordinarily fond of such places, which "just grew'd like Topsy", and mostly they make them work well enough. A disproportionate number of architects and planners, having done their best or worst in building from new elsewhere, for one reason or another make their homes in these "organically grown" bits of London.

A second kind of "London village" consists of residential quarters built outside the then built-up area of the city to provide more spacious living for the better-off than could be found in the crowded lanes and alleys of the Square Mile. These new quarters were built in the 17th, 18th and early 19th centuries, and built mostly in the fields and market gardens to the west of the City. They include Covent Garden, Soho, Marylebone and Belgravia to the west; Spitalfields and the now vanished merchants' houses of Swedenborg Square to the east. But these new quarters, at least to the west, catered for a wider social range than just merchants. As Chapter 21 shows, Soho's early residents included many parliamentarians, since it was convenient for Westminster – a fact which underlines the duocentric nature of the growing metropolis: the City proper as the commercial centre; Westminster, the administrative and legal centre. Between them, in the days when the Strand really was just that (the river bank), and the Fleet meant a somewhat murky tributary of the Thames or a murkier gaol rather than newspapers, there the town houses of the nobility spread themselves; the lawyers settled in the deserted groves of the dispossessed Templars; and members of an emergent civil service, like

Navy Secretary Sam Pepys, often made their homes there. Though originally suburbs in the word's true sense – outlying districts of the city – these have all now come to be regarded as part of the West End, which most people now instinctively regard more as "the centre" of London than the original Square Mile.

My third type of village really amounts to an extension and acceleration of the second type of development from Georgian into Victorian times: districts of terraces and squares, usually built speculatively, with the needs and aspirations of the growing middle classes of the capital in mind. It includes districts like Barnsbury and Pentonville to the north, parts of Southwark and Lambeth to the south. Often this orderly townscape of terrace, square and villa rubbed shoulders with an existing village, as Barnsbury does with Islington; sometimes, like De Beauvoir Town, to the east of Kingsland Road, it exploited a family landholding adjacent to one of the main highways out of London.

De Beauvoir Town is, of course, not a town in the sense that those of my fourth category are: places like Woolwich and Enfield, which had and still have an economic as well as a social existence of their own, distinct from the suburbs around them; and people who live in them tend to talk of "going to London" rather than (as in most suburbs) "going to Town". They are *in* London and yet not *of* it; significantly Enfield which, though within the fief of the Greater London Council since 1965, still with a perverse pride carries the postal address "Enfield, Middlesex". And in Chapter 15 you can read how a polytechnic lecturer from Stoke-on-Trent, arriving to live and work in Woolwich, recognized immediately that here was "a northern Industrial town set down, as it were by accident, on the south bank of the Thames".

My fifth type of village is the product of 19th- and 20th-century transport systems. A notable example (which does not feature among the two dozen villages in this book) is Golders Green. When that great entrepreneur of the London tube system, Charles Tyson Yerkes, was planning his Charing Cross to Hampstead and Highgate tube (now part of the Northern Line of the London Underground), he is said to have driven in a private hansom cab with his engineer, H. H. Dalrymple, out to Hampstead, then on up across the heath and through the fields to an open and empty crossroads. "This is where we'll end the line," he said; and indeed for fifteen years after its opening in 1907, Golders Green remained the terminus. The prosperous district which now spreads round

Golders Green station was thus the direct result of a new tube line, and not built on any pre-existing village centre.

More often, of course, railway, tube and tram lines sparked off or accelerated the expansion of existing villages into suburbs, or led to development of new suburbs close to existing villages. One case in point brings us to my sixth type of village, the planned *rus in urbe* type of suburb. The pioneer here, Bedford Park, dates from the 1870s, and its trees and buildings (many of them with the characteristic long-pitched roofs of the great Victorian architect Norman Shaw) have developed a pleasant maturity, attracting back not only (see Chapter 2) such *cognoscenti* as Reading geography professor Peter Hall and the headquarters staff of the Victorian Society, but many others for whom roomy, robust houses, tree-lined roads and a distinct sense of community exercise considerable appeal. Bedford Park, with its church, its Tabard Inn, and shops clustered conveniently round Turnham Green station, came about largely because one man, Jonathan Carr, believed that the new, aesthetically minded middle classes of his day should be able to live in houses and in a community which reflected their developing artistic and social values. Carr, the enlightened (if often precariously under-capitalized) developer, influenced what Bedford Park became just as much as his architects. He believed, for instance, that the Victorian habit of banishing domestic staff to the basement was wrong. Bedford Park kitchens are, as a result, invariably on the ground floor, often in a back extension – though it may be noted that, in the servantless 1960s and 1970s, working middle-class housewives wanting to install dishwashers and freezers and wanting also the added convenience of having the family eating in the kitchen, have often found them not nearly large enough. They have had to extend the extensions.

The best known of the villages in this category is, of course, the considerably later Hampstead Garden Suburb, where, though working through a charitable trust, the individual personality and ideals of Henrietta Barnett influenced the character of the place (just as Carr did at Bedford Park) at least as much as the architects. Hampstead Garden Suburb does not feature in this book; but it is a fascinating place with a fascinating story, and if and when the time comes to produce either another *Illustrated London News* series or a sequel to this book, the Garden Suburb would clearly be a front-runner for inclusion. It, together with Letchworth and Welwyn Garden City, greatly influenced the whole pattern of suburban

development; and, though in many respects their imitators aped the
superficials and missed the essentials of these planned settlements,
the creations of Henrietta Barnett and Ebenezer Howard and their
architects greatly influenced the pattern of London's expansion,
and influenced Londoners' expectations and aspirations. In
particular, it and the expanding public transport network encouraged people to expect scattered, low-density suburbs and gave
rise to the assumption that house-plus-garden is the norm in housing, which Rasmussen so admired in *London: the Unique City*. And,
though the Londoner's conception of "village" has more to do with
social and commercial focus than with height or denseness of buildings, a preference for "human scale" and for buildings which are
mellow and to some extent higgledy-piggledy, rather than all of the
same recent vintage, certainly play a part in village consciousness.

Certainly, changing public attitudes towards redevelopment have
played a great part in both Londoners' consciousness of local
identity and place, and the care and concern that now goes into
conserving and strengthening the distinctive local character of
London's villages. I remember, when on the *Middlesex Advertiser*,
the first newspaper I joined as a young trainee reporter in 1960,
looking with some excitement at the then Uxbridge Borough Council's far-reaching plans for redeveloping that town centre. To be
sure, some old buildings like the market hall, old coaching inns and
the 15th-century parish church were marked out for preservation;
but broadly the approach was to sweep away the old and sub-
standard and replace it with a new, efficient and functional shopping
precinct in concrete and glass. And at that time most people probably approved or acquiesced in such a clean-sweep approach.
Today, such is the public's dislike of standard, "shoe-box" commercial buildings that most developers try quite hard to give their
new developments a distinctive or local character; and at Uxbridge,
the London Borough of Hillingdon's new and very expensive civic
centre was deliberately designed as a complex confection of pitched
tiled roofs and reddish-brown brick walls expressly in order to
counteract what public and councillors now perceived as the
dreariness and inhumanity of the neighbouring shopping precinct.
Whether so large a building really provides an antidote, even with
its "vernacular" architectural dress, is an issue on which both
architectural critics and local people disagree among themselves.

Large-scale redevelopment, therefore, whether of shopping
centres, office blocks or high-rise flats, fuelled Londoners' distrust

of change and awoke their dormant affection for their particular localities. These changing public attitudes came through very clearly during the marathon public inquiry into the Greater London Development Plan. The GLDP was in principle the prototype of the now nationwide system of strategic *structure plans*; but the filter Parliament has since inserted, which enables inquiries to select strategic issues for debate, had not then been devised; and so any member of the public could in practice come and tell the GLDP panel about the qualities and problems of their bit of London, provided they could hang it on some reference in the plan. Moreover, though *local* planning was (and is) in principle the concern of the boroughs, the GLDP contained references both to historic buildings (which are a GLC responsibility) and to areas of special character or metropolitan importance; and this gave conservationists a very strong justification for arguing for greater protection and enhancement of particular localities. What came out of all this was a growing sense of the diversity of London, and people's sense of belonging to a particular bit of the capital. The Glaswegian might justifiably sing that he belonged to Glasgee and Glasgee belonged to him; the GLDP inquiry became used to a rather different chorus. London, witnesses seemed to be saying, certainly belonged to them, in the sense that they had a right to influence its future planning; but they belonged rather to Chiswick or Islington, Camden Town, Camberwell, Blackheath or Greenwich. Their first loyalty was to their individual villages. This, indeed, has reflected itself in a growth of local amenity societies: the number of local civic and similar groups in Greater London registered with the Civic Trust rose from a mere eighteen in 1958 to more than a hundred in 1978 – and that took no account of scores, perhaps hundreds of more narrowly based residents' associations and *ad hoc* action groups, such as those opposed to (or, just occasionally, lobbying for) road schemes affecting their districts.

The reasons why people turned against large-scale change in their urban surroundings during the late 1960s and 1970s have been examined elsewhere (see, for example, the Introduction to my *Goodbye, Britain?**); but clearly in recent years the rise of the conservation movement, the propaganda impact of European Architectural Heritage Year, and the general trend of legislation and government policies, have all contributed towards a greater concern and affection for particular localities. Conservation architect Donald

*Sidgwick & Jackson, 1975.

Insall, himself a Kew "villager" (see Chapter 4), has put it well in urging that conservation's aim should be "to make every place daily more itself". This is a very different approach from that followed in the 1960 Uxbridge plan mentioned above, when only a few obviously important listed historic buildings were to be preserved. Now planners tend to look at overall townscape; and that is obviously in keeping with the public's real wishes and expectations. What makes a village is not two or three architecturally splendid set-pieces, but the whole shape and feel of the place, its odd quirks and eccentricities, and even what were formerly regarded as ugly excrescences such as Victorian drinking fountains and Jubilee clocktowers.

London villages, it should be said, resist the impositions both of municipal bureaucracy and municipal boundaries. Some of the most thorough-going villages with the strongest physical unity and the most robust sense of community are cut by artificial boundaries. Of those to which this book devotes chapters, Highgate, Blackheath, and Bedford Park are cut down the middle by borough boundaries – Highgate, indeed, is split among three or four different boroughs; and, as in other cases, the borough boundary which principally offends against reality (between Haringey and Camden) only perpetuates an older boundary (between Middlesex and the old County of London) and still more ancient parish boundaries. Of course, the reality of a village and people's perceptions of it are much less rigid than municipal or postal boundaries. "Highgate" and "Hampstead" are fashionable labels to which people in N19, NW5 or NW6 may well aspire. I live in SE13 (which means not Blackheath but Lewisham), but our house is in the Blackheath conservation area, and over my typewriter as I compose this introduction I look directly on to the open space, Blackheath.

Fashions also change. As remarked in Chapter 16, the families of both my parents left Islington in the 1930s for the more up-and-coming suburbs of Highgate and Muswell Hill. Now Islington is the up-and-coming place, but Edwardian Muswell Hill, having sagged in public estimation, is certainly now "coming" if not quite "up". Such fashions are not by any means always or entirely rational. Chance and individual determination have a hand in them, with journalists' expressions of local patriotism and party chit-chat playing some part. It is, however, fairly clear that local awareness, concern and pride help to push neighbourhoods up in public estimation, and help to keep them up. Practical concern for the environment is catching. One fence repaired in a street, one porch restored, sets other people caring for their houses in the same way. And local authorities themselves are now often better attuned to local needs and local feeling, so that they refrain from imposing the standard solution and look for something that suits the particular case – whether it is a matter of paving or lamp-standards or trees.

But are they well enough attuned to do the right thing by London's villages? Many people doubt it. Chapter 24 reports that Hampstead people distrust or feel hard done by Camden, and lament the loss more than a decade ago of their own borough council. Greenwich often feels the same way about a local authority which, though it bears their village name, is largely run from (and, they suspect, *for*) Woolwich. The GLC, of course, is remote; but often the boroughs seem hardly less so. London, I believe, needs something like a system of urban parish councils, representing real, cohesive communities – the villages of this book, no less. They should exercise four kinds of power. First, the right to be consulted and to advise on behalf of their communities on the wider actions of borough and GLC as they affect those communities; second, a right of veto over purely local questions, with no real wider ramifications; third, the ability to exercise devolved powers on behalf of the boroughs, thus bringing a finer local tuning to the implementation of policies decided elsewhere; and finally, the power that would rest on having an assured budget, probably a specified poundage on rateable value. In areas where a village is, indeed, split among two or more boroughs, the village or parish council would straddle those boundaries, its activities relating to each of the boroughs concerned. An unacceptable dichotomy? Not a bit of it! The virtue of this arrangement would be the forcing of local authorities to accept in practice that real life does not conform to notions of administrative tidiness.

If at the outset of my *ILN* series I had doubted the strength of village communities, the ensuing twenty-four months could not but have remedied that doubt. People cared – particularly people in local civic and amenity societies – and they showed themselves prepared to walk me round, talk me round and answer endless ill-informed questions. Members and officers in local authorities also gave willingly of their time, as did many others who helped me, often with little or no notice, to resolve doubts and mitigate my ignorance. When it came to updating the articles, everyone I asked responded both willingly and quickly. The rationale of updating was, by the way, to leave the original articles very much as a record of what people felt and said at the time they were written, rather than to attempt to chase the will-o'-the-wisp of absolute up-to-dateness. If, however, it became plain that the original text was faulty, or the situation so altered as to render that text misleading, then I changed it.

In particular I would like to thank the following: for Camden Town, Ellen Farquharson; for Bedford Park, Tom Greaves; for Bermondsey, Nigel Haigh; for Kew, Alison Williams; for De Beauvoir Town, Stuart Weir; for Clapham, Hermione Hobhouse and Stephen Beavan; for Spitalfields, John Earl and Bob Chitham; for Mill Hill, Dulcie Rispoli; for Marylebone, Richard Bowden and John Harris; for Fulham, Patricia Talbot; for Bloomsbury, George Wagner and Brian Woodrow; for Southwark, Betty North and Stanley Osborn; for Putney, Peter Gerhold; for Enfield, Carinthia Arbuthnot-Lane; for Woolwich, Cliff Pollard-Britten and Bryan Harris; for Islington, Mary Cosh and James Ogilvie-Webb; for Limehouse, Bob Gilding and John Bacon; for Highgate, Ion Trewin and Patrick Lawlor; for Camberwell, Charles McKean and Jim Tanner; for Chelsea, John Yeoman and John Head; for Soho, Bryan Burrough; for Blackheath, Neil Rhind; for Covent Garden, Leslie Ginsburg, Jim Monahan and Geoff Holland; and for Hampstead, Nan Farquharson and Gerry Isaaman. To anyone omitted I apologize; to all those I met and who helped me, best thanks. The exercise was a long but very enjoyable one. To you must go much of the credit; for me alone should be reserved any brickbats.

Tony Aldous
Blackheath, October 1978

1

Camden Town

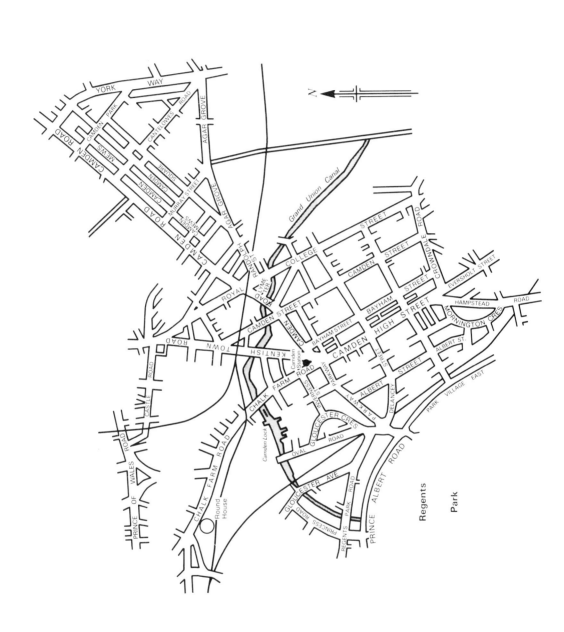

1

Camden Town

When I was a child in Highgate, Camden Town was that seedy, scruffy, traffic-battered place between us and the West End, with what seemed the draughtiest tube station on the Northern Line. These days the tube is still draughty and the traffic a good deal worse. But much of Camden Town is now anything but scruffy. Middle-class professionals have moved in to colonize the likelier streets and crescents, and – with some tongue-in-the-cheek help from Alan Bennett – give the postal district NW1 a social cachet it scarcely aspired to thirty years ago.

Camden Town developed mainly in the 1840s and 1850s, when the invasion of bricks and mortar crossed "the New Road" (Euston/ Marylebone Road) into the fields and farms of the manors of Cantlowes, Rugmere and Tottenhall. Dickens lived for a time in Bayham Street, and to many who now inhabit the area Camden Town's lingering Dickensian aura has great romantic appeal. Jonathan Miller, for one, revels in its Dickensian links and atmosphere.

The Millers live in a tall, thin Victorian terrace house in Gloucester Crescent, just behind Parkway. They have been there fifteen years, and Miller claims that he is not an outsider who moved in and colonized a hitherto working-class area. "I've lived within a mile of here all my life," he says, adding that Camden Town's nearness – within easy cycling distance – to the West End and the hospitals where he and his wife trained made it an obvious place to live.

Even eighteen years ago those tall, faded but grand Gloucester Crescent houses were not cheap. The Millers paid £8,500 for theirs in 1961. It seems cheap only by comparison with the £50,000 that such houses, much "improved", have recently been fetching. For today's Gloucester Crescent is very different from that of the early 1960s. Then many of the houses at the Parkway end of the crescent

3

Inverness Street, one of London's liveliest street-markets.
Bargains are to be had in fruit, poultry, veg, and good old-
fashioned junk.

were lorry-drivers' pull-ups. Houses in single-family occupation
were the exception. Now a single family with perhaps a student/
baby-sitter in the attic is the rule. Cheerful paint and large numbers
of bright (and noisy) middle-class children have replaced the
peeling plaster and quiet, middle-aged bachelors of the old multi-
occupation régime.

Not everyone welcomes the change whole-heartedly. Most
Camden Towners are ambivalent. Derek Jarman, thirty-one-year-
old postman and Labour councillor for the Chalk Farm ward,
which reaches to within a stone's throw of Camden Town tube
station, was born and has parents who were born in the neighbourhood. He dislikes the way in which "gentrification" has tended to
push out working-class residents, but concedes that the bricks and
mortar of much of the area are in a healthier state as a result. As a
postman, he grumbles that professional families take in tons of mail
compared with the "football coupon once a week" of their predecessors, but adds: "It all means jobs for postmen." He is at one

with the gentrifiers in saying that Camden Town is an exceptionally friendly place, an accessible place; and, with Regent's Park, Primrose Hill, the Regent's canal towpaths and Hampstead Heath all within walking distance, it is a good place to bring up children.

One of its attractions is the open market in Inverness Street, just off the High Street. It has been there for about eighty years, with some of the same families and (it is said) the same barrows as in Victorian times. It is still a real market selling vegetables, food, clothing and household junk of the workaday kind. It forms part of a shopping area where you can buy a range of produce from shark steaks to pheasant and grouse, from good Greek bread to Asiatic herbs and spices.

Mr and Mrs John Haral, who came to Camden Town from Cyprus in 1946, have run their Greek food shop in the market since 1953. Their shop is typical of the kind new Camden Towners delight in, giving personal service and selling foods like *pourgouri* (a sort of Greek semolina made from crushed wheat, prepared by the Harals themselves), just one of the specialist, minority lines they stock, based on long experience. But several family businesses like these, sold on retirement or pushed out by rising rents, have been replaced by newcomers (often multiples) who will stock only "safe" lines and threaten to impoverish the variety that makes Camden Town a joy to shop in.

On the eastern borders, overlooking Primrose Hill, lives Ben Whitaker, former MP for Hampstead and now director of the Minority Rights Group. He told me he thought Camden Town an agreeable and convenient place to live, and that it would, happily, never become as smart as Hampstead. He, like others, has derived a good deal of amusement from detecting "writers using each other as material". This rather incestuous quality in parts of Camden Town is well exemplified by a resident of Gloucester Crescent who found herself nodding to familiar faces without being able to pin down where she had encountered them. Only later did it dawn on her she had seen them all in the columns of *The Times'* Marc cartoons: Mark Boxer draws some of his striving-to-be-with-it left-wing intellectuals from the life of the crescent.

Whitaker points to three great success stories in today's Camden Town. The Camden Lock complex of craft workshops and eating-and-drinking places on the canal; the Round House; and Marine Ices, opposite the Round House. Marine Ices, which in the 1950s used to be a small but excellent Italian ice-cream parlour, has grown modestly but not sacrificed the quality of its sorbets, which stand comparison with the new American invaders. But what is more important, say the Camden Towners, it is one of the few places in London where you can take the kids for a cheap Sunday lunch of pizza or spaghetti and have a child treated like an important customer.

The Round House was built as an engine shed. The *ILN* recorded in 1847 the construction of "this vast accommodation for the engines and tenders for the luggage department" of the North-Western Railway. Designed by Robert Stephenson and others, it held twenty-three engines round a central turntable. But railway locomotives got bigger and in 1869 Gilbey's took it over as a liquor store. Since 1968, after a struggle to raise money to convert it, it has been a theatre and arts centre.

When I talked to him in December 1976, George Hoskins, then its administrator, quoted Peter Brook as saying: "Give me £50,000 for improvements, and you can have in the Round House a better National Theatre than the one they are building so expensively on the South Bank." Be that as it may, the Round House provides a magnificent, flexible covered space for experimental theatre. This was notably demonstrated by Théâtre du Soleil's production of *1789* in which the audience sat in the middle and the show went on around them.

Despite subsidies from the Arts Council and Camden borough (in recognition of its regular children's activities), the Round House still, said Hoskins, has to struggle to make ends meet. Yet when it turned property developer and built a new block, now let out as offices and recording studios, it was attacked for being commercial. Its refusal to stay pure but poverty-stricken has, however, given it new offices in place of makeshift huts, and the 150–200 seat Theatre Downstairs.

The third success story, Camden Lock, also arouses mixed feelings among local people. This complex of craft workshops, restaurants and cafés, opened four and a half years ago in old warehouses round the canal basin, is now a huge success. It draws both tourists and local people at sunny weekends. Its open-air antique and craft market is as "artificial" and "trendy" as Inverness Street is "real". Almost everyone who goes there finds it great fun, but locals like Jonathan Miller and Derek Jarman worry that the tourists may take over Camden Town and make life less convenient for residents, crowding pavements and buses and encouraging

The Regent's Canal at Camden Lock: a pattern of water, boats, stone, brick, and 19th-century ironwork.

boutiques and antique marts to take over from useful shops on which the residents of Camden Town depend.

Though they would mostly dismiss this fear, Camden Lock craftsmen have their own worries. A doubling of rents has had the effect, feared by craftsman/jeweller Jackie Jones when I talked to her in late 1976, of forcing craftsmen to go into repetitive lines to the detriment of the creative crafts that were the *raison d'être* of the complex. Although the buildings are zoned for light industry, units have increasingly taken on the role of retail shops rather than productive workshops. Another threat – the landlord's plan to redevelop the lock – was turned down after a public inquiry; but that has not stopped his architects from putting in further applications for redevelopment which the tenants regard as destructive of the spirit and the purpose of the place.

Though Camden Towners are often critical of their council in detail, especially at rate-paying times, the London Borough of Camden enjoys a pretty good reputation in the urban village that is at its centre. This is true of its social service and recreational provision, and its environmental planning. Architect Hugh Morris, who lives in Albert Street, south of Parkway, and is chairman of the Camden Town Amenity and Transport Group, says they were

Camden High Street: the one-way system mostly keeps traffic moving but, many people believe, has damaged both trade and Camden Town's sense of community.

Park Village East, dating from the 1820s, with which Nash established the tradition of suburban villas and rounded off his Regent's Park development, Camden Town's more elegant side.

pleasantly surprised to find the borough's local plan for Camden Town broadly in line with their own thinking. "No drastic comprehensive redevelopment, no tower blocks, but a careful tidying up."

Morris welcomes the proposals for small-scale in-fill housing. His only major reservation concerns industrial redevelopment of railway goods yards towards Chalk Farm. The borough's insistence on keeping housing and industry rigidly separate, even when the industry is small-scale and quiet, is unnecessary and out of date, he thinks. He believes that one-way traffic in Camden High Street has made it less usable and attractive as a shopping centre, and welcomes proposals for an against-the-flow lane for buses and taxis. Traffic can be dealt with only by steadily increasing the tourniquet of restraint on commuters, he believes.

A rather different view of Camden Town comes from Mrs Annabel Rowe, who lives in a tall corner house in Camden Square, on Camden Town's borders with Holloway. Deprived of the use of both legs in a car accident ten years ago, she gets about either in a specially converted car or, for short distances, a battery-powered wheelchair. Since she has two children aged six and four, at primary and nursery school respectively, this mobility is very important to her. She told me she likes Camden Town because it is near enough to the West End for her to drive there easily.

The Camden Square locality is one of the borough's "environmental areas" with through traffic kept out by blocked ends of roads and "no entry" signs. This means some of her car journeys take longer, but on the other hand the streets are relatively empty when she goes out in her electric wheelchair. Mrs Rowe has been campaigning for easier access for the disabled. Since her accident she has come to realize that a kerb without a run-up, which is nothing to the pedestrian and merely irritating to the pram-pushing mother, is impossible for a wheelchair user.

Our last view of Camden Town is from the window of the studio at the top of artist and designer David Gentleman's five-storey house in Gloucester Crescent. It looks out over gardens and a council depot towards Arlington House, the red-brick doss-house where tramps and winos, among others, seek nightly shelter. Most people think it ugly. Gentleman thinks it rather fine. He came to Camden Town twenty years ago because it was cheap and central and, like many others, now seems half in love with it. "It isn't pretty in the way little Hampstead streets are pretty but it's a nice mixture – fairly unpretentious, fairly solid and with a good balance of brick and painted surfaces."

He and his wife Sue explained that they like the social mixture and the different nationalities, the liveliness of the street market, the variety of shops and restaurants – though regret that the place round the corner where they once went for egg curry at 3s 6d now charges West End prices. They live on five floors, with ninety per cent of family life going on in the opened-out basement. Like scores of other families they have knocked through the wall between front kitchen and back scullery. That was the origin of Alan Bennett's Knocker family of NW1: they knocked through to make a light, comfortable, big, family living space where once Victorian cooks and kitchen maids laboured in the gloom. "Knocker" may sound like a term of derision. To those who have tried it, knocking through means children's bedtime stories, relaxed Sunday lunches and a practical sort of family togetherness. You might choose a much worse symbol than that for the life-style of the new Camden Towners.

2

Bedford Park

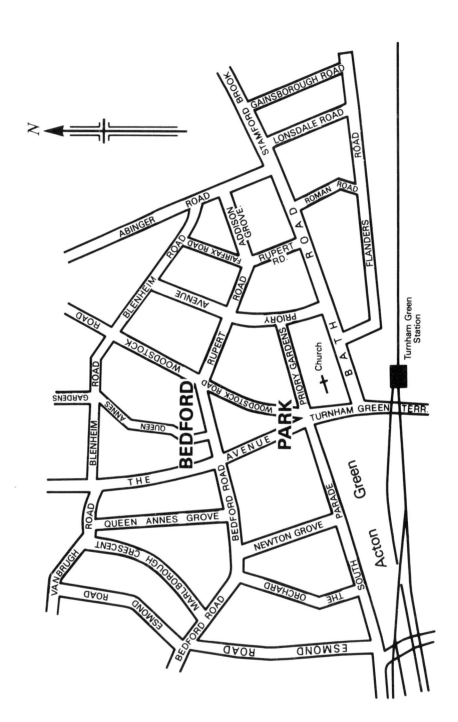

2

Bedford Park

Bedford Park was our first garden suburb, pre-dating Hampstead Garden Suburb by thirty years. It was also until recently London's forgotten garden suburb. Even today people tend to look blank when you mention it and think the place is somehow connected with Woburn Abbey, or Bedford College in Regent's Park, or even Duchess of Bedford Walk in distant Kensington. It is, in fact, just over a mile west of Hammersmith Broadway, straddling the borough boundary between Hounslow and Ealing, and near the station misleadingly called Underground – the platforms are twenty feet above ground level – and anomalously named Turnham Green, for the green of that name is closer to a station even more anomalously labelled Chiswick Park.

Bedford Park, called after the late-18th-century Bedford House (built by brothers named Bedford) was the creation of an artistically minded cloth merchant, Jonathan T. Carr. He set out in 1875 to give the London middle classes with aesthetic leanings houses to their taste at prices they could afford, to buy or to rent, with the added advantage of easy access to town by railway. Tom Greeves, architect, has lived in Bedford Park for twenty-seven years and is one of the founders of the Bedford Park Society. He is a leading authority on the history of the place and tells us in his book, *Bedford Park: the first garden suburb* (Anne Bingley, £4·25), that the development "took the form it did as a result of the Aesthetic Movement of the 1870s when – in reaction against the High Victorian vulgarity of mahogany, wax fruit, gilt frames, crinolines and stucco – 'art' furniture, things Japanese, dadoes, peacock feathers, flowing dresses and red brick 'Queen Anne' revival style came into their own."

Or as a satirical ballad-writer in the *St James's Gazette* put it:

> " 'Tis there a village I'll erect
> With Norman Shaw's assistance
> Where men may lead a chaste, correct
> Aesthetical existence."

The ballad misleads, however, in implying that Norman Shaw, designer of the old New Scotland Yard building on Victoria Embankment, was Carr's first choice of architect. Initially Carr commissioned E. W. Godwin, but his early houses, such as No. 1 The Avenue, were much criticized, and he found Carr's cost limits impossibly tight. So, in 1877 Carr engaged Shaw, who set the character of the place with light, airy, generally three-storey houses of red brick in a Queen Anne Revival-moving-towards-Arts and Crafts style, of which the distinctive features include Dutch gables, some handsome shell porches, sun balconies in white-painted joinery above large bay windows, generous gardens and, as deliberate social policy, no basements. Servants, Carr held, should not be forced to slave away in dark, airless kitchens below ground.

He had chosen a good spot. Apart from public transport facilities (thirty minutes to the City when the District Line extended its service to Richmond in 1877), there was the fact that much of his

Both the distinctive fences and bay windows topped by white-painted balconies are characteristic of Bedford Park's houses for the aesthetically minded Victorian middle-classes.

original twenty-four acres had been laid out as an arboretum by the eminent, but later bankrupt, botanist, Dr John Lindley, FRS. Preservation of fine groups of mature field trees also seems to have dictated the informal, curving layout of all but the three principal roads and, though the original trees have gone, this leafy informality remains one of Bedford Park's great attractions.

Though Carr always lacked capital, financing one operation by a mortgage on the last, and Bedford Park never made him or the company which succeeded him huge profits, it was a success socially. It attracted many artists, some of whom became famous and then moved elsewhere. Early residents included W. B. Yeats and his artist brother Jack, Pinero, Lucien Pissarro, William Morris and "the Noble Anarchist" Sergius Stepniak who, having eluded the Tsar's police, died under a train on a local level crossing. G. K. Chesterton came to visit and court his future wife, Frances Blogg, who lived at No. 8 Bath Road. But on the whole the many artists of one kind or another among the early Bedford Parkers were mostly struggling or only middling successful. They were enthusiastic aesthetes, often revelling in art and eccentricity for their own sakes, and with more assurance and enthusiasm than cash. Yet they were active and enjoyed themselves, with concerts, plays, fancy-dress dances lit by chinese lanterns, and a great spawning of

The Tabard Inn by R. Norman Shaw (1880) was, with the Church, the Club, and the School of Art, one of a group of public and community buildings designed to establish Bedford Park as a distinctive community rather than just a dormitory suburb. The inn contains tiles by de Morgan and Walter Crane; the Stores, originally in the same building, provided "everything from groceries to livery stables" (T. A. Greeves).

societies. Their pub, The Tabard, had (and still has) decorative tiles by de Morgan and Crane; and their environment and their taste were better by far than those of most of their contemporaries.

The 1880s and 1890s were the peak; then Bedford Park went slowly downhill, with an additional lurch when the Edwardian age was shattered by war. Two maids to a house, with starched aprons and caps, ceased to the normal régime. The artists and their houses grew progressively scruffier; more and more houses were split up or rooms let off. After the Second World War, mend-and-make-do and local councils' preference for pulling down and rebuilding in 1950s' municipal style threatened the Park's homogeneity.

Then in 1963, in the face of an act of outstanding aesthetic beastliness by Acton Council – a five-storey old people's home in yellow brick in Bedford Road – the worm turned. A Bedford Park Society arose; its founders worked hard to get local and Whitehall planning authorities to appreciate and protect Shaw's legacy. In 1967 something of the old spirit rekindled with the first of a series of Bedford Park festivals – music, dancing, art exhibitions and a fair on the little patch of Acton Green that abuts the shops and Turnham Green station.

It was soon after this demonstration of concern by a reawakening community, with an exhibition featuring both Bedford Park's quality and its plight, that the society got its message through to Whitehall. A sympathetic official saw the exhibition, realized the urgency, and at last managed to break down the refusal to see reason from which the Minister's advisory committee had suffered. As a result 356 individual houses were listed – virtually the whole of Carr's and Norman Shaw's surviving architectural legacy. And since then the environmentally and artistically minded middle classes have progressively been rediscovering Bedford Park. The drift from single family houses to multi-occupation has been reversed; and money has been lavished not only on repairing roofs, putting in damp courses and applying gallons of fresh white paint, but in restoring the distinctive fences and the terra-cotta balls which crown their supporting pillars.

Who are the new Bedford Park people, and why have they come to live there? Some, like literary agent Andrew Best and his graphic designer wife Gemma, came because they wanted to be west of London, and a study of six-inch maps showed up some roads with generous gardens. Others, like Peter Hall, professor of geography at Reading University, came because he knew of (and indeed had

The treescape along the curving line of roads like, here, in Queen Anne's Gardens, are as much an ingredient of the Bedford Park scene as the architecture.

lectured on) the first garden suburb, and of all the places roughly half-way between Reading and Bloomsbury, where his wife works, this was the one they wanted to live in.

The Halls' approach was remarkably single-minded. When agents failed to deliver, he and his wife Magda went out one Sunday morning armed with four hundred duplicated letters asking to be informed of any house for sale, and popped them through letter boxes. The result: a Norman Shaw semi-detached house in tree-lined Bedford Road, with the characteristic first-floor sun balcony.

Jane Fawcett, for thirteen years secretary of the Victorian Society, brought to the district not only herself and her husband Ted, the National Trust's public relations director but, after a long and vain search for reasonably priced premises nearer the centre, the society itself. The Victorians are now established at No. 1 Priory Gardens, an attractive house near the church and the station, by E. J. May. The previous owner bought for £45,000 at the top of the market in 1970, then when prices collapsed went bankrupt. The Victorians, having opposed his unacceptable plans for building in the garden, bought from the receiver for £28,000. "A case of virtue rewarded," comments Mrs Fawcett.

Marcus Edwards, a barrister specializing in commercial law, has lived in Bedford Park for ten years. He lives in one of the few pre-Carr buildings, a Georgian house dating from 1790 at No. 1 South Parade, and he moved there "because it was the only place we could find". He likes the area for its mixture of artists, musicians and others, but says that among his own outside contacts "nobody really knows about Bedford Park" – which is partly its attraction. His house has a very large garden, which he and his wife enjoy throwing open, in rather the way Jonathan Carr did his, for public occasions.

His wife Sandra explained that she is a relative newcomer, and is still to some extent reserving judgment. She says she is too busy to have joined in much: her commitments included national chairmanship of the Pre-School Play-Groups Association and of Fair Play for Children, and membership of Westminster City Council, as well as looking after her own three children aged ten, nine and seven. She enjoys her garden being used for parties by various organizations and just giving a hand, and felt she was made most welcome by local Tories when she helped at a council by-election. American by origin and accent, she showed when I talked to her a practical impatience with the two councils' – Ealing's and Hounslow's – failure to put right the tattiness of the crossroads and green at the suburb's focus. She has since got herself elected to Ealing council.

On the other side of the political fence is Jim Daly, former chairman of the GLC's transport committee, who bought his Norman Shaw house in Bath Road, Bedford Park, in 1963. A west Londoner for much longer, he says he moved there not because of any First Garden Suburb, Norman Shaw charisma, but because the house was pleasant and at a price he could afford. He welcomes the better care now lavished on the area, and up to a point the move back to single family houses, but is worried by certain aspects of these changes. He bought his house, he told me, for about £7,000, which he could afford while working as a research assistant for the National Union of Teachers; but by 1977, as a senior lecturer at the North Eastern Polytechnic, he could not afford it if he were starting again. And though he has fought, both as a GLC member and a Hounslow councillor, for the retention and suitable use of Bedford Park houses, he distrusts some people's assumption that elaborate restoration of Bedford Park architecture has automatic first claim on limited public funds without thought for more urgent social priorities.

And representatives of the arts? Well, mezzo soprano Laura Sarti discovered Bedford Park while travelling to rehearse *Die Fledermaus* with soprano Madge Stevens, liked what she saw, and found a Woodstock Road house by Shaw admirably adapted both for family living and, by knocking two rooms into one, for musical rehearsals.

Activities like the thirty-year-old House of Arts and the annual fortnight-long festival have great attractions. The festival, started in 1967 on the initiative of a new vicar, the Reverend Jack Jenner, has restored Shaw's gothic-cum-Renaissance church and raises some £1,700 a year for the fabric and for various charities. Father Jenner coordinates the Fair on the Green with which the festival kicks off and which leavens the artistic diet with a day of coconut shies and roundabouts. He told me he believed there was more of a sense of community than twelve years before when he first arrived; and most Bedford Parkers would probably agree.

But is Bedford Park becoming too preciously arty middle-class? Irene Coates, immediate past chairman of the Conservation Society, says she loves her adopted village for its trees and its roomy, adaptable houses, but thinks it suffers from a self-appointed ruling clique which is "almost medieval". Bedford Park is definitely snobbish, she says.

Others laugh at any such notion, and would say with Marcus Edwards: "We haven't an élite. There's no wealth at all, and no fame." Compared with a Kensington or a Hampstead, no doubt that's true. It depends on your standpoint. Though dishwashers and deep-freezers have replaced the cook-generals, Bedford Park today is as solidly middle class as it was a century ago.

The attraction of the Bedford Park scene depends greatly on detail, whether it is the way in which fence rails rise elegantly to each post, or the careful preservation of features of the street scene like this octagonal Victorian pillar-box on the corner of Bedford Road and The Orchard.

3

Rotherhithe and Bermondsey

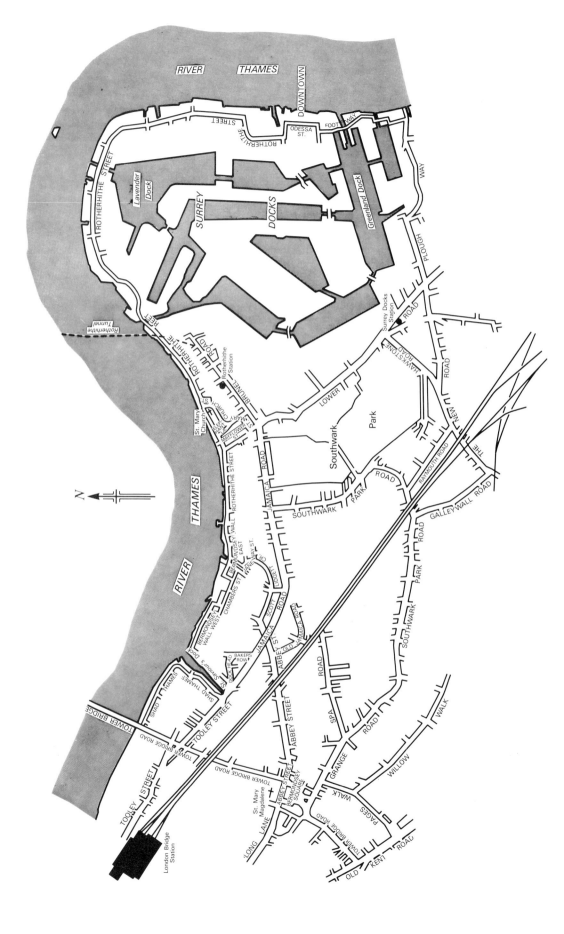

3

Rotherhithe and Bermondsey

In a little public garden just behind Guy's Hospital stands a shelter with a plaque. It reads: "This shelter was erected to commemorate a lifetime of service by Dr and Mrs Alfred Salter to the people of Bermondsey." Salter's story is not widely known or remembered these days, even in Rotherhithe and Bermondsey. He was the outstanding student of his time at Guy's Medical School, won all the prizes and seemed set for a brilliant career in medical research and Harley Street. But as a Guy's student in turn-of-the-century Bermondsey he had seen how the poor there lived – and died – in the squalid, overcrowded district.

The area that had then just become Bermondsey borough – Bermondsey, Rotherhithe and the Surrey Docks – had long been a Cinderella district. In medieval times most of the land caught in that bend of the river between London Bridge and Deptford was marshy. Three places stand out as early settlements: Horselydown – the high ground which is the eastward extension of the southern bridgehead; Bermondsey Island (or Beornmund's Eye), the higher ground where now Tower Bridge Road crosses Abbey Street, and where a great Cluniac foundation grew up from the 11th century onwards; and the village of Rotherhithe, on the riverside opposite Wapping.

Rotherhithe means "the place where cattle were shipped" and the tradition is that cattle destined for Smithfield, brought up river from farms in Kent, were unloaded there and driven to a point near the Bricklayers' Arms, to be fed, watered and rested before going on to London. In the 19th century, with the growth of docks, wharves and manufacturing, Bermondsey's population shot up rapidly, from 46,000 in 1801 to 102,000 in 1871; but the houses built for them behind the river wall were not salubrious places.

By Salter's time, conditions had improved, but not much. Tuberculosis was rife; the average life expectation was lower than almost anywhere else in London. Salter saw, grieved, debated with his conscience – then threw up his career, moved permanently to Bermondsey, became a poor man's doctor and, because medicine did not cure basic social conditions, a politician. Under his leadership, a crusading, infant Labour party, its propaganda financed by a flourishing co-operative bakery, eventually captured the borough council in 1922 and set about building a New Jerusalem in the dockland slums.

They established a pioneering health service, and the five years after 1922 saw the death rate cut from 16.7 per 1,000 of population to 12.9, new cases of TB from 413 to 294. They planted 9,000 trees in two years, so that the *Daily Chronicle* wrote enthusiastically of "Bermondsey's boulevards". Salter's housing policy now looks strangely modern, for he wanted those grim, unhealthy tenements replaced not by barrack-like blocks of flats but by cottages with gardens. In two little roads just north of the new Jamaica Road dual carriageway – Wilson Grove and Scott Lidgett Crescent – you can see the "garden suburban" terraces that an enlightened Bermondsey borough built in the 1920s by direct labour at around £500 a time, before Whitehall, County Hall, land shortage and cost problems forced them into building flats.

Salter and his wife Ada lived all their lives in Bermondsey. They sent their daughter to a local school and identified themselves with local people. The daughter died when, against all the odds, she caught scarlet fever for the third time. The tragedy only strengthened her parents' commitment to their adopted district. As its MP Salter fought unremittingly for a new deal for his people. Yet today (given that it is healthier and more prosperous) Bermondsey is not a New Jerusalem. It has its achievements, its historic corners, its breathtaking river views, but for the most part it is a drab, decaying segment of the inner city, down-at-heel, and with a declining, ageing population.

One man I talked to who has lived in the midst of change and regretted it is sixty-four-year-old Henry Hoffman, who keeps one of the two remaining eel pie shops in Tower Bridge Road, Bermondsey. His mother and father started the business around the time when Salter was a medical student. Hoffman sold me pie and mash for 26p. while talking sadly of the large-scale demolition that had swept away his former customers' terrace houses and the factories where they worked, and destroyed three streets to make room for a roundabout and a flyover. His customers, he said, used to take a twopenny tram ticket ("Twopence in the old money, mind you!") to Abbey Wood and back. Now their sons and daughters sweep by in Fords and Maxis to homes in Catford or Thamesmead.

Up the road, nearer Bermondsey Square, Charlie Secular, one of the few London fishmongers who cures his own mackerel, haddock and bloaters in "smoke-holes" treacle-black from fires of oak sawdust, declares he would never live anywhere but Bermondsey, above the shop. His clientele has changed – more people come by car from other areas – but "they're nice people, still". His daughter and son-in-law, who run the business with the Seculars, commute from another part of London. Seculars have sold fish in south-east London for three-and-a-half centuries, but tradition does not necessarily convince the new generation.

One business that does thrive in Bermondsey, at least on Fridays, is antiques. The Caledonian Market moved there when it was bombed out of Islington, and now in Bermondsey Square and its surroundings antiques and what pass for them outnumber fruit and vegetables and less pretentious wares by 20 or 30 to 1. Several warehouses are let out in stalls, often on a weekly basis; and such a rendezvous for the trade has narrow, picturesque Bermondsey Street become that lorries now roll up on Thursday nights and

Totters at work. Amidst widespread demolition and the decay of unused land and buildings "awaiting redevelopment", it has sometimes seemed to Rotherhithe and Bermondsey folk that junk and antiques were the area's only two thriving industries.

dealers trade across the pavement by torchlight. Few local people are involved.

In a 1960s rectory alongside 17th century St Mary Magdalene I met the Reverend Mervyn Wilson, his wife and their four children. He has been Rector for seven years and is now convinced that Salter's dream of a healthier, happier Bermondsey has gone badly awry. He believes that the borough, now part of Southwark, has been knocked down too much, with damaging results both to the familiar townscape and to people's sense of community. But worse, the municipal solution to appalling housing which Doctor Salter and his colleagues adopted with pioneering enthusiasm had become a rod for Bermondsey's back.

For eighty per cent of the area's homes are council properties and the authority's criteria of need have progressively forced out younger people. Young couples have virtually no chance of buying their own place there, and small prospects of a house with a garden for children to play in. So more and more of them have gone elsewhere, and Bermondsey, like other inner city areas, has become increasingly inhabited by the elderly, the less skilled, and the underprivileged.

Bermondsey Square, where from early Thursday evening to well into Friday afternoon the New Caledonian Market is a bustling centre of the London antiques trade. In the background, St Mary Magdalene Church.

Rotherhithe, which must once have been a riverside village standing amid low-lying marshy lands, is now regaining something of its old, pre-Victorian aspect, thanks to large-scale clearance. The GLC is gradually turning the area to the west into parkland, though many of the jigsaw pieces are at present corrugated-iron-encircled waste lots. Here a visual disaster was narrowly averted. The original plan called for the demolition of almost everything except the parish church, St Mary Rotherhithe, with its distinctive Corinthian-columned spire. The clear-and-rebuild reflex led councillors and officials to assume that the wall of 19th century warehousing should be swept away: those dirty old warehouses where their forebears worked for less than sixpence a day must not stand in the way of progress! That course would have been disastrous. The church would have remained, alone in a windswept expanse of little-used greensward, and the local people been left visually even more rootless than they are.

Len Hatch, a docker who works at one of the few wharves still active on the Rotherhithe riverside, Thames Rice Milling, says: "To me, the warehouses and the church go with one another. The church would have looked naked without them." Hatch, in his late forties and born in Rotherhithe, is vice-chairman of the Bermondsey

St Mary's Rotherhithe, seen from the Thames surrounded by its cluster of Victorian warehouses, now being conserved and given fresh life, in many cases as small workshops for craftsmen.

and Rotherhithe Society, which campaigned for and won conservation areas round the old village centres of Rotherhithe and Bermondsey.

But freeing fine old industrial buildings from the threat of demolition is only part of the conservation battle. They must also be given new rôles and at Rotherhithe the transformation has started. The Industrial Buildings Preservation Trust, which took a lead in converting warehouses at Clerkenwell Green into craft workshops, has begun a similar process at Hope Sufferance Wharf, adjoining the churchyard. Michael Murray, a silversmith from near the British Museum and the Hope Sufferance project's part-time director, hopes that it will achieve two useful objects in addition to giving the buildings a new use: cheap working space for self-employed craftsmen; and, with luck, some jobs for local people.

In a pair of adjoining warehouses, linked by a bridge across winding Rotherhithe Street, film-maker Richard Goodwin, the co-producer of *Murder on the Orient Express*, has a combined home and picture research library which will be open for public reference. "My wife and I are conservationists," he told me. "We wanted these warehouses to be preserved. And in the end the only way to make it happen seemed to be to come here and make it happen."

A charitable trust is providing financial assistance for the Goodwin project and its architects have managed to achieve a marriage of style and economy. The trust had spent by early 1977 over £150,000 on the scheme, which will create a number of jobs and which includes craft workshops, a shop selling craft wares made in Rotherhithe, and a two-storey studio which can be used as a hall by local people.

A hundred yards down Rotherhithe Street in another timber-and-iron-framed, tall brick warehouse, a former film editor, Mike Canty, is engaged on a similar project. It is a shoe-string operation and the group of craftsmen include violin and harpsichord makers, potters, woodworkers, a silversmith and textile and graphics specialists as well as a girl who dyes wool to match and mend Persian carpets.

Canty, who took over the Waterside warehouse from an ailing film animation company called "Crunchy Frog", builds on self-help and self-sufficiency. His father was a bricklayer: the tenants pay half their £8 rent in labour. That is why their new staircase, required by fire regulations, has cost nearer £500 than £5,000. One tenant has a joiner boy-friend. "When we have forty quid or so in

Linsey Pollak, one of the craftsmen at Waterside, a craft co-operative in Rotherhithe Street. He makes early woodwind instruments such as flutes and bagpipes, and every few months he and his colleagues put on a lively and informal musical evening when they play the instruments they make.

the kitty, he comes down for the weekend, works like crazy and makes us ten new windows at £4 a time."

Two of Canty's Waterside tenants run a theatre at the bottom of the building and there is also a hall. Both have achieved much in winning over local people initially suspicious of and hostile to middle-class outsiders. But Canty is cautious. He believes the integration of craftsmen newcomers will take a decade, and argues that two-year renewals of his GLC lease are too short to build on. Waterside has since put proposals to the GLC for development of its and neighbouring buildings on a longer term basis; but despite backing from Southwark, was still at the time of writing awaiting a response. Canty still suspects that most local councillors would at heart like to bulldoze the old warehouses and conservationists and craftsmen with them.

Ron Watts, chairman of Southwark borough planning committee, disagrees. He concedes that some councillors had taken that hard line at public meetings, but points out that local people had supported the craftsmen newcomers. He personally regrets the wholesale clearance of handsome, potentially sound streets like Storks Road where Salter lived. Time and time again, he explains, the housing committee had urged demolition, the planning committee rehabilitation – and housing had always won, because that was the way the sums were done. The financial basis of decisions has since been changed, but too late to save many attractive 18th- and 19th-century buildings. He says that the borough now recognizes and is trying to respond to the need to have a more local, personal presence. It is also trying to recast its housing policies – partly perhaps because it foresees a housing surplus in a few years, and prospective tenants who will be more selective in their choice. One sign of change are the low-rise houses going up in Bermondsey to the wonder of local people.

Mervyn Wilson welcomes the revised policies but, like many others, is sceptical whether the bureaucratic leopard can really change its spots. Wally Fletcher, greengrocer, market rent collector, and chairman of the Downtown Tenants' Association, is optimistic. He is one of the dwindling population of an island now surrounded by the now idle Surrey Docks network. Although Trammell Crow's giant trade mart scheme has been shelved, the council seem intent on pressing on with housebuilding and renovation and many councillors, like Watts, want to see provision made for young couples who might otherwise leave the area.

From a jobs standpoint, the trade mart carries potential benefits. If postponement becomes a final withdrawal for want of finance, Southwark and the GLC will have to think again. They might just – with the arguments of the Inner City Studies before them – espouse the "small is beautiful" cause. After all, small businesses like Leslie Crips' ironworks, founded in 1837, find their services much in demand. Crips told me he constantly receives the small specialist or rush orders ignored by the big firms.

Bob Mellish, MP for the area, provides a wry postscript. "I'm called the dockers' MP, but almost all the docks have gone," he says. He has long campaigned for radical action to revitalize London's redundant docklands, and urges strongly that new housing provision should cater especially for young married couples – for if they went Bermondsey would languish and come near to death. Yet, despite its ageing population and drastic physical change, Bermondsey and Rotherhithe, says Mellish, still has its "village atmosphere", and Bermondsey folk "are grand people to talk to".

Those are qualities which bulldozers have not destroyed, and which, with care and luck, more responsive policies than those of the past twenty years will conserve and foster.

4

Kew

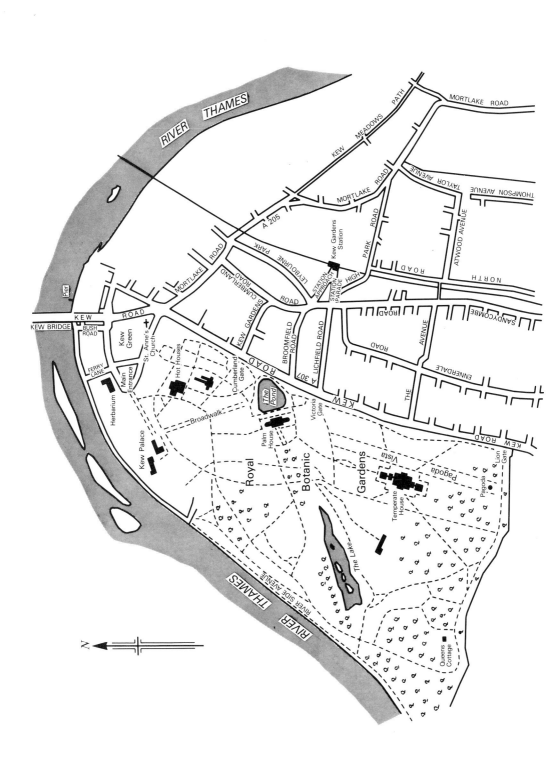

4

Kew

Kew means different things to different people. To some, the "wonderful show" – herbaceous borders *par excellence* – put on for the public's benefit in the Royal Botanic Gardens; to others, "wandering hand in hand with love" in the "summer's wonderland" of Alfred Noyes' lilac time; for some, the gardens as a world-renowned centre of scientific learning and research; and for others, Kew is not primarily the Gardens at all, but a place to live, or a traffic jam on the South Circular – the queue at Kew.

We can identify at least three separate Kews. First, the Gardens and the royal palace round which they grew. Second, Kew Green: a bright necklace of mostly Georgian houses fringing a blunted triangle of turf, with St Anne's parish church sitting, like some large, broody, orange hen, untidily but charmingly off-centre. And finally, Kew Gardens, the Victorian and Edwardian suburb, which developed round the railway station of that name from the late 1860s onwards, spreading north to the green and west to Kew Road and the long, brick boundary wall of the Gardens.

Kew came into prominence in the 1730s when George II's eldest son, Prince Frederick, got William Kent to rebuild an existing house there for him. This building, the White House, like the later New Kew Palace, "a medieval, fortress-like dwelling" designed by James Wyatt for George III, has long since disappeared (they were demolished in 1802 and 1828 respectively), leaving the more modest but charming Dutch House as sole inheritor of the title "Kew Palace". Built in 1631 for Samuel Fortrey, a merchant of Dutch descent, it served George III, Queen Caroline and their children as a country house; and the Department of the Environment have recently refurbished and rearranged it to re-create the royal domestic style so vividly described by Fanny Burney in her diaries. The inadequacy of the Dutch House as a royal establishment prompted the building of many of the houses fringing the green, where some of the royal children were boarded out.

The Dutch House, built in 1631 by a rising London merchant and later used by George III and his family.

The Georgian period also gives us Pope's epigram, engraved on the collar of a dog he gave Prince Frederick:

"I am His Highness' dog at Kew;
Pray tell me, sir, whose dog are you?"

as well as the scandal of his son the future George III's putative morganatic marriage to a Quaker's daughter, one Hannah Lightfoot, which one local historian believes took place in Kew Church. Kept secret at the time, the affair is said to have produced offspring including a son, known as George Rex, who was packed off to the Cape. But it rumbled on into Victorian times and seems to explain a mysterious break-in at Kew Church in the 1850s: for the only items taken were the parish registers of marriages and births covering the period of George's affair with the young Quakeress.

As to the Gardens, Kew figures in botanical history as early as the mid-16th century, when the Rev. William Turner, father of English botany, had a garden there. Prince Frederick's wife, Augusta of Saxe-Gotha, continued to develop the gardens after her husband's death, though in a romantic-picturesque rather than a botanical manner. To this period we owe William Chambers' Great Pagoda and Orangery, as well as the establishment of the first nine-acre botanical garden, now grown to three hundred acres. Under George III, Capability Brown took a hand in the landscaping; and the king personally supervised, numbering among his labourers one William Cobbett, radical journalist to be, who was apparently then in straitened circumstances.

In 1820 both the king and Sir Joseph Banks, the gardens' un-official director, died, and a period of decline ensued. The royal gardener Green saw his precious orange trees die for want of adequate hothouses, though he offered £250 out of his own pocket for their extension and repair. It was squeeze and freeze with a vengeance, and faced with suppression of his own post, presumably without benefit of redundancy pay, this long-suffering horticul-turalist killed himself. In 1838, however, the Government appointed a committee of inquiry which paved the way for the establishment three years later of Kew as a national botanic institution.

What of Kew now, as a place to live in? It possesses, more than most London suburbs, a remarkable sense of village-like community – perhaps its position in a loop of the Thames helps. The name Kew derives from the words *caye*, for quay, and *ho*, meaning a spur of land, which run together formed Cayho. Kew has always had a quite separate identity from Richmond and, even more so, from places across the river. After a period of decline in the 1930s and 1940s, Kew is now undergoing a rebirth. Mrs Evelyn Badger, who has lived in a house on the north side of Kew Green for more than forty years, told me: "Kew has gone up in the world. Many of these houses were empty for years." In the 1920s and 1930s the Green had quite a different character. Four of the houses on the north side were restaurants, with awnings and signs proclaiming watercress teas with a pot freshly made for every customer. Like houses in Kew generally, those on the Green tended to be occupied by several families. Now the single-family house, alive with children and with, at most, a couple of baby-sitting students in the attic, is the rule.

Robert Kee, author and TV broadcaster, lives a few doors away in the one Victorian house on the Georgian north side of the Green. He and his wife Cynthia came to Kew in 1963 from a two-room flat in Notting Hill. "We'd been looking everywhere for a house we could afford. I bought this one at an auction for £11,500, having taken two strong brandies beforehand. It had been a restaurant. We discovered that when John Freeman came to dinner with us. He

Kew Green, with houses Georgian, Victorian, and variegated half-timbered. Jo Grimond once, when he lived here, came out and ordered parked cars off the grass.

said, 'I know I've been in this house before.' Then he remembered. It was before the war, when it was tea-rooms.'' The things Kee likes about Kew are the open space – a great chain of public green areas including Richmond Park, Old Deer Park, Syon Park and Wimbledon Common as well as Kew Gardens – and of course just looking out on Kew Green. What he detests are aircraft noise and the traffic on the South Circular, which he regards as a monstrous intrusion. It has, he maintains, been diverted through Kew away from its obvious dual carriageway route not far away at Chiswick.

The South Circular is one of the unifying causes which has brought Kew people together. The GLC had plans to widen the residential stretch of Mortlake Road, which forms the South Circular's approach to Kew Green, and to create a one-way system through residential streets to the south. An *ad hoc* resistance group called Kewtac (Kew Traffic Action Committee) presented a well argued case at a public inquiry, and defeated the one-way scheme. Though the road widening won ministerial approval, the GLC has no funds for it at present and it seems that Kewtac's and the Kew

Society's drip-drip-drip of reasoned argument may now have convinced the politicians that such an "improvement" would be as futile as it would be environmentally ruinous. The queues at Kew are in fact tailbacks from a congested junction north of Kew Bridge and a recently rebuilt narrow railway bridge farther south.

David Blomfield, one of the band of Liberal councillors who, building on their original support in Kew, until recently held a majority of the Richmond borough council seats south of the river, says the only real answer is the completion of the M25 orbital motorway. While only a small proportion of cars may be by-passed, the M25, he believes, would divert a much larger proportion of heavy lorries. Kew can live with cars, but not with the environmental punishment inflicted on the place by the heavies.

Blomfield and his wife came to Kew in 1965 to live in an Edwardian detached house in Leybourne Park, in the part of the suburb that grew round the railway. "When we moved there, we were the only family out of sixty houses in the road with children under sixteen," he recalls. "Now there are something like forty children in the road."

As Richmond's once appalling reputation as an education authority has markedly improved, so these parents, says Blomfield, have

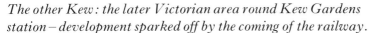

*The other Kew: the later Victorian area round Kew Gardens
station – development sparked off by the coming of the railway.*

felt that "the local state schools were the natural local schools for our children". Kew is now not the kind of suburb where wives tied by toddlers lead lonely, isolated lives. There is much contact and mutual aid; friendships develop from contacts made at the school gate.

One can see why the Liberals thrive in Kew. It is the kind of close-knit parish, proud of its separate identity, in which "community politics" in the broadest sense are natural. Blomfield cites the case, which everyone is talking happily about in Kew at present, of the sub-post office on the Green. The Post Office proposed to close it as uneconomic when the former postmaster retired. Everyone protested, including people who lived close to the Crown branch office at Kew Gardens station. They signed the petition because they cared about old people living near the Green who would have a mile to go to draw their pensions. Tory MP and Conservative-controlled council backed them to the hilt; the Post Office changed its mind. Now Mr and Mrs Uday Kapadia, from Bombay by way of Mitcham, are installed and paying out pensions with a friendly smile.

Kew people have another running grumble against the Post Office. Their phone numbers are in the Outer London (Surrey) book, which is all the Post Office gives them. A high proportion of the numbers they want to ring are in the London postal area. There is much begging and borrowing of London directories from friends in Chiswick, Mortlake and beyond. Some people feel they get the worst of both worlds: they are London for the GLC, which they don't like, but not London for phone numbers, which would be useful.

Parking is another cross Kew has to bear, particularly round the Green and in the streets that lead up to the Victoria and Lion gates. Over a million people a year pay up their 1p (reduced from a pre-decimalizaton 3d) to enter Kew Gardens, and as many as 30,000 do so on a single peak Bank Holiday. An increasing number come by car and even an expanded riverside car park near the main gate cannot cope with these peaks. On the whole those who live by the Green share the philosophical view of their local bobby, PC Webb (who comes by bike, not by Panda car): "If you choose to live in one of the loveliest places in London, you can't expect people not to come and gape at you." On the whole the visitors behave well. Once or twice they have begun parking on the sacred greensward. Some residents cherish memories of Jo Grimond, until recently resident

View down the Victorian Lichfield Road to Kew Gardens'
Victoria Gate.

at No. 71, descending wrathfully like Moses from the mountain and
remonstrating with the transgressors – but to more effect, for they
took heed and desisted.

The Kew Society, though it has joined forces on occasion with its
local Liberal councillors and its distant Tory council, is non-
political. One recent battle concerned land between the river and
the backs of houses on the Green, where the Boathouse, a tatty pub-
cum-dance hall of somewhat violent reputation, once stood. Successive owners proposed multi-storey hotels and gross over-develop-
ment with mini town houses. The society, and Kew as a whole,
fought them; adjacent householders put in a second planning application, designed to demonstrate the unacceptability of the plan,
proposing comparably dense development along the matching
sections of their own back gardens. The opposition succeeded in
reducing the scheme both in density and bulk, and the society's
chairman, solicitor Tony Sheffer, told me he regarded the outcome
as a qualified victory. Others, like Robert Kee, still feel bitter about
it, and believe that the opposition simply ran out of steam when it
ought to have gone on fighting.

The affair demonstrates, however, the way in which Kew can call on the expertise and resources of professionals such as former Kew Society chairman Bruce Coles QC, who represented it at the Boathouse inquiry. Many lawyers, bankers and above all architects live at Kew, including conservation architect Donald Insall; university and church specialists Bob Maguire and Keith Murray; Kenneth Wriglesworth, former assistant to Sir Albert Richardson, who has practised conservation by turning a redundant Wesleyan chapel into a home; and George Cassidy, the Kew Society's president. Cassidy, hospital architect, local historian and JP, steered the society away from outright opposition to the proposal for a bail hostel in Kew, an issue which split local people. Some predictably said, "Why should we have it?"; others urged that well-heeled Kew ought to make its contribution to a wider social good.

Kew, the community, and Kew the Botanic Gardens, remain curiously detached from each other. Of course Kew residents enjoy the Gardens; many of them, like Libby Insall, were drawn by them. Yet Kew Gardens, with its Herbarium of approaching five million dried plant specimens and its unparalleled library, has its consuming task; and, while not aloof, it is, behind its walls and gates, distinctly detached. Scholars like Nigel Hepper, Assistant Keeper for Floras, pursue knowledge, publish, and develop international contacts the world over. How to get a Land Rover in Kenya across closed frontiers to botanical sites in Tanzania may for the staff appear a more pressing problem than that of local people who would like to continue a towpath walk through a gate closed by labour shortages and security fears.

Over thirty of Kew's staff actually live in the Gardens – dedicated horticulturalists like George Brown, just retiring after twenty-one years at Kew. He told me: "You tend to live with the plants and not have so much time for outside contacts." This is true, too, of Kew's birdkeeper. Cornishman Harold Allen, who rears birds as well as controlling pests which threaten the plants. Though he cycles daily from a home outside, Kew for him clearly means the Gardens and his work there.

Kew the Gardens and Kew the community, however, suffer from a common blight – aircraft noise. In summer, people who love gardens have their pleasure shattered by being under Heathrow flight-paths, with an aircraft going over every fifty-four seconds and the shadow of the plane falling across the house each time in exactly the same place. Hacan, the Heathrow Association for the

Kew Bridge seen from Strand-on-the-Green. Kew Pier is on the left.

Control of Aircraft Noise, started in Kew as Kacan in 1967, and ten years later had 2,500 individual members and forty affiliated amenity groups. Its vice-chairman Mrs Alison Williams can point to some real relief as a result of its typically (for Kew) professional lobbying and pressure. Improved landing systems free the Kew and Richmond area from aircraft noise for at least half the day, and in January 1977 further changes cut the noise levels to which the area is subjected. "The difficulty," says Mrs Williams, "is to make those in authority aware of the effects of aircraft noise on the environment and to inspire them with a feeling that something must be done about it."

But now the spectre of Heathrow expansion haunts Kew and Hacan. The plans being made could jeopardize all the progress so far achieved, she says. They threaten not only streams of 700-passenger Jumbos lumbering over Kew Gardens on what should be quiet Sunday afternoons, but M4 and M3 motorways so overloaded as to make car travel virtually impossible for local people. No wonder the talk in Kew increasingly favours a fresh look at least at an economy-style Maplin.

5

De Beauvoir Town

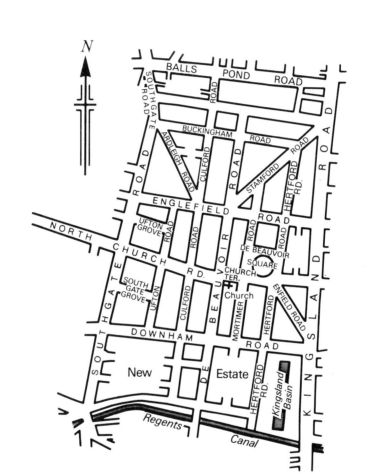

5

De Beauvoir Town

De Beauvoir Town is not a big place: not much more than a quarter of a square mile. Nor is it well known. It has no tube station, and its name does not appear on the destination blinds of any London bus. When I asked one south Londoner, steeped in the local history of his own area, whether he knew where De Beauvoir was, he rather thought it was somewhere to the left of Provence. There is in fact a town called Beauvoir in that area, but the London "village" called De Beauvoir lies north of Shoreditch between the Regent's Canal and Ball's Pond Road. Even Cockneys from Clapton, a mile farther into Hackney, have been known to scratch their heads and say they have never heard of it; yet it is a remarkably attractive area of inner London, with a past and a present that mark it out as somewhere special.

De Beauvoir Town is to be found behind the western side of Kingsland Road, whose straightness gives a clue to its origin as a Roman highway north out of London. One of the earliest developments hereabouts was a mansion, Balmes (or Baumes) House, built about 1540 by two Spanish merchants named Baulm, which became a private lunatic asylum in the early 19th century where unscrupulous guardians sometimes incarcerated heirs to large fortunes. Ball's Pond Road, De Beauvoir's northern boundary, has a fine terrace of 1812; that name derives from a disreputable public house, whose landlord, Mr Ball, provided, among other entertainments, duck shooting on his pond.

To the south lay White Mills Common, where lead mills existed as late as the 1820s; and here the Honourable Artillery Company, first promoted by Henry VIII, traditionally had the right to practise archery. In 1786, during one of their periodic forays to break down fences and hedges that interfered with these rights, members of the company encountered a newly built brick wall erected by the proprietors of the white lead mills, Walker, Ward & Company.

They were about to knock this down as well when a Mr Maltby, a partner in the firm, ran up to apologize. He had not known of the archers' royally established rights, he said, but if the wall were spared would certainly accommodate them. So the archers contented themselves with shooting an arrow over the wall and, honour satisfied, left it standing.

By the 1820s, however, more serious development threatened the rights of the HAC. The canal had opened to the south in 1818, and a successful but unscrupulous local entrepreneur, William Rhodes, extracted from the absentee owner of the estate, the eighty-three-year-old Reverend Peter de Beauvoir, an extraordinarily permissive ninety-nine-year building lease on the estate for a fraction of what it was really worth. The lease was obtained from the clergyman on his sick-bed, and Rhodes built relatively little before the heir, Richard Benyon de Beauvoir, started a twenty-two-year-long court case which ended in the setting aside of the lease.

The successful heir then had fresh proposals drawn up for the development of his estate of a rather more straightforward character than Rhodes' ambitious ground-plan, which had envisaged four squares linked by diagonal streets to a central octagon. What then resulted, in the 1840s, was development with an air of spaciousness and architectural quality; and the one square Benyon de Beauvoir built (originally to be called Park Place but in fact named De Beauvoir Square) later formed the corner-stone of the conservation area and of the area's rescue from municipal bulldozery. That square dating from 1840, with its neo-Jacobean villas with ornately shaped "Flemish" gables, is a unique architectural set-piece, a pioneering piece of town planning. Yet only ten years ago Hackney council still intended to demolish it, as part of a massive redevelopment excercise that would have razed every building from the canal to Ball's Pond Road. Stuart Weir, who moved to the area in 1967 and founded the De Beauvoir Association to fight the plan, remembers talking to a Hackney councillor.

"We're planning to keep the square," said the man, who represented the ward but did not live there. "Oh, that's good," replied Weir, brightening. "They're in poor repair, but they're really very attractive houses." "Oh, no. We're knocking down the houses," rejoined the councillor. "We'll just keep the square."

For perhaps eighty years after it was built, De Beauvoir remained a well-to-do and reasonably well-thought-of district. Two miles from the Bank of England, yet on the edge of the Middlesex countryside, it attracted prosperous City folk; its spacious, tree-lined streets had an agreeably well planned air; and, unlike the part of Islington immediately to the west, its houses were in pairs or fours rather than the long, high and rather overbearing terraces of the 1860s. In Southgate Road, its western boundary, the houses had tiled drives where carriages would wait to take householders to the City; and Charles Furby, nearly eighty years a De Beauvoirite, recalls that three local authorities were responsible for maintaining this street: Hackney for the east side, Islington for the west, and the London County Council for the strip along the middle.

Two world wars, dilapidations, multi-occupation and, from the 1930s onwards, creeping backyard industrialization, set De Beauvoir on the path of decline. The well-to-do progressively moved out to smarter, greener suburbs such as Stamford Hill (1880s), Wood Green (1880s) and Palmers Green (1920s). The Benyon Estate, which still owns much of the area, found itself forced by death duties to sell off blocks of freeholds; and the requisitions, bombs and lack of maintenance of the last war left De Beauvoir in poor shape to withstand fifteen years of planning blight which followed the publication of Hackney's wholesale redevelopment plan in the early 1950s.

De Beauvoir Square; behind it the towers of the Hackney Council redevelopment originally intended to replace the whole of De Beauvoir.

Mrs Mabel Hall, who has lived in Ufton Road, De Beauvoir, since 1911, remembers the shock and disbelief when residents from the southern part of the area, facing the first wave of demolition proposals, knocked on her door for help. She and some neighbours clubbed together to pay for leaflets, and the case which residents put up convinced the inquiry inspector that southern De Beauvoir should be spared. Unfortunately the Minister who took the final decision, Henry Brooke, seems to have been more influenced by the political game of housing numbers than by consideration of architectural or social worth. Something between a quarter and a third of De Beauvoir Town, including such streets as Benyon Road, Balmes Road and the canalside De Beauvoir Crescent, was razed to the ground to make way for municipal tower blocks nineteen storeys high and slabs of maisonettes.

By 1967 the climate was changing. People in the rest of De Beauvoir were now all too conscious of the inhumanity and enormity of the redevelopment plan; the Civic Amenities Act had

Racked by heavy traffic, but still elegant and comfortable homes, these early-19th-century terrace-houses in Ball's Pond Road were among the first to be built in De Beauvoir.

familiarized the public with the concept of conservation of areas as distinct from preservation of individual buildings; and two young journalists working on *The Times*' newly created PHS diary column (as I was at the time), had moved into attractive but down-at-heel Regency houses in Ball's Pond Road. Robin Young, sometime Liberal candidate for Orpington, came first "because it was an attractive house and it was all I could afford"; then Stuart Weir.

They and a number of others, including an architect, Graham Parsey, gave the residents' fight an extra punch and *savoir faire* which it previously lacked; they unearthed and presented the facts, argued and goaded; and councillors and officials, accustomed in Hackney's traditionally one-party state to steam-rollering opposition, began to groan at the very mention of De Beauvoir.

De Beauvoir fought resourcefully, arguing that improvement and conservation were the right answer, not destructive, sterilizing demolition. The climate in Whitehall was indeed changing; and the GLC's historic buildings men, alerted by the association, set in motion the machinery for listing at least the square and the best adjoining streets. But in 1968 came the local government election landslide which swept the Conservatives to power in Hackney as in almost every inner London borough. This political aberration was timely for De Beauvoir, for during the Tories' three years of control they stopped the bulldozers and set up two general improvement areas. When Labour, once more in power, attempted to retreat from this, the De Beauvoir Association – aided by surveys of the area made by students from the Central London Polytechnic – was able at a further public inquiry to show itself better briefed and in command of the facts than the men from the Town Hall.

Just as the initiative for a general improvement area came from the residents, so did the plan for road closures designed to cut down the use of minor roads to avoid traffic. But the association, in concert with two tenants' associations on the new council estate, has firmly held to the view that blocking roads is not enough. Advantage must be taken of closures to provide much needed play and amenity space. The residents elected a steering group for the general improvement area, whose improvements sub-committee took the initiative in drawing up plans for a "mini park" and community centre carved out of closed roads and empty sites and buildings close to the new estate. Hackney council is paying for the park, and work has started on converting a disused factory into a community centre, which residents will equip from their own resources. A separate association representing both council tenants from the New Town Estate and residents of old De Beauvoir are now managing this scheme. Local people have also been pushing proposals to turn over Kingsland Canal Basin for children's boat clubs along the lines of the successful scheme at Islington's nearby City Basin.

Some residents and firms objected when it was proposed to make permanent experimental road blocks designed to remove through traffic. De Beauvoir generally backs the plan, however. People recognize the justice of the case argued by tenants' leader, Reg Crowfoot, that the New Town Estate, built to densities of around 130 persons per acre with little play space for noisy, energetic children, has a claim on whatever amenity can be created without destruction from the more spacious Victorian acres immediately to its north. This and other road closures will provide amenity and play space which De Beauvoir as a whole sorely needs. The inquiry inspector accepted the case for the closures, which have now been made permanent.

Indeed, what distinguishes the De Beauvoir Association from most other amenity bodies is that, having won its initial battle, it has not sat back and contented itself with self-congratulation and environmental cosmetic. To the annoyance of some newcomers, it ran a campaign for tenants' rights and raised the temperature in the area enough to discourage "winklers". Easing tenants out was simpler in other areas, so they curtailed their depredations in De Beauvoir. Compared with Barnsbury or Islington, gentrification here has been limited and of a mild variety. Weir started a free newspaper, *de Beaver*, which circulates to 3,000 households as well as to councillors and officials, again informing, arguing, goading. Launched in 1971, it must be one of London's longest-running community newspapers.

Improvement progressed in the area for two other reasons. The Benyon Estate, which still owns much of the area and is managed by a solid, long-established firm of agents, Brown & Brown, of Islington, entered into the improvement plans with enthusiasm. Eric Brown, senior partner in the firm, told me: "The trustees had the imagination to see what should be done, and to say: 'Go ahead and do it'. They haven't had a penny back from it yet." Naturally, they hope to reap their material reward in the longer term. The estate has returned many of the more attractive houses to single-family occupation on remunerative leases, but has matched this by converting other houses into self-contained flats for tenants. Improvement

The Hackney council estate which covers the southern part of De Beauvoir, seen from the Regent's Canal.

has succeeded so well and parts of the area now look so smart and elegant that two members of the Benyon family – Tory MP William Benyon, of Abortion Bill fame, and a cousin – returned to live at least part of their lives in De Beauvoir.

The other big factor in improvement was the foundation of a housing association, the De Beauvoir Trust, run as a part-time operation by Robin Young. In its six years of independent operation it bought forty-two houses, some of them as cheaply as £500 or £600 each, for conversion into some hundred rented flats and maisonettes. The trust has now been absorbed into the bigger and more professional Circle 33 Housing Trust, but its rescue operations undoubtedly filled a vacuum which would otherwise have been filled only by decay or the attentions of speculators.

What is it that attracts people to De Beauvoir and holds them there? Derek Humphry, a journalist on the *Sunday Times*, used to commute from a village in Wiltshire. Moving to London, he concluded: "If we were going to live in the city, we should really live right in it." From his attractive, end-of-terrace 1840s house, it takes him ten to fifteen minutes to cycle to his Gray's Inn Road office. He likes De Beauvoir, he told me, because it is handy, attractive, but unpretentious. His wife Ann, who comes from Boston, Massachusetts, generally dislikes London but finds De Beauvoir an exception in its friendliness.

Round the corner, her neighbour Mabel Hall, De Beauvoirite for sixty-six years, agrees. "We don't live in each other's pockets," she says, "but if anyone needs help, it's there." She cites recent instances of children looked after while mothers were in hospital; a blind woman helped daily by another tenant in the same house; and regular visiting of old people in nearby almshouses. But she also pays tribute to relative newcomers like Weir, Young and Parsey, who have devoted a staggering amount of their spare time and effort to the interests of their adopted village.

Weir, who left *The Times* to work for Shelter and the Child Poverty Action Group, also became a (very independently minded) Labour councillor. His grass-roots "community" politics are, locals tell you, of the kind that has him taking a deserted wife to the supplementary benefit office before he goes to work in the morning. Parsey, as chairman of the general improvement area's sub-committee and co-editor of *de Beaver*, reckons to devote fifteen or more evenings a month to voluntary activities in the area; his wife, Jo, in between looking after three children, has managed also to raise some £3,000 worth of advertising to keep *de Beaver* running as a free newspaper. Long established De Beauvoirites cannot but admire the wholeheartedness of this effort, even when, like printer George Shephard, they oppose particular policies such as the road closures.

Shephard, in his fifties, comes from a family of printers – though his son went to university to study dentistry. His printing workshop with its linotype machines stands alongside his house, bounded on two other sides by gardens, and exemplifies the generally happy mixture of homes and employment in the area. He and his wife Betty point with pride to their prolific back garden: there are owls in the area these days, they said, and the summer tree cover in some De Beauvoir roads is really quite rustic. But the Shephards do not think the place is quite what it once was, and regret that local opposition blocked the Benyon Estate's management proposals when freeholds were enfranchised.

Not all industry, however, is as inoffensive as George Shephard's printing shop. Steve Allen, a BBC radio producer, can point from the windows of his charming 1840s house near the blocked end of Hertford Road to three neighbouring firms. One, which reconditions sewing machines, is quiet and totally inoffensive; a second, a car sales firm with a floodlit compound, is tolerable; but the third, a glass factor, who has spread his operations into empty lots all about, causes resentment.

Allen, a founder member of the De Beauvoir Association and chairman of the general improvement area steering group, draws a distinction between quiet, job-creating pockets of industry which the inner city should welcome, and industry which, either by its nature or because of the way it operates, is unacceptable as a neighbour. De Beauvoir suffers he says, from some "cowboys" who service vehicles and spill oil across pavements or carry out noisy activities such as stapling packing cases at weekends and late into the night.

A De Beauvoirite since 1952, Allen is not really an outsider: he grew up in Highbury and his wife Diane hails from Shoreditch. They do not have the airs or accents of "gentry". Though Mary Toomey, who keeps a general store and off-licence in the middle of De Beauvoir, remarks that the area is smartening up and there are "surgeons and solicitors moving into the square", on the whole the incomers are keeping a low profile. Many of them like the area just because it is not "smart". Thus, although it has a wealth of pubs – eleven in the square quarter of a mile, a recent *de Beaver* survey showed – happily none of them has yet succumbed to brewers' formica and gimmickry. At least one, the Sussex, does a good line in lunches, but without fancy Islington menus or prices. Another, the Duke of Wellington, boasts a small amateur theatre-cum-music hall behind its fine and recently redecorated high Victorian bar.

The Duke of Wellington public house, kept by former Irish banker Jerry O'Neill, who created the Sugawn Folk Kitchen and Theatre at the back.

The landlord, Irish former banker Jerry O'Neill, created the theatre and wrote one of its recent plays, a piece which dealt with the problems of housing stress in the area; it won an enthusiastic review in *The Stage* and rejoiced in the title *God is dead on Ball's Pond Road*. Yet the success of his Sugawn Theatre, of the De Beauvoir Association and the improvement programme, all go to show that God is *not* dead in De Beauvoir Town. Some property advertisements have talked recently of "fash de Beauvoir Town". Mercifully, De Beauvoir is still far from being "fash". That is one of its chief assets; long may it remain that way.

6

Clapham

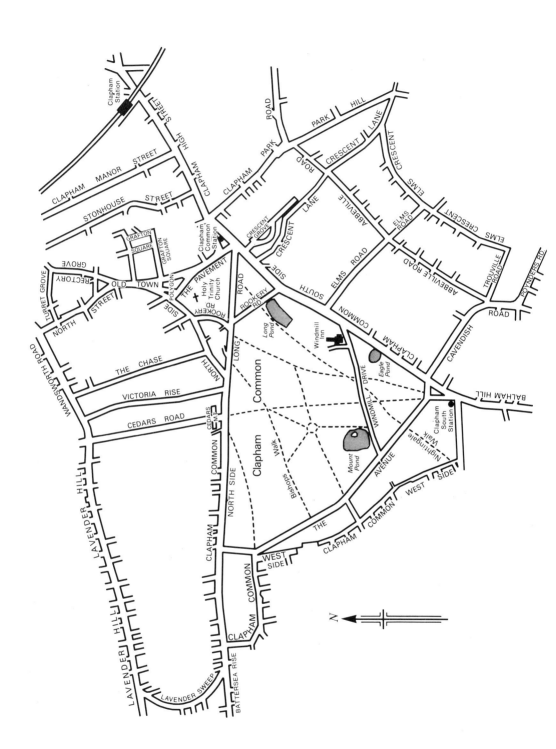

6

Clapham

Clapham? Three stations on the seedier, southern end of the
Northern Line; a large triangular Common, criss-crossed by traffic,
and with clusters of red buses and a sad little Edwardian clock-
tower in the north-east corner; the transport museum local people
fought (but failed) to keep – these are perhaps the main ingredients
in the outsider's mental picture of the place. But there is much more
to Clapham than these. It has an illustrious past, and its present is
lively and full of change.

The name Clapham seems to mean simply "the village or manor
on the hill", and until the 19th century Clapham was still largely
rural. Pepys spent his last years there, a sick man relishing its rustic
quiet and good country air. In a letter to him John Evelyn talks of
"your Paradisian Clapham". In the 18th and early 19th centuries
the district thereabouts was famous for growing asparagus and for
the lavender now found only in the name Lavender Hill.

Clapham's grandest days were in the Georgian and early Victorian
eras. A few great houses set in spacious grounds dominated the
parish, which was the home of wealthy merchants and bankers such
as the Thorntons and the Barclays. But it also became the base and
powerhouse of a group of zealous Anglican evangelicals known as
the Clapham Sect. These proselytizing and reformist Claphamites
founded the Bible Society, as well as a shorter-lived African
Academy to educate former slaves from Sierre Leone; and they
gave their backing, through the Thorntons' kinsman neighbour
William Wilberforce, to the Anti-Slavery movement.

From the late 18th century onwards, however, the Clapham
estates were increasingly broken up, and round the fringes of the
Common appeared parvenu "villas" of a mere thirty rooms or so.
The wealth and influence of the leading Victorian Claphamites
seems to have kept the railways at bay, diverting a line proposed to
run from Victoria via Clapham Park instead through Wandsworth

Common; but the arrival of the City and South London tube in 1900, with its cage-like, gate-ended carriages, paved the way for a further social revolution. The humbler terraces of lesser Londoners covered the gardens and grounds of the great houses and robbed Clapham of its social cachet. A municipal boundary still cuts the Common in two, but there is no longer much fire in the dispute which once led Battersea men to build banks and dig ditches across it, and Clapham men to take them down and fill them in.

By the 1930s the place was, indeed, regarded as very plebeian-suburban. Miss Alice Crossthwaite, who lives in an early-18th-century house with panelled interiors on North Side, remembers the response of well brought up folk in Kensington in the late 1930s when she admitted to living there. "They looked down and shuffled their feet in embarrassment; then softened it by saying 'Ah, one of those lovely houses on the North Side!'" But Clapham was still not one of those places where "people lived". She remembers that, when driving over Chelsea Bridge, one had the sensation of entering a different and totally unfashionable world. And yet Miss Crossthwaite, whose former ambassador brother lives across the Common from her in secluded and still private Crescent Grove, clearly loves

The gargantuan Victorian terraces by Sir James Knowles on the north side of the common, with Saturday footballers in the foreground.

Clapham. Its assets for her are its fresher air, greener vistas and (despite continuing demolitions and depredations) fine buildings. She also enjoys its cosmopolitan classlessness.

Farther along North Side, on the site of a former mansion, The Cedars, and forming a gateway to the later Cedars Road, stand two gartantuan Victorian terraces by Sir James Knowles, architect of the Grosvenor Hotel, which share that edifice's mansard roofs and overall architectural grandiloquence. Mrs May Cristea, whose husband came from Romania, told me she had lived in one or other of these ten huge houses since 1930. She once had a flat in the mansarded tower of the eastern terrace, with its splendid views across the Common to the south and to the heights of Hampstead and Highgate to the north. During the Second World War, she recalls, a high ranking army officer came to visit her there with a view to mounting an anti-aircraft gun on the roof – from which intention fortunately he was dissuaded. Eventually Mrs Cristea had moved into the one house still retaining its original 1860s interior, with gilded mirrors, scagliola columns, classical mythological paintings on the fourteen-foot ceilings and everywhere the ivy-leaf motif in iron and stone with which Knowles was obsessed.

Boating on the pond near south side attracts boys and girls of all ages. The Henry Thornton comprehensive school is seen through the trees in the background.

The house, now lovingly restored and maintained, was, when the Cristeas bought it in 1958, a squalid multi-occupied slum; and Mrs Cristea strongly criticized Lambeth Council's policy of buying other such houses only to earmark them for use by the homeless and by problem families who are, on the whole, unlikely to cherish them.

Clapham's attractions for her are its fresh air – local legend holds that it comes straight from Brighton – its fine trees and buildings and its proximity to central London ("By car, only nine minutes to Sloane Square"). Her worries and irritations include Lambeth's policy of acquiring and using (or misusing) listed historic buildings such as these two terraces, and a feeling of growing violence and social instability in the area. She mentions with wry amusement her terrace's brief spell of notoriety in 1976 when the police uncovered an IRA bomb factory there.

Another Clapham resident is John Letts, a director of the Folio Society, who founded National Heritage after the Clapham Transport Museum saga had convinced him that museums needed encouragement and protection from the bureaucracy. His house, which dates from 1795, is one of the few survivors of more than ninety such houses fringing the Common. It faces the garden rather than the Common and has a verandah and a bay stretching the whole height of the house. He and a friend split its twenty-nine rooms into two maisonettes: his top half of the house makes a spacious home for him, his wife and their four children as well as books and the paperwork of National Heritage. He bought the house from two old ladies, one of whom – the mother, in her nineties – he remembers seeing lying mob-capped in a four-poster.

For John Letts much of Clapham's attraction lies in that house and its garden of about an acre with mature trees, so that in summer, whether you look in the direction of the Common or towards the garden, there is scarcely a house to be seen. He also likes Clapham for its neighbourhood shops, both in the Old Town area and down the hill to the west at Northcote Road in what is, strictly speaking, Battersea.

Aspects of his adopted London village that sadden or worry Letts are the growing violence (ranging from purse-snatching to assault and murder on the Common), official destruction of some of the most attractive houses, the creation of a one-class council flat "ghetto" along the low-lying former marsh from Wandsworth to Waterloo, and what he regards as the GLC's war of attrition on motorists – aimed at the commuter, but making life increasingly difficult, he says, for local people who, in the present state of public transport, are dependent on cars.

Clapham these days seems full of laundries and trade unions and civil servants. Tom Jackson's Union of Post Office Workers has its headquarters in Crescent Lane with a back door to, and a stake in, the management of the still private Crescent Grove; the Seamen's Union head office, Maritime House, an endearingly pretentious 1930s classical pile, just manages not to dominate Old Town. Both the chairman and secretary of the Clapham Society were civil servants; while the redoubtable Miss Crossthwaite, besides taking on three children when her sister died, had a career in the Factory Inspectorate.

But small businesses also thrive. Susan Collier, daughter of actress Patience Collier, lives in and runs a successful fabric design studio in Old Town. She and her sister Sarah Campbell design for a number of leading shops, including Liberty, Heal's and Habitat. Mrs Campbell and her husband Alastair live in a nearby street of 1860s terrace houses which she told me she likes because they are small enough not to be either pretentious or split up. She enjoys the area because it is friendly and not striving to be smart (as a teenager, she disliked Kensington); approves of Lambeth Council because its social services department provided her with Louis, her two-year-old adopted son; but hates the phenomenon of "dead" houses, emptied and officially vandalized by the local authority while endlessly awaiting demolition. Pluses for Clapham as far as she is concerned include a good new bookshop, Tetric, in the High Street, a newish delicatessen, and a food store that sells bulk muesli. Minuses: "No fishmonger" and "dog shit on the Common".

Stephen Beaven, former secretary of the Clapham Society and when I first met him Tory councillor for one of Clapham's three-and-a-half wards, is a research executive with a leading retail chain. He lived in Clapham for twenty years, then moved just down the road in Kennington, but was involved from the start in the Clapham Society. The spur to its formation in 1963 was a desire to improve Clapham Cross, the tatty patch of green adjoining Clapham Common tube station and the clock-tower. Although the Council commissioned a townscape consultant to prepare designs, it remains unimproved.

The Society – one of whose principal begetters, Hermione Hobhouse, later became the Victorian Society's secretary – has however

*The busy heart of Clapham: the Alexandra Hotel and its
neighbours, opposite Clapham Common tube station.*

chalked up some successes. It opposed with others three Lambeth
comprehensive redevelopment schemes – at Iveley Road, Rectory
Grove and Acre Lane – and saw its opposition upheld by public
inquiry decisions. Beaven stresses that the Society's aim was not to
oppose redevelopment as such, but to oppose misguided redevelopment in the wrong places, which would destroy potentially attractive areas including houses and street patterns laid out by Thomas
Cubitt. Lambeth's new Stonhouse Street redevelopment west of
Old Town, for instance, although visually quite attractive, is open
to criticism because it destroyed the existing street pattern, some
houses which were both attractive and capable of improvement,
and above all, because it was a clean-sweep solution which created a
solid block of new, council estate development, instead of infilling
the gaps between sound and attractive houses. Hermione Hobhouse
argues that this finely tuned approach to redevelopment is now seen
to be not only preferable visually and socially, but also more
economical.

Lambeth seems to some extent to have accepted this argument,
and rehabilitation and renovation are now the order of the day in

Clapham. The state of the area's housing is reflected in two shop premises standing opposite each other in North Street, Old Town. One accommodates the architectural practice of Robert Watts, who moved there from Bloomsbury and reckons half his work now consists of local rehabilitation and conversion; the other is a "Community Shop", grant-aided by the Urban Aid Programme but started on local initiative, which provides advice to local people, especially on housing problems.

Compared with problems of homelessness, such matters as tree-felling may seem to be unimportant. To many Claphamites they are not. Dutch elm disease has robbed the Common of some 300 mature trees, and the Clapham Society has been much involved with the Council, which now cares for the Common, in selecting replacements. Replanting started in 1977 in The Avenue. The Society has also over the years taken the lead in getting historic building listings extended to take fuller account of the Victorian era; published its own survey in the late 1960s, which it has recently updated; and supports plans by the residents of the Georgian Crescent Grove to restore its South Side gateway to the splendour it enjoyed when such wealthy merchants as Julius Caesar Czarnikow lived there.

The Crescent in Crescent Grove, dating from 1827 and still a private street.

Traffic bothers different people in varying degrees, according to location and their sensitivity to noise. Because the Common is bounded on all three sides by A-roads, there is no easy solution. Stephen Beaven concedes that, though they seemed a good idea at the time, the one-way race-tracks in both the north-west and north-east corners of the Common, the product of the high tide of Traffic-Management-To-Ease-Traffic-Flow, have brought more disadvantages than advantages.

More broadly, Clapham seems to him to represent a basic mistake of British planning and housing policies in the 1950s and 1960s. Sincere planners and politicians, with a burning resolve to answer with radical solutions the problems of substandard housing and environment, concentrated on the broad stroke, the clean-sweep solution. They sought to knock down whole neighbourhoods and build from scratch. We know, with hindsight, that the sweep is rarely clean, the hiatus between the beginnings of blight and demolition and the final completion often wounding.

Meanwhile, as they kept their eyes firmly on the long-term objective, the planners paid all too little attention to apparently minor matters such as the decay of Victorian terraces or the uninspiring state of the Clapham Cross "mini-village green" by the clock-tower. Money and attention for such "inessentials" were lacking; and although Lambeth has clearly had a change of heart, it may nonetheless be significant that the Council still has not found the money or determination to improve that little triangle of grass which tens of thousands of people pass and look at daily. When Stephen Beaven argues that such environmental improvements are also "essentials" because they create a climate of confidence and well-being among ordinary people, he is speaking not as a Conservative politician but as a conservationist with pride in his particular London "village".

7

Spitalfields

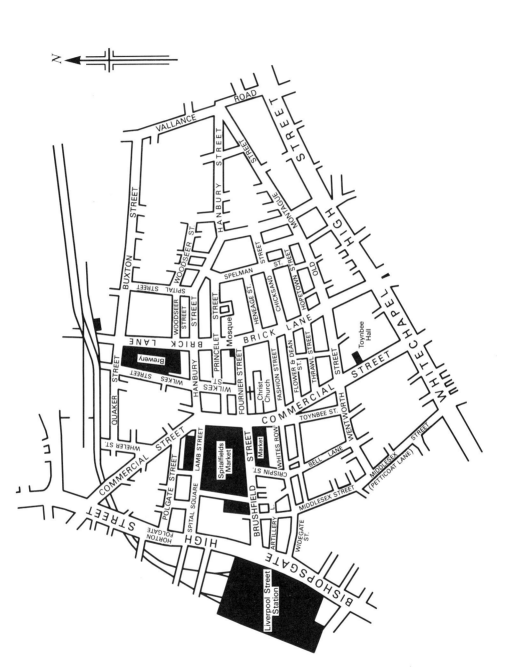

7

Spitalfields

Spitalfields has always meant immigrants, ever since the land had houses on it. Close to the City's eastern edge, it was also near the wharves and docks of the Pool of London. The first sizeable influx came 290 years ago – Protestant Huguenots from France, seeking refuge in a more liberal land after the revocation of the Edict of Nantes. There followed the great 19th-century waves of European Jews, driven from their native lands by pogroms, houndings and religious and economic constraints. Finally, mainly in the last six or seven years, has come the most recent immigration of them all, and the most desperate: Bengalis fleeing the starvation and strife of their overcrowded, poverty-stricken homeland.

Those first French Protestant immigrants were silk weavers, and the earliest and (potentially) most attractive houses in Spitalfields were built for them, on a hitherto largely green-field site, between about 1715 and 1730: tall, thin, elegant 18th-century houses with fine doorcases and panelled interiors, as well as the characteristic, spacious and well-lit weavers' garrets. Paradoxically, because Spitalfields "went down" socially in the 19th century, there was little redevelopment and whole chunks of 18th-century London have survived.

The quality of what is left of 18th-century Spitalfields comes through well from the London Borough of Tower Hamlets' recently published draft local plan. "Within the mixture of bustle, confusion, industry, noise and vitality . . . there are three small areas of outstanding Georgian buildings. Over 130 buildings are statutorily listed and they are contained within approximately ten short streets. Individually the buildings represent some of the finest small 18th-century houses in London, not least internally, and together they form a domestic townscape of exceptional quality, remarkably unchanged by modernization or conversion."

Unchanged, but not undamaged. For, more and more, the 20th century has used these premises as the 19th century began to do – for industrial and commercial purposes. One hundred years ago Spitalfields had become a quarter of sweat-shops; and today the pattern of small-scale, economically marginal, rag trade and skin trade enterprises persists. Early 18th-century houses built for single-family occupation by the gentry have taken, and are still taking, a colossal hammering from heavy-duty sewing machines and intensive human wear.

Stair treads are worn through, 18th-century balusters missing, panelling covered with asbestos; roofs leak, floors sag, brickwork bulges. GLC Historic Buildings staff cite cases of houses occupied by as many as five small businesses: half a dozen sewing machinists in one room, two or three trouser-pressers or fur-dressers in the next. Contrary to popular belief, old buildings do not often wear out. But, lack of maintenance apart, pressure of activities they were never meant to support, and sheer intensity of use, are destroying their fabric.

Spitalfields is a place of contrasts. On one side of the sluggish stream of container lorries that is Commercial Street, we find all the

Having a breather. Like most vegetable markets, Spitalfields starts and finishes early. View through market buildings to Hawksmoor's great Christ Church – now less well patronized than the nearby Great Mosque.

bustle and apparent chaos of the great vegetable market; on the other the Fashion Street conservation area, centred on Fournier Street. At one end stands Hawksmoor's noble Christ Church dating from 1729, and at the other what was originally the New French Church built in 1743.

This building tells the district's polyglot history well. First it housed the Lutherans; then, after the purely domestic immigration from English rural shires, the Wesleyans. Next it became the Great Synagogue, which it remained until the 1960s when, most of the Jewish Community having migrated once more to Golders Green and other airier suburbs, it fell empty. Now it is the Great Mosque which, as its new congregation needs no pews, packs in 800 or 900 for services.

Diagonally opposite at the other end of the street, in his high-porched 18th-century rectory, lives the Reverend Eddie Stride, rector of an empty Christ Church which needs $£\frac{1}{4}$ million for its repair. His less numerous faithful worship in an even older church in nearby Hanbury Street; but Christ Church, its roof secured by wise use of the proceeds from the sale of St John's, Smith Square, is not totally unused. Its crypt houses a shelter for some of the vagrant alcoholics who gather at the foot of the church's now railed-off front steps.

In two other ways, Christ Church is now being used more than it was. An ancient bell-ringing fraternity, the Society of Royal Cumberland Youths, has restored the belfry and installed a peal of eight bells from a demolished church in Clapham, with an $8\frac{1}{2}$-ton concrete ring-beam to support them. The ringers drive in from places like Orpington and Tunbridge Wells to change-ring and to ring for services. The "youths", incidentally, won their name in 1746 by ringing a peal for the Duke of Cumberland as he returned to London after his bloody victory at Culloden.

The other encouraging use is of the body of the church for music-making. Following a trial concert in November 1976 which demonstrated that this grimy, peeling interior was acoustically superb, the Friends of the church, with other musical and conservationist bodies, mounted two successive summer concert seasons. The 1978 season included a week's festival of lunchtime and evening concerts which the music-loving public greeted with enthusiasm. Eddie Stride's view, though sometimes misunderstood, is, as he expressed it to me, once again clear and forceful. Restoration is quite beyond his congregation's resources, and in Spitalfields the church has

Street-market in Brick Lane – these days as cosmopolitan and lively as an Eastern souk.

anyway more urgent social priorities, but Christ Church can and must be saved. "What is a £¼ million to preserve a thing of beauty when as a nation we spend £4,000 million a year on gambling?"

Behind Spitalfields' decaying 18th-century façades, and perhaps even more in the areas of Victorian housing outside the three small conservation areas, human problems abound, eating into the social and economic fabric of the community. Poor housing, high unemployment, low levels of skill, low educational standards, inadequate incomes – these are some of the "indicators of deprivation" which led the Home Office, the GLC and Tower Hamlets borough to set up a special community project with £200,000 of extra funds. When I talked to the project's director, Dr Richard Smith, it had been running for two years and he could point to some limited achievements: for instance, the provision of playground space in an area almost devoid of it, the planting of trees, provision of a local law centre, and the opening of two community centres, one of which caters specially for the needs of the Bengalis.

Working alongside Richard Smith is an ILEA project, the Montefiore Community Education Centre, housed in a Victorian three-decker former primary school and headed by Brian Merton. Sceptical of the chances of eradicating Spitalfields' social and economic problems because he believes areas like this to be endemic in our present society, Merton can nonetheless point to some real progress on a palliative level. "We administer first aid to casualties," he says.

First aid ranges from pre-school play-groups to adult education classes, and Montefiore has also made a valuable contribution to community development. Thus, for instance, its photographic workshop enables community action and tenants' groups to argue their cases graphically, in at least one instance persuading the borough to rehabilitate 19th-century cottage housing instead of demolishing it. Dr Smith points to parallel results from a grant given to one group to mount a traffic noise survey. This convinced the GLC that a tower block near busy Commercial Street really did need protective double-glazing. One of the disappointments has been that the indigenous population moved in and used the Montefiore facilities so intensively that the Bengalis were shy of

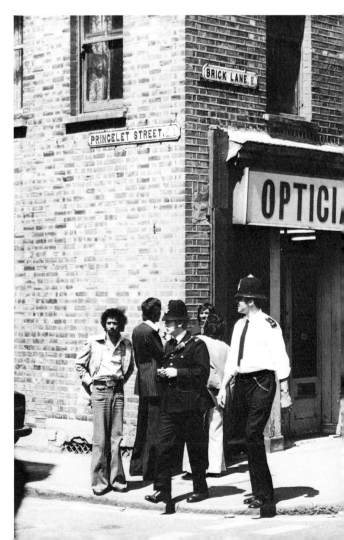

Bengalis in Spitalfields have recently had cause to complain bitterly of gangs of National Front supporters beating up lone youngsters from their community. Scotland Yard's response has been to establish a new police post in Brick Lane.

seeming to butt in. Hence their demand, now met, for a community centre of their own.

The main wave of Bengali arrivals in Spitalfields filled something of a vacuum. Many of the 18th-century houses round Fournier Street, typically with gardens built over as workshops or a row of lavatories – the minimum the Factory Acts required – lining what had become a small yard, were falling empty as the Jewish rag trade proprietors moved out or closed down. The Bengalis stepped in with their own small rag trade and skin trade enterprises; and, though 18th-century houses (whose interior walls are often only inch-thick wood panelling) provide at best unsuitable and hazardous premises for light industry, they are a source of local jobs. Gap sites in the area ought to offer scope for erecting suitable replacement premises, sometimes behind replica façades, but that has not yet even begun to happen.

Proximity to the City has provided other entrepreneurial and job opportunities for Asian immigrants. For instance, Mr Ataur Rahman Choudhury, a committee member of the Bengali Action Group, has lived there since 1962 and runs an Indo-Bangladesh restaurant whose customers are mainly City businessmen. Spitalfields is a friendly place, he says, but housing is often bad and overcrowded.

What of the district's previous wave of immigrants, the now indigenous Jewish Cockneys? Michael Morris, forty-eight-year-old taxi-driver, member of the Spitalfields Project's consultative committee, its steering group and of one of the confusing array of action groups, likes his native London village because it has a sense of community, is not anonymous, and is beautifully central for a cabby to operate. It has, he thinks, suffered from the upheaval of the huge Gardiner's Corner road scheme at Aldgate East and the associated redevelopment; and from the loss of local amenities like cinemas, eel-pie shops and, more recently, an invaluable neighbourhood Woolworth's.

On the plus side, the community has been learning to flex its muscles, speak out clearly, and teach the authorities a thing or two about what it wants and needs – whether a longer green time for pedestrians on the Commercial Street pelican crossing, or local housing policies more attuned to local people's preferences and less disruptive of existing communities. Morris expressed himself worried and angry at attempts to blame all the area's ills on the Asian immigrants. His family had seen it all in the 1930s, when the

Jews were the target. A bachelor, Morris lives in a 19th-century tenement block due for demolition and thinks he may move out of Spitalfields when rehoused, "though I shall always be involved in the area".

In contrast, economist Eric Elstob – half his family were Swedish but he hails from the West Country – had in 1977 only recently moved into Spitalfields, and is intent on staying there. He came looking for possible office premises for the investment trust firm which employs him, looked at the houses and "came to the conclusion that the one thing they should *not* be used for was offices. They should be lived in again as houses." Backing this conviction with action, he bought his Fournier Street house in 1973, set about restoring it with the aid of a local builder, and then moved in to finish the less basic work himself.

Elstob revels in Spitalfields, from the genteel vagrant "Onion Lill", who sweeps the pavement with a broom made from newspaper and dosses on his doorstep in wet weather, to the Bengali pub where even the juke box titles are in Sanskrit. His own house is superb, having been built as a "showhouse" by an 18th-century master carpenter and owned for several generations, until Elstob bought it, by a Bath architect and his forebears. He welcomes to it a succession of foreign students and other visitors who come and camp amidst DIY chaos and drink his China tea. Elstob says he believes

This early-18th-century doorway in Fournier Street shows the architectural quality of the best Spitalfields merchant houses. In the 17th and 18th centuries Spitalfields was a smart address.

passionately that what Spitalfields needs is not the reinforcement of a working-class – still less a white – ghetto, but a healthy admixture of social classes and nationalities.

He pays warm tribute to both the GLC and Tower Hamlets for the encouragement and aid they have given him in restoring his Fournier Street house, but he disagrees with those councillors who think turning houses like his gradually over to single-family occupation would drive out much valued local employment. It need not do so, he argues, for there is room on empty sites in Spitalfields and its surroundings for purpose-built premises for the rag trade at rents no more than those paid by many Bengali entrepreneurs for their present unsuitable workshops.

Others, while sharing his enthusiasm, are less optimistic. They see 18th-century Spitalfields as teetering on the brink of collapse. As one GLC Historic Buildings official has put it, "Our system of historic buildings laws and grants can work very well when there is an economic head of steam which only needs topping up. But at present we have no machine that can begin to tackle a Spitalfields situation, least of all in a time of recession."

He and his colleagues speak from a decade and a half's experience of patiently trying to put together packages of grant aid and planning consents that would encourage companies or individuals to take on the restoration of Spitalfields houses. There have been some successes, but not enough, and they have not come fast enough. Spitalfields can still be saved: the decay is controllable, the gaps few enough to be filled in replica.

More recently a comprehensive survey of about seventy houses has investigated in detail the special interest, state of repair and injuriousness of use of each. This has allowed the official conservationists to draw up priorities for remedial action. One conclusion to be drawn from the results was that Spitalfields needs a special package on the conservation front just as urgently as it needed urban aid. The solution GLC Historic Buildings men have been moving towards is this: the conservation apparatus should be used only to restore the houses as shells, at what will still seem a reasonable cost. Others, such as housing associations, can then turn them, internally, into acceptable homes with the use of a different kind of public funding, and again at what will appear a reasonable cost. Probably only in this way can these tall, panelled, thin-staired and still beautiful structures be saved and made once more fit for the only purpose that really suits – as people's homes.

8

Mill Hill

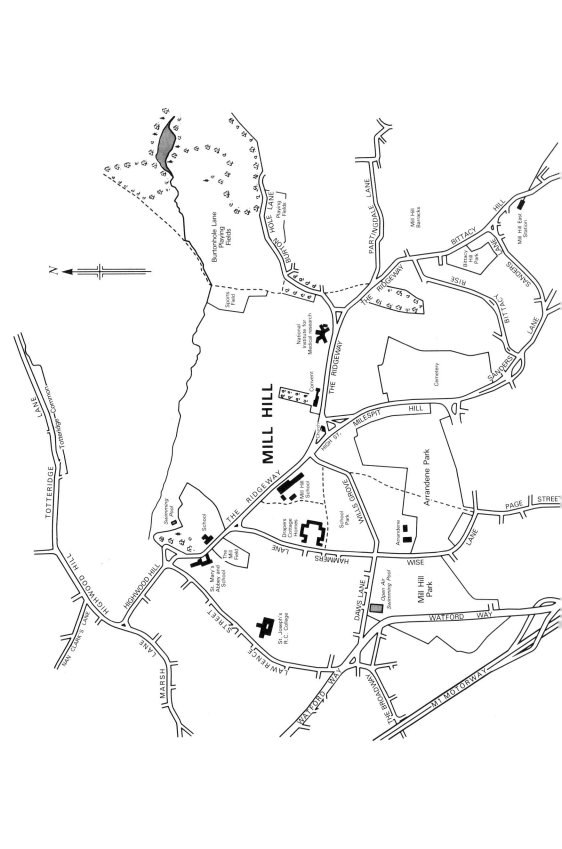

MILL HILL

N

Burtonhole Lane Playing Fields

Sports Field

BURTON HOLE LANE

Playing Fields

PARTINGDALE LANE

Mill Hill Barracks

BITTACY HILL

Mill Hill East Station

Bittacy Hill Park

National Institute for Medical research

THE RIDGEWAY

RISE

BITTACY

LANE

SANDERS

SANDERS LANE

Convent

Cemetery

TOTTERIDGE LANE

Totteridge Common

Church

High St.

MILESPIT HILL

HILL

Arrandene Park

PAGE STREET

Swimming Pool

School

THE RIDGEWAY

Mill Hill School

Drapers Cottage Homes

School Park

WILLS GROVE

Arrandene

HIGHWOOD HILL

St. Mary's Abbey and School

The Mill Field

LANE

HAMMERS LANE

WISE

LANE

MARSH LANE

NAN CLARK'S LANE

LAWRENCE STREET

St. Joseph's R.C. College

DAWS LANE

Open Air Swimming Pool

Mill Hill Park

WATFORD WAY

WATFORD WAY

THE BROADWAY

M1 MOTORWAY

8

Mill Hill

Mill Hill is perhaps the nearest to a "real" village of any place so far visited in this series, which may surprise anyone who knows the name only from sign posts on the A1 or M1. Indeed Mill Hill Broadway, squeezed between the rush and roar of these two major highways, is one of at least three places that bear the name. Another is Mill Hill East, a station on a truncated limb of the Northern Line, surrounded by rather grey streets of comfortable 1930s and 1950s semis, with a fair suburban tree cover and, dividing it from Finchley, the green space bounded by the Dollis Brook.

Neither of these is the real Mill Hill. That lies between them on and around the heights of The Ridgeway; its foliage is of an altogether more luxuriant kind, its spaces are more spacious, its vistas longer. Large institutional landholders – Mill Hill School, the National Institute for Medical Research, the Roman Catholic Church, the Army – have provided as valuable a barrier to urban sprawl as formal Green Belt policies. Mill Hill has stayed a village girdled by woods and green fields.

Arnold Bennett in one of his novels once described a small, mid-European principality as having a population nine-tenths composed of inn-keepers and charcoal burners. At first sight on a sunny day Mill Hill's population seems to consist nine-tenths of girls on horses; but as you dig deeper you discover among the foliage considerable numbers of lawyers (Lord Justice Sellers and Lord Gardiner among them); film and show-business people; doctors and medical research workers; Roman Catholic fathers, sisters, brothers and others; and, of course, schoolmasters.

Mill Hill School does not, however, dominate. Its classical main building (1825, by the architect of the Royal Exchange, Sir William Tite) is assured but modest behind its greens and fringe of trees. The lawns behind the Tite building abound with splendid and exotic trees, many of them planted there by Peter Collinson, the

*From The Ridgeway, Mill Hill School may keep a low profile;
but to the south Sir William Tite's great classical portico looks
out boldly towards that Other Place on its distant hill – Harrow.*

Quaker botanist whose house the school's founders bought to
accommodate their first pupils. From these same lawns the views
southwards are wide and long, taking in, among other places, that
Other Place, Harrow on its distant hill. So self-effacing is the public
school these days that bus conductors whose vehicles were stopped
outside it have been known to look blank in response to the
question, "Where is Mill Hill School?"

The school began in 1807 as a "grammar school for Protestant
dissenters", but was never exclusively Non-conformist. Its doors
were opened to compensate for those of Anglican public schools,
which were slammed rudely in the faces of dissenters. Nowadays
some of the stricter brethren rather frown on its officially sanctioned
un-Sabbatarian activities.

Dissent of many kinds has prospered here on the heights of Mill
Hill, as well as longevity and, it is said, ghosts. Richard Seifert,
architect of Centre Point and many less known but socially more
useful buildings, lives in a modest but marvellously sited 1930s
house on Milespit Hill, which he bought in 1946 for £3,000, helped
by his colonel's gratuity on leaving the army. All his family – his
wife, their three children and three grandchildren next door – have
heard the cries of a young girl who, local legend has it, was thrown
alive into a pit there in pre-Roman times.

Seifert told me he has never wanted to move either out of his
green-roofed 1930s house or away from Mill Hill. The Green Belt
protects the view from his garden, where the wildlife includes a

visiting red fox and a nuthatch; and, though he is possibly London's busiest architect, he does his civic duty as a magistrate on the High Barnet bench. With three generations of Seiferts, he was, he quipped, something of a local Forsyte, and "almost the oldest inhabitant". In these parts this sometime builder of unloved tower blocks ranks as a committed conservationist; he said he fervently trusted that Westminster City Council would not try to cover land it owned farther down the hill with council housing; and modestly admits that the award-winning infill cottages next to the 17th-century Nicoll Almshouses were designed by his firm.

Just along The Ridgeway and out of the tiny High Street, said to be the shortest in London, is white weather-boarded Rosebank, a Quaker meeting house from 1678 to 1719; and, representing a different kind of dissent, there stands on or near The Ridgeway a number of Roman Catholic institutions, the most impressive being St Mary's Abbey, close to the Mill Field; St Vincent's, with its long, tree-lined vistas towards Totteridge; and St Joseph's, the college and headquarters of an international missionary order

Richard Seifert's house in Milespit Hill, which he bought in 1946 for £3,000 but has been much extended. In Mill Hill, Seifert ranks as a strong conservationist.

which in the more than 110 years of its existence has sent more than 1,000 young men out to distant lands.

The building, which dates from 1871, is more impressive from afar than close to. Its hundred-foot tower is topped by a statue of St Joseph which was recently taken down for repair by a specially hired crane on a lorry. Father Peter Dirven, who showed me round the college, explained that the strength of the Roman Catholic community in Mill Hill derived from the benefactions of Cardinal Vaughan, later Archbishop of Westminster. Since his day things have clearly changed: the missionary students normally go about, like most other young men of their age, in jeans or corduroys, and the bar in the student wing of the college serves Newcastle Brown. Around the college lies a small farm, run by a lay brother who has in his care some forty milk and beef cattle and several hundred chickens. A place so huge is difficult to keep up, despite some modernization; and the Fathers recently had to cope with the expense of installing a sophisticated new fire detection and alarm system. Brothers and students have also been working hard to replant a landscape denuded by the felling of some eighty diseased elms.

So much for the Roman Catholic seminary. What of the "Protestant dissenters' grammar school" up the hill? Alan Elliott, then headmaster, told me how he had come there "from another village – Marlborough" in 1974. He said that Mill Hill School kept a low profile these days and was not at all stand-offish. The older boys did their bit by way of social work – he talked of Mike, a head of house, and the old lady whose home he cleaned from top to bottom. "He was the only person she would let inside. Mike is dyslexic, but wing-three-quarter for the XV."

Mill Hill now takes ten to fifteen girls each year into the Sixth Form, both as boarders and day pupils. Its roll of 520 pupils includes 310 boarders who pay £2,000 a year. For what? Social cachet, a caring community, good manners, small classes, good teaching, a tailor-made curriculum? All these, but also for the kind of adventurousness that has pioneered O-level teaching of the geography and history of France in the French language, and a Field Centre at Dent in the heart of the Pennines.

Mill Hill is seen by many as a friendly, truly village community. Several families have been there since before the Second World War, and in some cases even longer. One new arrival was told by a friend from the other side of the world, "You're going to Mill Hill.

You'll be a customer of Vincetts." Vincetts is a picturesquely housed and excellent village butcher, a family firm of several generations, which Millhillians like to claim as the best in London. And Mill Hill is the kind of place that both appreciates such quality and carries its fame to the four corners of the world.

Another anecdote concerns the Elliott family's ginger kitten, which strayed while they were away in Wales for the weekend. They eventually recovered the errant cat and were, he said, able to retrace its movements over the preceding two days, accounting, by reference to people who had fed, looked after or simply noticed it, for every single half-hour of its absence. That, he said with pride, is the kind of place Mill Hill is.

Not everyone has so glowing a report. Denis Rothwell, a Yorkshireman, came to Mill Hill via Cambridge University and Pye. Head of the engineering department at the National Institute for Medical Research and one of about 600 people who work there, he has lived in Mill Hill for six years. He says it is a beautiful place combining the best of living in London and the country, but that "it lacks corporate spirit". Of Mill Hill East, he comments: "We don't like to talk about it! It doesn't look or feel like the other Mill Hill." Of the Broadway area, he remarks that as a shopping centre it has gone down of late, partly because it has felt a commercial draught from the new Brent Cross shopping centre. "There is no pub on The Broadway, and a bakery that used to serve good, cheap lunches has now become a building society branch." The Broadway has plenty of potential, but it is largely unrealized, says Rothwell. The whole area "seems to have no focus".

On the other hand, Mill Hill does have some thriving musical activities, and this is important for Rothwell, who is an accomplished

Mill Hill Broadway, which now lives in the shadow of the elevated M1 and is said to be losing some trade to the new Brent Cross shopping centre.

pianist and plays chamber music with the Barbican Music Group. In the great battleship of a research station that towers up at the eastern end of The Ridgeway, he arranges a charity concert each year on a professional or semi-professional level in aid of the Imperial Cancer Research Fund. Once, recently, April Cantelo came to sing; on another occasion they had a musical version of Tolkien's *The Hobbit* – which sounds all very Mill Hillish. Another resident, Wilfred Ransome, has brought top-flight musicians like Alfred Brendel, Rubinstein and the Amadeus Quartet to play in Mill Hill at charity concerts, and continued to do so after moving to the South Coast. But the ghosts of Mill Hill do not let go that easily. Ransome moved back after only a year or two's exile, so strong was the spell of these healthy northern heights.

Lack of shops and lack of buses are two frequent complaints on The Ridgeway. Another is the price of houses; for though, superficially, there is a range of house sizes, from near stately home to tiny cottage, young married couples of modest means often find Mill Hill beyond their grasp. Thus Rothwell points out that, though the older among the technicians in his department may have bought houses in Mill Hill when they first came to work there, more

Rural Mill Hill. It is green-belt views and footpaths like these that draw people to Mill Hill and hold them there.

recent recruits to NIMR are forced to commute from towns farther out in the green belt, such as St Albans.

At the northern end of The Ridgeway the road swoops down under St Mary's Abbey, then climbs again up Highwood Hill to join the end of the Totter*ridge*. Here, round Nan Clark's Lane, is another little community hidden away, of farms and film people's romantic residences, thick spinneys, wading birds and yet another tortured spirit. For the lane gets its name from poor Nan Clark, a servant girl strangled in its deep shadows who still, they say, cries out in terror on suitable moonless nights. At a cottage on the corner of the lane I met straight-backed seventy-nine-year-old Miss Freda Weedon, who with her father and sister Elsie ran the dairy farm set up by film director Sydney Box. Ah, what a milk round was that for celebrities! Ian Carmichael, and Peter Rogers, producer of the *Carry On* series, from the world of entertainment, Judge Sellers and Lord Gardiner from the law, Sir John and Lady Laing from the world of business. "Lovely people," said Miss Weedon, "and they live so long up here. It is very healthy, you know!" To prove her point past the window trotted Lady Sellers, silver-haired, pink-cheeked and riding side-saddle. Shoppers in The Broadway are still once or twice a year vouchsafed the sight of this venerable lawyer's wife shopping in the shadow of the M1 – in horse and trap.

Round the corner from Miss Weedon live Dulcie Rispoli and her engineer husband Peter. He is one of those happy Mill Hill residents who have no need to commute even the twenty-five minutes it takes to drive to the West End, because he keeps his work at home. In his case, work consists of making the apparatus that simulates waves in the tanks used to test models of the machines that may one day extract our energy needs from wave-power. Mrs Rispoli told me that she was, in any time she has left from running their Hampstead hi-fi shop and bringing up children, secretary of the twenty-eight-year-old Mill Hill Preservation Society. Unlike some amenity societies, it finds itself most often fighting shoulder to shoulder with the local authority, the London Borough of Barnet, in defence of the Green Belt, historic buildings, unfelled woodlands and unspoiled vistas. Footpaths in this area are well known and well trodden, and only very determined developers try to wear down the planning authority's defences.

For not only is Mill Hill village protected by conservation area status, numerous tree preservation orders and its deterrent Green Belt, but an "Article 4 Direction" forbids householders to do, without prior approval, even those minor extensions and alterations permitted to the residents of less favoured districts. Two recent planning issues in which the Society took a hand concerned proposals for a giant "leisure park" at nearby Edgwarebury, scotched for the moment by borough refusal; and the restoration by a family export/import business of the near derelict Lawrence Farmhouse, a charming 18th-century rural fragment in the otherwise dully urban world of Mill Hill Broadway.

Down Nan Clark's Lane, in a thatched but strangely curving 1930s cottage, live the Hobsons: Marina, her businessman husband Ron and their three children. They have lived in this house for more than sixteen years, but had been in Mill Hill four years "before we even knew this place existed". Though the lights of the distant M1 and some traffic noise reach the house, it is a remarkably tranquil, sequestered spot, and they have fought to keep it so. Mrs Hobson runs a farm bought from Sydney Box, and a bird sanctuary in the wooded area known as Wilberforce Walks, part of the grounds of the now demolished house where "the Liberator" once lived. (Wilberforce also built St Paul's Church as an Anglican chapel of ease on The Ridgeway, right opposite the handsome, classical Nonconformist chapel provided for that "dissenter school".)

The Hobsons bought the land round the tree-fringed pond at Wilberforce Walks after fighting, alongside the Preservation Society and Mill Hill as a whole, proposals to infiltrate this tranquil wooded area with speculative housing. It was then full of car bodies. They cleared and fenced it, and then, almost before she knew it, Mrs Hobson found herself running a convalescent home for ailing wild fowl, mostly birds hit by cars. She said that many neighbours, such as Miss Weedon, now had keys, and sitting in the sun surrounded by now very tame wild fowl is a favourite afternoon recreation with some of Mill Hill's older people. Mrs Hobson also shows round visitors interested in birds, and sometimes has requests at Hallowe'en from ghost-watchers who want to sit up all night there for the return of Nan Clark and her anguished fellow-spirits. Of the feathered population, Donald, a drake found injured after a collision with a car by a woman in Welwyn Garden City and nursed by her in her council flat, is the most engaging. He is personable, greedy, very tame, well-preserved for his age and, said Mrs Hobson, had bred three families. Clearly it is not only longevity and ghosts that the air in Mill Hill encourages.

9

Marylebone

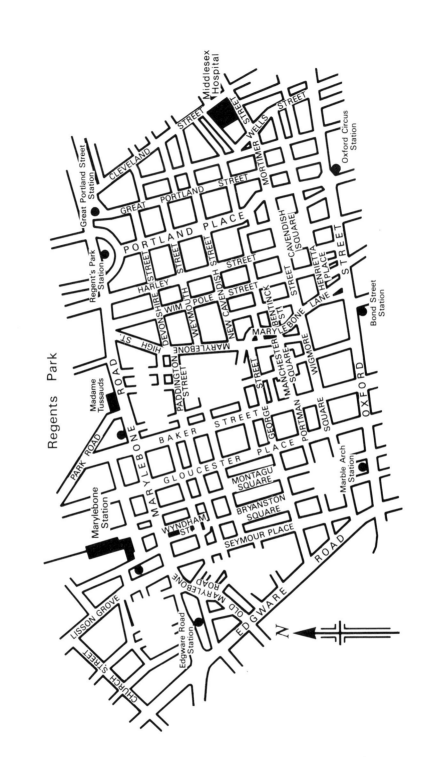

9

Marylebone

Marylebone is in and yet in a curious way not of the West End. When the Russian ambassador went hunting in Marylebone Park in 1601, the village of St Mary-le-Bourne ("bourne" being the Tyburn brook) was still very much a village surrounded by fields. In 1650 the gardens of the manor house were separately leased to some entrepreneur in the 17th-century leisure industry, who opened them as a public pleasure garden. Pepys, on his first visit there in 1668, wrote: "Then we abroad to Marrowbone, and there walked in the garden . . . and a pretty place it is."

At that time the metropolis stretched barely as far as Soho Square, so that a gap of half a mile or so separated "Marrowbone" from London. Urbanization began after John Holles, Duke of Newcastle, bought the estate in 1708. Cavendish Square (1717) was the start; adjacent streets dating from the 1740s onwards commemorate members of his family: Henrietta, his daughter, is remembered by Henrietta Place; her husband, Edward Harley, Earl of Oxford and Mortimer, by Harley and Mortimer Streets; and their son-in-law, William Bentinck, Duke of Portland, by Bentinck Street and Portland Place. The successors of the Portlands, the Howard de Walden Estate, still own the freeholds of large chunks of the parish.

Cavendish Square and the developments that followed were not only urban but urbane: streets and squares, spacious and rectilinear, a well-ordered Georgian town plan of well-ordered, gentlemanly houses, discreetly expressing the assurance and wealth of their age. Their survival is one of the features that those who live and work in Marylebone today delight in; another is the narrow, curving line of Marylebone Lane as it wiggles its rustic diagonal from Oxford Street across Wigmore Street to Marylebone High Street.

The High Street itself appeals by virtue of contrast: by its bustle, animation and intensity of business activity, which are the more

Park Crescent, the fulcrum of Nash's great vista through Regent's Park. The architect was better at overall design than contract supervision. In recent years the Crown Estates Commissioners found themselves obliged virtually to rebuild these and other terraces behind their beautiful façades.

marked after the sobriety of traditionally residential streets and squares to east and west. But what do we mean by "Marylebone" today? Not all the old borough, for St John's Wood, remote and comfortable beyond Regent's park and Mr Lord's cricket ground, is distinct and suburban, which Marylebone most certainly is not. Local consensus seems to take Oxford Street as its southern, Edgware Road as its western and the zig-zagging diagonal boundary with Camden as its eastern limit – including, most appropriately, the Middlesex Hospital, but excluding such dubious haunts of publishers and poets as Fitzroy Square. To the north, one must be arbitrary. Regent's Park, though architecturally indivisible, cedes only its southern and western Nash terraces to Marylebone; but

Marylebone the railway station we must include, and the whole chunky proletarian salient straddling Lisson Grove.

Who lives and works in this London "village"? Its character has changed a good deal in the last forty years from stately residential to sometimes hugger-mugger professional. Dominant activities today include medicine, dentistry and diplomacy. Though not as rich as Belgravia in ambassadorial presences, Marylebone can boast a dozen embassies and high commissions, among them the Chileans, the Polish, the Swiss, the Kenyan and, inscrutable behind the peeling and shuttered Portland Place façade, that of the People's Republic of China. A Chinese diplomatic post for well over a century, this was the building from which Sun Yat Sen escaped while waiting to be shipped back by the Imperial Chinese government to imprisonment in Peking; it was also the scene in the late 1960s of a bizarre battle between club-wielding embassy staff and London policemen. Later it was the battlefield in a conservationist cold war; for the Chinese, who moved their main operations a few doors farther south, proposed in the early 1970s to demolish this James Adam building and redevelop the site with offices for embassy use. There was argument about whether our historic buildings laws or an embassy's extra-territorial status prevailed, but it seemed until recently the Chinese were dissuaded or prevented. Nonetheless, conservationist-minded souls in the Royal Institute of British Architects just opposite (and there are such among its staff!) have watched in anguish as this fine Georgian building crumbles and decays. In October 1978 the Secretary of State for the Environment gave the Chinese permission to rebuild, but stipulated that they must keep the Portland Place façade and at least the appearance of its side elevation in Weymouth Street.

One of Marylebone's attractions is Maison Sagné in the High Street which is reputed to sell the best croissants in London. The original M. Sagné was a Swiss. Nowadays, still a private business, it is run by two partners – Roy Hall, the baker and pastrycook, and his *alter ego* in the shop, Stanley Comras – who still produce such specialities as Mont Blanc (chestnuts and cream) in the original kitchens used by Sagné when he founded the business in 1921. "Old-fashioned, but very clean," says Mr Comras. The business, he adds, is now catering for the fourth generation of the same families. He says he notices two changes: first, whereas in the 1930s Maison Sagné's customers occupied the tall Portman and Howard de Walden estate houses as family houses, now they tended to be doctors, dentists, diplomats and others who only worked in the area; second, the range of people who are able to indulge a taste for Sagné's particular kind of luxury has broadened. "We still sell very much the same lines," Comras told me. "You might have expected dieting to make a difference, but we haven't noticed it. I suppose more people can afford the things we sell."

Fashions *have* changed, however, in the waxworks world. In the 1930s Madame Tussaud's, the collection of waxworks brought to Baker Street by that famous lady in 1835 and moved round the corner to its present location in Marylebone Road in 1884, was visibly languishing. The arrival of the cinema had, it seems, made people consider waxworks dull and old-fashioned. Now, partly thanks to refurbishment and initiative by the present management, it has more than recovered its old popularity. In 1976 for the first time more than two million people visited it.

Juliette Simpkins, publicity officer at Tussaud's, told me she had worked there since 1965. She does not live in the area, but would like to do so if she could find a flat there. From her office window she has observed over two years the rebuilding of the Nash terraces behind their famous façades. Cream-painted, elegant Nash and the green, bosky park are a combination she regards a "superb".

Close by is another view which Kenneth Williams, actor and television funny man, used to enjoy when he lived in nearby Harley Court. He looked down on Thomas Hardwick's columned and classical parish church, St Mary's in Marylebone Road, with its cupola and statues of virgins picked out "in real gold leaf", all lit magically by the afternoon sun. Tranquillity, views of the Regent's Park lake – what more could a weary actor ask? It was a veritable paradise until the air pump or giant extractor fan on the roof ran amok. "Instead of a gentle purr, it started to go b-bump b-bump," continuously, day and night. So Williams gave up and moved in with his mother in Osnaburgh Street.

The things Kenneth Williams told me he likes best about Marylebone are "first and foremost the amount of green in the parks and the squares, which really is magnificent"; second, the quality and variety of local shopping (somewhat eroded, he said, by high rents forcing useful shops out); third, the area's geographical convenience and accessibility; and fourth, its cosmopolitan character.

Another Marylebone personality, who gets some 8,000 people in and out of his building every day, is Arthur Spicer, British Rail's

*Stanley Comrass at Sagné's, founded in 1921 and reputed to sell
the best croissants in London.*

area manager at Marylebone Station. Born and brought up in
Highbury, he started his railway career as junior booking clerk at
Marylebone in 1937, served in the forces and returned twice – once
in 1945, to the booking office, then after graduating elsewhere to
station-master and assistant area manager status, to become Marylebone's station-master. The area manager's writ runs not only in the
station; he also rules over 128 route miles of track to Aylesbury on
one line, on the other to Wycombe, the Risboroughs, Bicester and
Banbury.

Marylebone was, before Beeching, a main-line terminus, connecting through lush Edwardian shires and Chiltern halts with the
Midlands and the north. Though Spicer's 700 trains a week are all
suburban diesels, his territory, he told me, had been slightly
extended, with Banbury added on to the end of the Bicester service.
Another change concerns the scene to the north of the station.
There the Victorian railway builders swept away great tracts of
artisan housing for their marshalling yards. Now the local authorities have, not before time, been putting houses back again.

The climate has also changed in another way at Marylebone. Across its cathedral close of a taxi yard, by way of the decorous cast-iron *porte-cochère* if it's raining, lies the former Great Central Hotel, for some years past headquarters of British Railways. BR's chairman, Sir Peter Parker, glimpsed now and then from across the way, has shown rather more of an eye for our railways' architectural heritage than his predecessors. At least he gives that impression, and the anathema which the Victorian Society and its fellow-travellers have bitterly tossed at BR since the Euston Arch debacle have of late been softened.

Marylebone and Baker Street Stations were essentially creations of the late Victorian and Edwardian age, bringing money and taste from lush Lutyensesque pads in the Chilterns to make more money and spend it in this agreeable part of the metropolis. The district itself remained a fertile patch for men of property to cultivate. Folkard & Hayward have been estate agents in Baker Street since 1899; a Folkard, though retired from partnership, was, at least until recently, still consultant to the firm; and its senior partner now, John Stacey, is son of Albert Stacey who joined the original Folkard & Hayward as an office boy.

Partner Albert Harrold, who came to the firm in 1926, told me he had watched its practice change from largely residential to include a large proportion of commercial buildings, and seen a post-war

Marylebone station, quietest and most cathedral-like of London termini.

generation of newly affluent businessmen step in in the wake of the traditional upper-middle-class families. Comparisons on rents and prices are difficult, he said, because, for a start, in the 1930s you never sold a flat or maisonette. In those days he might have been able to offer you a maisonette on three floors with six rooms plus kitchen and bathroom for £150 a year – less than £3 a week. Now the same space would probably be divided into three flats each of which, if you could get hold of them, would cost you £800 a year plus quite heavy rates. Much has changed in his time: more traffic, Marylebone Road widened, new office blocks, Baker Street to a great extent redeveloped; but large areas are physically unchanged, thanks at least partly to good estate management by Portman and Howard de Walden.

Sometimes the estates' beneficent controls seem a shade too stringent. In the north-west corner of Portman Square a fine Georgian house now provides quarters for the Royal Institute of British Architects' unrivalled collection of drawings and for an exhibition gallery provided by Mr H. J. Heinz II of 57 varieties fame. Its doorway is round the corner in Gloucester Place, and the absence of even the most discreet notice on the railings in the square has confused many and defeated some; but, until recently at least, the Portman Estate has been reluctant to sanction such an aid to discovery. John Harris, curator of the collection, was lately elected president of the well-established St Marylebone Society, an amenity society which not only fights environmental threats, but seeks actively to promote improvements. One of its pet schemes recently was the paving over and barring to traffic of a section of Wyndham Place round Smirke's St Mary's Church, which Westminster City Council has welcomed, is ready to carry out, but lacks the cash for. The society commendably set about raising the £8,500 needed for it. A first stage has recently been "pedestrianized".

Doctors really began to move in to Harley Street and Wimpole Street in the mid-19th century, originally using ground floor dining-rooms and libraries as waiting and consulting rooms and living "above the shop". These were the frock-coated surgeons whom Joseph Lister (for thirty-two years resident in Park Crescent) sought so long in vain to convince of the need for sterility under the scalpel. In an elegant stucco building in Chandos Street is probably the oldest medical society in the world. Founded in 1773 by a Quaker physician, Dr John Coakley Lettsom, the Medical Society of London sought, evidently with some measure of success, to bring together the three warring factions at that time: physicians, surgeons and apothecaries. Originally limited to twenty of each, the Society now has about 600 members.

It was perhaps in the 1930s that the area bounded by Portland Place, Wigmore Street, Marylebone High Street and Marylebone Road earned the nickname "Pill Island", but only in the 1940s and 1950s that the consulting room in a family house largely gave way to multi-plated establishments, with ten or a dozen medical men sharing the same front door. If Harley Street and the streets about it still retain some residential character, it may be partly because of a Howard de Walden restriction limiting professional use to ground, first and second floors; partly because a few stubborn or quixotic medical men still allow themselves the luxury of living on the premises. Doctors like Harley Street not only for its reputation (notice how Harley Street numbering runs fifty yards and three doors down some side streets), but also because there are many clinics and hospitals in convenient proximity. But doctors are on the defensive. One physician I talked to, who had been in Harley Street for thirty years, bemoaned the fact that solicitors and accountants were taking up new leases at figures which poor medical specialists in private practice can no longer afford. Moreover, he added, the present tally of about 2,000 private medical practitioners in the Harley Street area is also dropping because newly qualified doctors and surgeons increasingly choose a salaried, pensionable and broadly nine to five existence.

East of Pill Island is the polyglot, cultivatedly Bohemian but essentially Establishment world of "the Beeb", centring on Broadcasting House itself and its big and nasty extension which so overshadows Nash's All Souls'. Round the corner in Wells Street lurks upstart but successful ITN; farther east is the dowdier area round Great Portland Street which paradoxically houses the rag trade and much that is smart and innovative in fashion design. Architects, as we have noted, have their headquarters in Portland Place, in a 1930s building by George Grey Wornum which also houses the splendid but hard-up British Architectural Library.

Portland Place is handy enough for architects from the Charlotte Street/Percy Street/Fitzroy Square area, where denim jackets and string ties are as common as CD plates further west. Fewer architects practise in Marylebone. One of them, James Melvin of Gollins Melvin Ward (who moved from Russell Square twenty-seven years ago), expresses well what so many people find attractive in this part of London: art galleries, shops, restaurants all within easy reach to make life pleasant and civilized; but, above all, for their bread and butter, accessibility to prospective clients at an address – 18 Manchester Square W1 – which may be reckoned confidence-inspiring.

Across the great divide of Marylebone Road, with its traffic spilling down alarmingly from the Harrow Road flyover, lies a very different Marylebone: not elegant or fashionable but with a vigorous life and community of its own, and one of London's liveliest street markets. Illtyd Harrington, bearded, larger-than-life Welshman, East End schoolteacher and, until the 1977 election turnabout, deputy leader of the GLC, lives with friends in a Westminster City Council maisonette in the part of Marylebone between Edgware Road and the station.

"I was always fascinated by this area," he says. "It was a Cockney village which on the face of it had no right to be there. It's an almost baroque working-class area with its kind of strong family ties and matriachal rule one associates more with Bethnal Green, where I teach." He has lived in the area since the mid-1950s, and told me of the *cameraderie* of the Church Street market, where in his early days in London one woman stall-holder used daily to sell this

Doctors and diplomats, old-fashioned chemists and Georgian ironwork, as well as orderly brick terraces, give Marylebone its character.

young schoolteacher in his twenties two apples, an orange and a packet of figs – because "You needed looking after".

Harrington likes the area both for its accessibility from central and east London and its proximity "to my beloved canal". (A member of the Marylebone-based British Waterways Board, he is a dedicated canal enthusiast.) If it has a drawback, he said, this stems from the failure of local authorities (and indeed society) to find a current answer to the anti-social activities of problem families. The old solution was the "Nan figure", who imposed standards and laid down the law.

His village has sharply drawn boundaries. Church Street east of Edgware Road *is* Marylebone just as surely as Church Street west of it belongs to Paddington Green. Harrington's Marylebone is different from the Marylebone of the doctors and diplomats, but, in the estimation of those who live there, Marylebone-juxta-Bahnhof is just as much Marylebone as Portland Place, attracts at least as much loyalty, and is reckoned by those who inhabit it a good "village" to live in.

10

Fulham

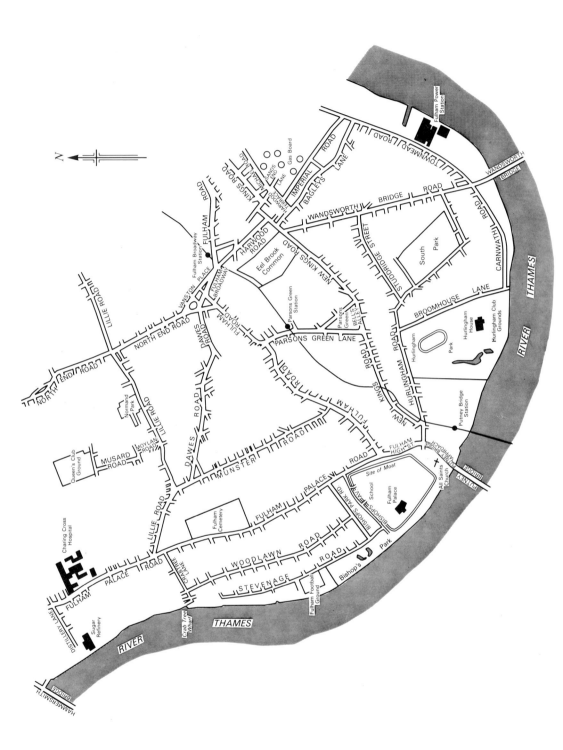

10

Fulham

To many Londoners Fulham is a dim, dull district somewhere beyond the World's End – a poor man's Chelsea at the unfashionable end of the King's Road, lately adopted by those with the wish but not the cash to live swingingly east of Stamford Bridge. But there is much more to Fulham than this, notably the Thames. The popular, outsider's view of the place forgets that Fulham has some $3\frac{1}{2}$ miles of riverside, running in a long loop down from Hammersmith Bridge along Fulham Reach to Putney Bridge and thence past Hurlingham to Wandsworth Bridge, Battersea railway bridge and Chelsea Creek. Almost half the boundary of Fulham is a centre-line in the tideway.

The reason why people forget Fulham's riverside is plain. Traditionally it has been walled in, a variety of industries hogging the tideway since late Victorian times; providing employment for the denizens of street upon street of red-brick terrace houses, but largely preventing them from seeing or enjoying their river. This the new borough, Hammersmith, which absorbed Fulham in 1965, has lately sought to remedy. In 1973 it published a *Plan for Fulham Reach* which aimed at ridding the north bank of the Thames between Hammersmith and Putney bridges of industry and replacing it with housing and pockets of open space connected by a continuous public riverside walk.

The success of the plan created other problems, however. In 1972 Fulham Reach provided 2,450 jobs; five years later only about 1,450 remained. In the context of high local unemployment and the national emphasis on the revival of declining inner cities, it seemed to Hammersmith councillors, as to local people and to the six-year-old Fulham Society, an alarming and undesirable loss.

The borough's response was two-fold. First it appointed a job hunter, industrial development officer Jack Stopforth, to bring in fresh employment. Second, in mid-1977 the council "formally revoked" its Fulham Reach policies for all sites still used by industry. The riverside walk remains an objective, but a long-term one. Firms, says the borough, should not feel under pressure to move.

While this about-turn may prove useful in keeping a few hundred jobs on Fulham Reach over the next few years, it is unlikely to affect more than marginally the general movement of industry out of the area. Belatedly pushing shut a rickety stable door, when you have already encouraged the horses to trot out to greener pastures and begun converting the premises to residential use, is a gesture rather than an action likely to bring results. Closures on Fulham Reach have generally resulted from take-overs, company rationalization and structural changes in the nature of industry. Tate & Lyle now own the Fulham sugar firm of Manbré & Garton. Cries from Hammersmith Town Hall of "Stay with us, industry. We love you!" were unlikely to alter their plans for closing Manbré's Sugar Wharf.

Besides, residential development has already gone too far and looks too convincing. At Crabtree Wharf the borough architect has produced an excellent and attractive scheme of houses and flats in red brick and with pitched roofs which is, visually and socially, an asset to the riverside. Farther south, architects Ted Levy Benjamin & Partners designed a large private development, River Gardens, also in brick but quite different in form. Its flats – £19,500 for one bedroom pad and £70,000 for a large penthouse – pile up in terraced form and serpentine plan, in order to give as many as possible of the homes a view of the river. Part of the roof of one flat is used as the spacious balcony of the next. Sceptics predicted that the flats would never sell; that no one with that kind of money would look at Fulham; that the public riverside walk would deter prospective buyers; and anyway, they asked, who would pay huge sums of money for a 999-year lease with industry and Fulham Football Ground as neighbours? Events confounded the sceptics. In the first eighteen months, the agents Bourdas told me, they sold all but one of the 117 flats. How encouraging that when a developer backs good design for once, the market upholds his judgment.

The same architects have designed a council development of sheltered old people's housing and family homes being built on an adjoining site; and the pattern of planning which is now likely to come into effect should leave Fulham Reach divided into three sectors. Farther downstream is Bishop's Park, a public park sur-

The "Italian Village", off Fulham Road: an attractive colony of studios set up between the wars by Italian artist Mario Manenti and his wife.

rounding Fulham Palace. Next, above Fulham Football Ground, is a stretch where wharves and industry are giving way to homes and small parks, and where the public riverside walk is being extended by over 500 yards. Finally, farthest upstream is a zone where industry can operate without any urgent pressure to move.

Concern about loss of jobs is accompanied by anxiety about the "Chelseafication" of Fulham. Mrs Patricia Talbot, a committee member of the Fulham Society, is herself an emigrée from Kensington. She found a reasonably priced maisonette in Fulham in 1970 after her husband died, but within two years, such was the new-found popularity of the area with young professionals, her insurance company asked her to double her premiums. When sons and daughters of long-established Fulham families marry, said Mrs Talbot, they cannot afford to buy even the humblest terrace house. But Chelseafication has not yet much affected the Sands End area of south-east Fulham, and the council's decision to declare it a housing action area – with more generous improvement grants – should help to sustain the existing community.

Fulham's popularity must be ascribed largely to an extension of the Chelsea cachet. Its red-brick hinterland is not outstandingly pretty, though it has some pockets of attractive Georgian and early Victorian houses. The village of Fulham existed at least as early as the time of the dyke-building King Offa: as a community it somewhat resented its 1960s takeover by upstart Hammersmith; but has lately been appeased by a council decision to rename the borough "Hammersmith and Fulham". Fulham's real suburban development dates from about 1870 to 1910. The houses included some designed for the lower middle rather than working classes – notably the relatively spacious Peterborough Estate, whose houses are distinguished by prolific prides of stone or imitation stone lions, gazing predatorily from every cornice. Local legend has it that there were to have been rather fewer: the developer's pen slipped and he ordered them not in tens but hundreds.

Historic buildings in Fulham are few. They include Sandford Manor, rustic, graceful and listed, but tragically decaying and vandalized within the grounds of Fulham's semi-redundant gasworks while plans for its future and the redevelopment of surrounding land are the object of intermittent debate; Fulham Pottery, of which only a bottle-kiln now remains, though fresh plans have recently been put forward for establishing a pottery museum; and, by the river, Hurlingham House and Fulham Palace.

The Palace was for four centuries the country residence of the bishops of London, but the present bishop, the Rt Rev. Gerald Ellison, has never lived in it. The Church of England recently leased it to Hammersmith Council, who plan to spend £175,000 of ratepayers' money, plus £35,000 in Historic Building Council grants, to restore it and make it safe for public use. The building has been much altered over the years, but its chief glory – the Tudor red-brick courtyard – is a place of beauty and character, like one of those rare faces which great age mellows rather than shrivels. Fulham Society chairman Patrick Ground expressed concern when I talked to him about the council's postponement of some of their spending on the Palace. At the town hall, they said that this would not prejudice proper restoration or the work of making the building safe. Because of the need for cuts in budgets, they had decided to take longer to carry out the restoration and thus avoided reducing expenditure on recreational facilities elsewhere in the borough. Impatient conservationists, however, have recently formed a Friends of Fulham Palace group to try to stir the council into swifter action.

Fulham's underlying neighbourliness came to the fore during Jubilee Year, 1977 – as witness this Union Jack painted on the surface of a road which held a successful street party, one of many in the district.

The surroundings of Fulham's little-known Palace hold some pleasant surprises: vines and a thriving herb garden; allotments much in demand from locals seeking to circumvent rising food prices; and a playground for handicapped children, with a cheerful tent-like building by architect and architectural writer Stephen Gardiner. Some preservationists thought it sacrilegious to place the playground cheek by jowl with the Palace and wanted the Fulham Society to oppose it. Others, like Mrs Talbot, thought such a stand would be selfish and, in public relations terms, disastrous. Their arguments swung the Society round to supporting the scheme.

On the corner of the Palace building the visitor spies a strange inscription: Ecclesiastical Insurance Office. If he has visions of reverend gents in gaiters and mitres writing out policies he is only partly wrong. Founded ninety years ago and with a head office now in Gloucester, the company exists to insure the fabric of churches and parsonages as well as a wide range of other risks, including the lives of both clerics and laymen. It has a bishop, a dean, an archdeacon and a vicar on its board, insures most of the Anglican cathedrals and abbeys including Canterbury Cathedral, and its turnover last year topped £8 million. Its chairman, Allan Grant, who was previously chief executive, says the office is more a place of pinstripe and bowler than cope and mitre. But he has known several recent incumbents of the See of London who lived at Fulham.

Though many of the newcomers to Fulham may be regarded locally as young trendies wanting to live near Chelsea but avoid the high rents and house prices, the biggest single incursion was by a group of people who were in many cases most unwilling immigrants. Charing Cross Hospital moved to Fulham Palace Road in 1973 because its old building, on a constricted island site close to Charing Cross Station, could not be extended nor any longer satisfactorily adapted to modern needs. The new building, designed by Ralph Tubbs, is seventeen storeys high, with ward floors going up to the fifteenth giving therapeutic views of the river to patients. The Hospital has 760 beds and, if its final phase is completed, will eventually expand to 1,000. At present shortage of funds has prevented that extension, so some departments are not as well off for space as was intended.

The hospital suffered its teething troubles, as does any building dependent on sophisticated technology, but working conditions are, says Miss J. M. Peggs, the hospital administrator, infinitely better than at the old building. Some 3,500 people work in the new

Street-markets in Fulham as elsewhere in London, provide both cheap fresh vegetables and a lively street scene.

hospital, including about 400 doctors and 1,000 nurses. Behind it, opened more recently, is a medical school with 600 students. Moving to Fulham – the only suitable site which the Department of Health could find in inner London – caused upheaval for many people who worked there. The old Charing Cross was splendidly central. By comparison, Fulham Palace Road seems dull and inconvenient. But the new hospital, with its ten operating theatres and Cass communication system connecting not only doctors but every patient with a continuously manned control centre makes such losses of amenity appear trivial.

A rather different view of Fulham is held by Clifford Tandy, a principal in a leading landscape and environmental planning practice, Land Use Consultants. LUC moved out of central London because of high rents, rates and overheads – first to Croydon ("which proved almost as expensive as central London, and instead of two rush-hours had four") and then to premises in the Fulham Road. Originally workshops, these had been indifferently converted

*The Hurlingham Club croquet lawns and tea on the terrace
under striped awnings – another world from the bustling 1970s
world of the Fulham Road.*

into offices. LUC have turned them into smart and practical
premises, and Tandy observes with approval the general process of
improvement and up-grading in the area. Shopping is now more
lively and varied; the area appears altogether in better heart.

Transport, he reports, is of mixed quality. Bus and tube services
are reasonably good, but buses not as reliable as they were five years
ago when the LUC moved there; taxis are much in evidence at
night, when they "stable" in the area, but "very rarely to be seen at
any other time; we've given up trying for them". Fulham does not
strike Tandy as being a homogeneous area at all. It is a number of
village centres rather than one, each with its own little group of
shops – for example, Fulham Broadway contrasting with Fulham
High Street. Restaurants are numerous and often good, but on the
whole expensive. "There is virtually nothing between fish and
chips and £10 a head." Other attractions are the various commons
and greens – Eel Brook Common, South Park, Parsons Green – and
the lively North End Road market. But northern Fulham is

desperately short of public open space, which explains in part the vehement local opposition to GLC development on the St Paul's playing field site.

Bishop's Park apart, the biggest green open space is a private one: the forty-acre grounds of the Hurlingham Club, which has 3,500 members, who pay £90 a year, and a long waiting list. Patricia Talbot is one of many local members who wave a pass, or are recognized, as they drive through the strictly patrolled gates, past the lake and carefully tended greensward to Hurlingham House. Originally a small and rather ordinary Georgian country house, it was given charm and style in 1797 by the addition of a grander stuccoed front and terrace facing out across the croquet lawns towards the river.

The Hurlingham Club (not to be confused with the tennis-dominated Queen's Club half a mile to the north) started life in 1869 as a live pigeon-shooting club. By 1905 a substantial group of members objected to this bloody and noisome pursuit, took the matter to the courts and won. Thereafter Hurlingham settled down sedately to polo until the LCC compulsorily bought its polo ground in 1951; it now offers tennis, bowls, cricket, putting, swimming in a heated open-air pool and, above all, croquet, for which it provides the national headquarters. The tranquillity of the tea-time terraces, with blue-and-white striped awnings and the gentle chink of cup on saucer, is scarcely broken by the click of mallet or the silent viciousness of an expert and ruthless roquet. "You could scarcely have anything else on those lawns," said the club's secretary, Mr D. F. A. Trewby. "Two people moving about is all right. Bowls would be a crowd!"

Hurlingham offers special memberships not only to wives and older children, but to visiting ambassadors and other diplomats. "We are very catholic," said Mr Trewby. "Our members include a whole range of professions." Yet no one would accuse Hurlingham of being proletarian or thrusting. It has style, spaciousness and peace – in many ways a contrast to the vulgar bustle that is the Fulham the world knows. It is an oasis of privileged calm and Edwardian good manners amid the frenetic, often bad-mannered but lively urban world that is 1978 Fulham.

11

Bloomsbury

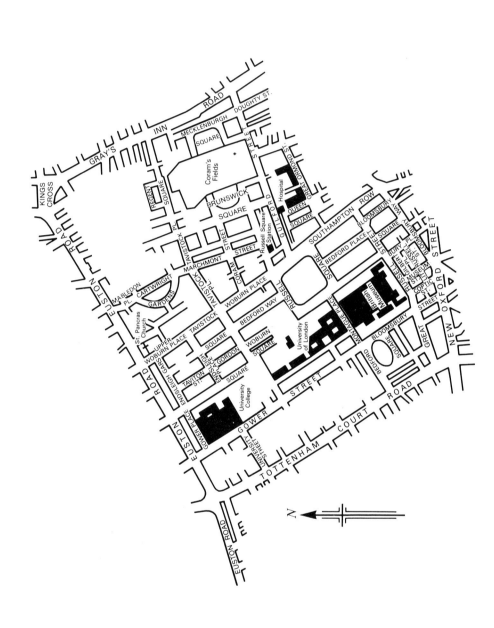

11

Bloomsbury

"Bloomsbury. District of WC London between Tottenham Court Road and High Holborn," states my old one-volume encyclopaedia baldly. "Contains British Museum, new London University buildings and Royal Academy of Dramatic Art. After First World War became known as home of a number of writers, artists, etc., and is popularly connected with a type of intellectual."

So much, in one estimation, for the "Bloomsbury Set", which actually began to exercise its influence on the arts a good decade earlier than that dismissive entry suggests. Yet in truth the term "Bloomsbury", whether used in approbation or uncomprehending derision, had (the proximity of the BM apart) not all that much to do with the place as a place. The brilliant aura of Lytton Strachey, the Bells, Fry, Woolf, and the rest might almost as easily have been attached to Marylebone or St John's Wood if two or three of them had happened to live there – though one may doubt if a "Marylebonite" or "John's Wooder" would ever have had quite the ring as "Bloomsburyite".

The geographical description is right, so far as it goes. East of Tottenham Court Road is a different village called Fitzrovia; south of High Holborn is unequivocally Covent Garden; while the grey, traffic-lapped wastes of the Euston Road are equally clearly no longer Bloomsbury. But how far east? Brunswick Square and Coram's Fields are surely Bloomsbury; and so too, in architectural character, is Mecklenburgh Square, or what remains of it. But surely Lamb's Conduit Street is Holborn?

Equally clearly Bedford Square (home of the Architectural Association and many publishers), although west of Gower Street, is as superlatively Bloomsbury as anywhere. We can make no authoritative beating of bounds because Bloomsbury fades by fits and starts into Holborn.

The name dates back at least to the 13th century, when the de Blemund family (probably from Blémont in France) held land there. It was Blemundisberi or -bury. Then consisting of fields and farms, it owed its development and still surviving Georgian character initially to the Earl of Southampton, who first laid out Bloomsbury Square, but then predominantly to the Russell family, Dukes of Bedford whose family names – Russell, Bedford, Woburn and Tavistock – adorn a high proportion of its streets and squares. The Bedford estates still own the freeholds of a large area of Bloomsbury, though their position as dominant landlord is probably now ceded to London University.

The university, in many people's eyes, has been the upstart cuckoo in the Bloomsbury nest. It began with University College, London, whose original 1829 building with the ten-columned Corinthian portico stands, tranquil and unexpected, at the back of its twin-lodged and gated courtyard off Gower Street. UCL came into being to provide a university education for non-Anglicans excluded by Oxford and Cambridge; it was known as "the Godless College in Gower Street"; and upright Anglicans established King's College to counteract this doctrinal permissiveness. The university, with its charter and power to grant degrees, followed in 1836, acquiring over 140 years a vast range of institutions and colleges stretching from Wye in Kent to Royal Holloway College in Berkshire, and with a total of some 60,000 students, internal and external – by no means all of them in Bloomsbury.

But Bloomsbury has borne the brunt of the expansion. Some say the rot set in with that white tombstone of a Senate House in Malet Street, designed in 1932 by Charles Holden, architect of several of London Transport's now statutorily preserved 1930s tube stations, and of the LTE's headquarters, 55 Broadway. Many of its critics concede that their view of it has softened of late. What seemed like a slap in the face for elegant, well-mannered Bloomsbury then, has lost its power to shock in the light, they say, of so many later acts of architectural vandalism. Senate House is Portland stone; large, dull and spacious, and, says R. G. Hutchings, deputy clerk of the university Court, who has worked there for thirty years, a very satisfactory building from a functional point of view.

But in the 1940s and 1950s the university could no longer afford Portland stone. The red brick boxes it put up then, including the students' union building, are among the ugliest and most vacuous architecture in Bloomsbury. By contrast, Sir Denys Lasdun's controversial concrete-and-glass wall of a law and education building, stretching along Bedford Way and eating into Woburn

Cosmo Place, which links the hotel world of Southampton Row to Queen's Square and Great Ormond Street with their hospitals.

Square, is intrinsically exciting and elegant. It suffers from one overwhelming defect. Bloomsbury was not the right place for it.

This view was put to me succinctly by Louis Bondy, antiquarian bookseller, Bloomsbury resident since he came to England in 1934 and former chairman of the GLC's Historic Buildings Board. "It's a fantastically interesting building, if only it had stood somewhere different – on a campus, in isolation. But facing Russell Square, which was a nice, interesting and varied square, it's like an axe beheading it."

Mr Bondy has observed with increasing regret the cuckoo university destroying its delicate Georgian nest – in the name, naturally, of educational progress. The rise of conservation as a powerful political force has in one or two places stopped it in its tracks, in others made redevelopment difficult and more expensive without actually preventing it. From the point of view of people like Mr Hutchings, this rearguard action is all rather unfair and un-fortunate. In the late 1950s they told the public what they proposed to do on the thirty-five acre university precinct, and took the ensuing silence (broken by protests from a few isolated Georgian cranks) as amounting to approval. Lack of cash delayed implementation; and then half way through redevelopment it pained them to find conservationist protests exploding like so many delayed-action mines in their faces, as they struggled to implement what they had believed was a generally agreed scheme.

Now public opinion rightly abhors the concept of huge institutional precincts encapsulated like alien bodies within the living tissue of a town. In the 1950s, recalls Mr Hutchings, some LCC planners were seriously urging them to concentrate much more of the university tidily in Bloomsbury – including for instance Queen Mary College, which they would have had Senate House prize out of the Mile End Road and transplant in Bloomsbury. A decade or so later GLC planners having labelled Bloomsbury an area of outstanding character, were expressing alarm at the loss of so many historic Georgian terraces, and began looking for ways of dispersing the all-too-dominant university presence.

Professor David Lang, vice-president of the Holborn Society, has been one of the livelier critics of redevelopment proposals, both by the university and, in southern Bloomsbury, by the British Library. He talked to me of "megalomaniac expansionism" on the part of his own university in the post-Robbins period, and of the "cataclysmic" effect of the new Lasdun buildings on Woburn Square. But Professor Lang is not a "150 per cent preservationist". He emphasizes that some buildings had reached a point when further patching-up was neither economic nor sensible. On the other hand, Connaught Hall of residence, of which he is warden, shows how a Georgian terrace can be adapted by a university to a reasonably satisfactory new use. Connaught Hall comprises most of Cubitt's 1830s terrace on the western side of Tavistock Square. Outwardly it appears unchanged – a row of narrow vertical Georgian houses; internally it is one integrated hall of residence housing 194 students and staff. In fairness to the "megalomaniacs" at Senate House, it should be added that this was one of the terraces they always intended to preserve.

Professor Lang, his wife and two teenage daughters form one of the few families living permanently in the university precinct. For shopping and entertainment it is wonderfully situated, he says; for education, paradoxically, less so. Primary schools are reasonable; but at secondary school age girls have to commute to Kentish

Town, boys to the other end of the Marylebone Road – and even that option, he added crossly, had now been removed by Mrs Shirley Williams. Other snags are the phasing out of the kind of homes which moderately off professionals can afford; the tendency of hotels, if the planners allow them, to eat up privately rented flats; and traffic. The road outside Connaught Hall once afforded residents somewhere to park their cars. Now it is yellow-lined on both sides "so that young men in company cars, with their jackets neatly hanging behind them, may use it as a new express way".

Russell Square, whose university-butchered western side marks the edge of the university precinct proper, is in some ways the centre of Bloomsbury. But it is also the point where two different Bloomsburys meet: to west and north the campus; to east and south hotel- and tourist-land. Woburn Place, Southampton Row, Bedford Place – streets which recall the landed aristocracy of two and three centuries ago – are lined by hotels great and small.

Of these the grandest now is the Hotel Russell, a late Victorian château-style pile in orange brick and terracotta, designed by Fitzroy Doll and opened on Derby Day, 1900. Like so many grand hotels of that period and scale, it became in post-war years steadily less and less economic, more and more difficult to maintain. In 1970 Charles Forte acquired it, and Trust Houses-Forte have lately

The Hotel Russell, seen from leafy Russell Square.

spent huge sums on restoration and modernization. What was a 500-bedroom hotel now has only 320 – but all those have private bathrooms. "The age of going along corridors in your dressing-gown to the bathroom is over," says general manager Harold Kruschandl. Every third bedroom has been converted to make a bathroom for its two neighbours.

But hand-in-hand with modernization has come true restoration – peeling off coat on coat of heavily ornate wallpaper and gloomy paint to reveal classical columns, friezes and cornices, now picked out in white and Wedgwood blue on magnolia. Public rooms where George Bernard Shaw on many occasions sat are now not only air-conditioned but returned to their former grandeur; the outside has been cleaned and repaired; and even the great lanterns which rise from those decorous Victorian railings now shine out newly bronzed. For the rest, Mr Forte is a hotelier, not a philanthropist. A single room cost even in 1977 £19 a night without breakfast, and, if you had an English rather than Continental appetite, that was £2.50 extra.

While the restored Hotel Russell now ranks as one of Blooms-bury's glories, the fate of Doll's other Russell Square Hotel, the Imperial, represents a double disaster: it was demolished, and has been replaced by surely the ugliest, the most tasteless of all the many tasteless modern hotels in London. Almost anything would improve it – purple paint all over as a job creation exercise; Virginia Creeper; or, best of all, dynamite.

Behind the Russell to the east lies a very different Bloomsbury where two large presences, one new, one old, attract our attention. First the Brunswick Centre, by architect Patrick Hodgkinson, provides sunny and generally very popular housing: a concrete ziggurat rising in terraces of greenhouse-like balconies above a

New homes and old: the Brunswick Centre, left, and Georgian terraces like those torn down to make way for it.

remarkably good little shopping centre, some restaurants and the underground Bloomsbury Cinema. It does not look quite as Hodgkinson intended; he meant it to be painted cream to match the neighbouring Georgian stucco. Now that it is there we must reckon it, socially and architecturally, a success. Whether anyone should have been permitted to tear down the Georgian and Victorian terraces that stood there before is a different question. They were not grand houses; but they were a harmonious townscape, as you can still see from the rest of Marchmont Street to the north – an area of social and commercial vitality, character and diversity.

Across Brunswick Square, behind trees and railings of a not-too-restrictive kind, we discover another, much older but no less beneficent presence: the Coram Foundation and all the activities concerned with children that have clustered about it. Captain Thomas Coram, whose statue by Macmillan you see on the north side of the square, went to sea in 1679 at the age of eleven, and made quite a thing of trade with the American colonies. On his return to England he was appalled at the plight of young children in London, many of them illegitimate, who were often literally "left to die on dung-hills". So Coram fought for seventeen years, and in the end successfully, for a royal charter to open what later became the Foundling Hospital. Its site is now safeguarded for the recreation and education of young people.

The foundation itself runs an adoption and fostering service from a house on the north side of Coram's Fields; its Coram Children's Centre provides day care for local children and their families, with a nursery and nursery school on the site; it also promotes research and vocational training in child welfare; and it is host to the Adoption Resource Exchange. Most of the ground on which the Foundling Hospital stood is now administered by a trust, the Coram's Fields and Harmsworth Memorial Playground; the colonnades and pavilions which fringed the site still stand, converted to house user groups ranging from scouts and guides to an ILEA play centre, a dance group and an organization called Kith and Kids. On a peak summer holiday between 400 and 600 youngsters may use Coram's Fields. Adults can also be seen there but, as a notice at the gate sternly points out, no grown-up may enter unless accompanied by a child.

Alongside the new, all-weather, bright green kickabout pitches stands the Wolfson Centre for Child Development Research, which studies children in, as it were, their natural play habitat. To the south are three other institutions concerned with children: the Great Ormond Street Hospital for Sick Children; London University's Institute of Child Research; and the Natal Centre, which is the local family health centre for the district. Can there anywhere else in any city be such a concentration of people and organizations devoted to child welfare? But what about customers? Official statistics appear to show that Bloomsbury and Holborn are rapidly losing population. Mrs Helen Hays, administrator of the Coram's Field trust, is sceptical. "That's what the figures seem to show. And yet round here I seem to meet more and more pregnant mums and under-fives every day." Unlike west Bloomsbury's university precinct, the area round Coram's Fields has a lively local community.

So too, in south Bloomsbury, has the $7\frac{1}{2}$ acres the British Library wanted, thought it had in its pocket, and then lost, thanks to changing tastes in conservation and a skilful and energetic fight by a remarkable *ad hoc* defence group, the Bloomsbury Association. "Bloomsbury" as far as this group is concerned is primarily the area bounded by Great Russell Street, Bloomsbury Way, Bloomsbury Street – and the west side of Bloomsbury Square. Most of this – let

Statue of Thomas Coram near the Coram Foundation in Brunswick Square.

Food for minds and food for bodies: ice-cream and hot-dog sellers outside the British Museum.

us call it "Little Bloomsbury" – the British Museum wanted for a new building to replace its hopelessly overcrowded library across the road. And it had every expectation of getting its way. The area appeared on every master plan from the 1930s onwards as part of the academic precinct; the buildings on the site, Hawksmoor's St George's Church apart, were considered mostly of indifferent architectural quality, tatty Victorian stuff which clearly ought to go!

But the Museum reckoned without Dr George Wagner, adult education lecturer, refugee from Hitler's Germany, sometime Holborn borough councillor and thirty-five years a Bloomsbury resident. He founded the Association, lobbied influential figures in government and refused to take Yes for an answer when Yes meant destruction of his beloved village. The Association drew support from residents and the small, specialist businesses (notably publishers and booksellers), in which the area is so strong. It mounted a social survey which showed that here was a thriving community of more than 1,000 residents and 200 businesses of various kinds; a community with an atmosphere that was attracting lively younger couples who would bring up families there; a community which lent a necessary and salutary leavening to the institutionalized academic Bloomsbury to the north, and indeed provided many academics with the specialist services they needed.

The Association argued, with increasing backing from Camden borough, local MPs and a courageous fifth column inside the academic ramparts, on four main points. First, "the village" was too important to be destroyed; second, the site was a bad one, forcing the architects of the proposed new library to go down much deeper, encasing their subterranean bookstacks in a concrete caisson to keep out an underground river; third, the library did not need to be next door to the Museum; and, fourth, a proposed alternative site at Somers Town, north of Euston Road, would be better both for most users and, in terms of social and commercial stimulus, for its host area.

The champions of the Bloomsbury site, notably Lord Eccles, chairman of the board of the new British Library, exerted enormous pressure on successive governments and twice appeared to have won the day. But Little Bloomsbury would not give up, and eventually won the right to survive. The library set its architect, Colin St John Wilson, to design a new and different building for the larger and more flexible site at Somers Town. Denys Parsons, press officer of the British Library, author and Bloomsburyite for thirty-six of his first forty years, says the British Library still regrets the Government's decision, but now concedes that librarians and academics from the north and midlands will find a British Library close to Euston, King's Cross and St Pancras stations considerably more convenient. Perhaps the chief loss is that the whole programme has slippped back a year or two. After thirty years of waiting the library nervously clutches Whitehall's half promise that its £100 million plus scheme may begin in 1979–80.

Meanwhile the reprieved $7\frac{1}{2}$ acres blooms and flourishes. The fight, comments Dr Wagner, has greatly strengthened the area's already considerable "social cohesion". People know each other, talk to each other, give time, money, energy and support to "the community". Each year the Association runs a Bloomsbury Fair; the healing of battle scars is symbolized by the Museum Choir singing in an eve-of-fair concert in St George's Church (whose Rector originally supported the redevelopment); and the junketings include a ceremonial pizza tasting at Pizza Express in Coptic Street, and a Bloomsbury Orgy in the courtyard of a block of 19th-century artisans' dwellings which the tenants have transformed with hanging and climbing greenery. The Association's takeover of the description Bloomsbury for their little patch is, of course, an outrageous piece of namebending. South Bloomsbury is not all or even most of Bloomsbury; it is not intrinsically the prettiest part of Bloomsbury, or perhaps the most important. But it is in many ways the most attractive and vital.

12

Southwark

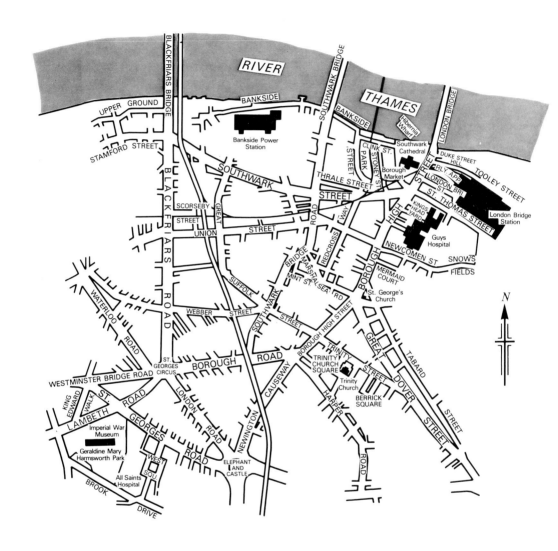

RIVER

BLACKFRIARS BRIDGE

SOUTHWARK BRIDGE

BANKSIDE

THAMES

LONDON BRIDGE

BANKSIDE

Hibernia Wharf

UPPER GROUND

Bankside Power Station

Southwark Cathedral

DUKE STREET

STAMFORD STREET

CLINK ST

STONEY'S ST

Borough Market

EARLY APP

DUKE STREET HILL

TOOLEY STREET

SOUTHWARK

THRALE STREET

LONDON BRI

BLACKFRIARS ROAD

SCORSEBY STREET

GREAT

STREET

PARK

STREET

LONDON ST

ST. THOMAS STREET

London Bridge Station

UNION STREET

ROAD

WAY

HIGH

KINGS HEAD YARD

Guys Hospital

SUFFOLK

REDCROSS

NEWCOMEN ST

SNOWS

WEBBER STREET

BRIDGE

MARSHALSEA RD

MERMAID COURT

FIELDS

BOROUGH

SOUTHWARK

MINT ST

St. George's Church

STREET

N

ST. GEORGES CIRCUS

BOROUGH ROAD

CAUSEWAY

BOROUGH HIGH STREET

TRINITY CHURCH SQUARE

GREAT

TABARD

DOVER

STREET

WESTMINSTER BRIDGE ROAD

LONDON ROAD

Trinity Church

STREET

STREET

KING EDWARD

WALK

ST GEORGES ROAD

LAMBETH ROAD

Imperial War Museum

BERRICK SQUARE

HARPER

NEWINGTON

Geraldine Mary Harmsworth Park

WEST SQU

ELEPHANT AND CASTLE

ROAD

BROOK DRIVE

All Saints Hospital

12

Southwark

That part of Southwark which Londoners know as "the Borough"
is as old as London itself. Even before the first wooden Roman
bridge linked it with *Londinium* on the north bank, here was the all-
important bridgehead. This point on the Thames, with its gravel
beds, offered travellers from the Channel coast their first reliable
fording place. In Roman times Southwark seems from the archeo-
logical evidence to have been a prosperous place. Not only did trade
from the Continent arrive there by way of Watling Street, iron from
the Weald, and travellers from the south by way of Stane Street; but
grouped around the bridgehead stood many spacious houses with
gardens running down to the river, and beyond them villas with
their country estates. Southwark was evidently to *Londinium* what
Gerrard's Cross and Virginia Water are to modern London.

After the Romans pulled out, Southwark seems to have had a
rougher time than its neighbour across the water. The bridge went,
and the link became a ferry between two separate and often hostile
kingdoms. But it was replaced in or soon after Alfred's time, and,
when London barred William of Normandy's progress over it, he
set fire to Southwark before turning westwards to ford the Thames
at a higher point.

The origins of the name Southwark first appear about AD 920 in
the Burghal Hidage (list of walled or defended townships) as
Suthringa Geweorche – literally, "the Surrey folk's defence-
work". But, unlike other military "boroughs", it failed until almost
1,000 years later to add municipal self-government to its undoubted
status as a military and mercantile borough. It and the City of
London were for centuries the only towns hereabouts to send
members to Parliament; and yet Southwark had to wait for its
mayor and corporation until 1899, long after the much later
settlement at Westminster had achieved them. The main reasons
for this were twofold: land ownership and manor jurisdiction by the

123

Church, than whom none was more zealous in holding on to rights and powers; and the importance of Southwark to the City of London, which eventually bought much of the Borough, establishing it as a part of its territory, the Ward of Bridge Without.

The proximity and influence of the City were, however, good for Southwark in two other ways. Its curfew shut the bridge as it did London's other gateways. Thus merchants arriving from the south and east at nightfall needed somewhere to stay while awaiting entry to London in the morning; and by the same token a City merchant wanting to journey south from London did not wait until morning to cross the bridge in the post-curfew rush-hour. He crossed on the eve of his intended departure, slept in an inn at Southwark and made an early start. So the High Street of the Borough became lined with inns which, following the old burgage plots, took the form of galleried wings opening on to long stable yards which ran back from arched entrances in the narrow frontages of the actual High Street.

In Dickens' day many old coaching inns remained. Now only one survives, and that only in part and thanks to the National Trust. The George, mentioned in *Little Dorrit*, does not leap to the eye of the casual passer-by in Borough High Street. Out of licensing hours great, spiked gates, closed under an archway, hide all but its Victorian front bar. But through the gates is the long coaching yard, with, on its south side, 17th-century balustraded open galleries and small-paned bar windows. The Great Northern Railway demolished the other two sides in 1889; their successors, the London and North Eastern, in 1937 made belated and only partial amends by presenting the property to the National Trust. Even after this, some unfortunate alterations took place; but the Trust and the GLC's Historic Buildings Committee are these days much stricter, so that recent alterations to cope with expanding trade have had to tread circumspectly and use much ingenuity.

At The George I talked to Mr Bob Pittman, the landlord, a stocky, matter-of-fact Cockney, of somewhat Pickwickian stature, who formerly presided over The Sherlock Holmes of Northumberland Avenue. Until 1977 his pub had one bar and one small restaurant. Now it has three bars and a much extended restaurant, and Pittman shoots up and down the narrow staircases with the energy of a steam engine. The tourists are, of course, the thing – American Pickwick enthusiasts particularly. (Mr Pickwick acquired Sam Weller at the White Hart, Southwark, now vanished.) But at

The George Inn off Borough High Street – the last fragment of the old, galleried coaching inns which used to be such a feature of Southwark.

present tourists tend to throng into the oldest bar, where thousands of pints weekly pass through the narrow "ticket window" servery hatch (which cannot be altered). In the back bars accents not of Atlanta or Arkansas but of Rotherhithe and Deptford prevail.

Southwark is still, as Chaucer's pilgrims and Mr Pickwick alike found it, an agreeable place for eating and drinking: Victorian pubs, whose archways still lead to the yards that once catered for the coach trade; the Anchor on Bankside, where Johnson used to meet his brewer friend Thrale, and among the most attractive of London's riverside pubs; and wine bars and cellars, like the excellent and atmospheric Boot and Flogger in Redcross Street – a free vintner's house which needs no normal licence and owes its name to two of the implements of the trade, the "boot", a protective covering for a wine bottle, and the "flogger", with which the cork is thumped into the bottle-neck.

Borough High Street itself has associations with three other activities: fruit and vegetables; hops; and surgery. Guy's Hospital, which lies to the east, owns much of the labyrinth of yards and

Entrance to Boot and Flogger wine bar – a free vintner's house which needs no normal licence.

THE BOOT & FLOGGER

alleys on that side of the High Street. Fears that it would pursue plans to redevelop here with the insensitiveness of its earlier tower block (known to locals as "The Spanner") have now abated. More recent plans have envisaged retention of yards and alleys and of the best Victorian façades, refurbishment and interior rebuilding, largely to provide much-needed accommodation for nurses, medical students and staff and other hospital employees. The small but active Borough Society, formed four years ago to fight destructive development in the area, believes the hospital's present proposals are on the whole acceptable and of benefit to the area.

On the other side of the High Street, Borough Market, the wholesale vegetable mart which has its origins in a medieval market in the High Street, has lost much of its trade to the New Covent Garden at Nine Elms. The future of the hotch-potch of market buildings under the railway arches is now under consideration. Southwark Council want to improve and revive the market. A Sunday morning furniture auction takes place there; and there is some talk of transferring the weekly "Caledonian" market from Bermondsey Square.

Another trade which has changed and waned is hops. I talked to Colonel Francis Richardson, once chairman of the hop merchants and, in his eighties, still consultant to his firm, Wigan Richardson. He recalled how in the 1930s there were more than thirty firms of hop merchants in the Borough, each with its own warehouse, and Central Buildings in Southwark Street housed a thriving Hop Exchange. Indeed the very telephone exchange for the area, before numbers took over, was HOP. Now only four hop firms remain. One reason was a disastrous fire of hop warehouses during the Blitz, after which the Hop Marketing Board (rightly, says Colonel Richardson) decided to consolidate warehousing close to the hop-fields, at Paddock Wood in Kent and Ledbury in Worcestershire. A second reason is the reduction of breweries from the inter-war 2,000 to 3,000 down to seven main and ninety lesser breweries today. A third reason is the more efficient use of the oils and acids in the hops which flavour our beer. But though warehouses in the Borough no longer hold hops in quantity, samples of the crop still come to merchants' offices, and to walk through the door of a firm like Wigan Richardson is to get a noseful of the rich, brown smell of hopfields.

The original Borough, and the City of London's jurisdiction within its Ward of Bridge Without, clung tightly to the bridgehead.

Boundary stones, such as those on the western edge of the cathedral churchyard, show how circumscribed it was. Actual development ran beyond it in two directions: south along the High Street to the point where the 18th-century church of St George the Martyr marks the junction of two age-old trading routes (now the A2 and the A3); and along and behind the river-bank, particularly to the west. Here ancient "liberties", such as Clink and Paris Gardens, afforded freedom from the rule of the Lord Mayor and Aldermen; which is why, in Elizabethan times, theatres, pleasure-gardens and brothels flourished in these parts of Southwark. Hence the famous Globe, which Southwark resident Sam Wanamaker is trying to re-create close to its original site. His present temporary theatre on Bankside, the summer Globe Fair, and his Bear Gardens Museum, are all steps in this direction.

But like every plan for development in north Southwark, the dream of a replica Globe with Shakespearean productions in authentic 16th-century setting runs into problems of cost. Though much of the area is under-used and decaying, land still holds a high value, supported by our anomolous compensation laws; and site conditions also make building expensive. Thus, in practice, socially attractive or useful development can only ride on the back of profitable commercial uses, such as offices. A current example is the huge Lloyds Bank computer centre going up just east of Blackfriars railway bridge. As the price for their planning permission, the developers have provided land and £300,000 for an associated development of 110 council flats, alongside a landscaped riverside walk. The development also includes shops and a supermarket, and a gallery for the Royal Society of Painters in Water-Colours.

This kind of planning deal has lately come under fire both from the courts and from local activists, notably the North Southwark Community Development Group, whose newspaper, *S.E.1.*, preaches a doctrine of Southwark for the locals; it opposes offices (which employ mostly suburban commuters) and wants more effective measures to bring back industrial jobs. Certainly north Southwark, which includes the whole riverside and its hinterland, from IPC's new King's Reach Tower in the west to the Surrey Docks in the east, has lost both jobs and people at a frightening rate in recent decades. The drop from around 450,000 in 1901 to about 110,000 in the early 1960s represented in large measure a population shift essential to rid the area of slum conditions; but the fall since then to about 60,000 stems in part from the disappearance of

Not all "The Borough" is being preserved. Elsewhere bulldozers are busy as here in Silvester street.

industrial jobs and the movement of people after them, seeking homes and work in towns beyond the green belt. Southwark borough planners, while anxious to retard or reverse this movement, have welcomed offices in some locations as a means of reviving the area's economy and getting something positive to happen in an area of economic and physical decay.

Development brings other types of planning gain. Alongside London Bridge, new infill offices have supported the restoration of some fine 19th-century buildings and are providing a public square on the riverside. This, for the first time in centuries, gives a view of Southwark Cathedral from the north bank and to City workers crossing the bridge.

One chunk of industry which is unlikely to move in the near future is the Central Electricity Generating Board's Bankside power station. When built in the 1940s it ranked as the largest generating station in Britain. Now, when 2,000 Mw is the norm, Bankside's 240 Mw no longer ranks as one of the system's giants. The fiercely contested planning consent which allowed the electricity authorities to build the present station, in place of the City of London Electric Lighting Company's pioneering 19th-century installation, stipulated that its flue gases should be washed before emission from its 300-foot stack. This condition is now an embarrassment to the CEGB. Normally hot gases rise and disperse; in warm weather washing may reduce the temperature to that of the ambient atmosphere, and so impede the gases' dispersal. The station's manager, Mr Alban Chase, told me he would soon, however, be in the happy position of needing only to run the station to meet peak loads on the national grid; new links in the grid's

London ring mean that newer and more efficient stations can supply the City and central London with more of their power requirements.

Mr Chase, who lives in Basildon and normally walks across London Bridge to work, readily admits that he and his 260 staff do not have much contact with what remains of a local community. They, like workers in CEGB's regional headquarters behind the power station, have their own canteen facilities. They expect, however, to gain from the arrival of shops and a supermarket, and from the landscaped riverside gardens on which work has recently started. A riverside pub with real ale from Young's should also be welcome. In the summer of 1977 Mr Chase and his staff helped the fund-raising efforts of the South London Industrial Mission by co-operating in a week-long Bankside Fête on land in front of the power station. With tugs of war, five-a-side football and other events, it brought life to a rather drab stretch of riverside and raised £500 to take children of one-parent families away on holiday.

Despite its proximity to West End and City offices, Southwark (the district as distinct from the modern London borough) has few sought-after residential neighbourhoods. One oasis of period owner-occupier smartness is West Square, an attractive and little-known Victorian backwater on the edge of the one sizeable open space, Geraldine Mary Harmsworth Park, in whose centre stands the for-bidding pile of the Imperial War Museum. West Square, claimed to be within division bell distance of the Commons, recently gained a new north side, with respectably matching neo-Victorian façades and a huddle of £37,000 freehold town houses tucked in behind.

But the district's two finest squares are not for sale. They belong to the Corporation of Trinity House, whose Elder Brethren administer lighthouses and pilotage services in UK waters. Its

The Imperial War Museum, set in this village's largest public open space, Mary Harmsworth Park.

Trinity Church Square with the church – now an orchestral rehearsal hall – on the right.

properties in and around Trinity Church Square and Merrick Square finance not lighthouses but charitable trusts which aid distressed mariners and their dependants. Here the Borough Society began, based on informal local groups who had fought to get an appropriate new use for the redundant early 19th-century Holy Trinity Church which is the centrepiece of that square.

Stanley Osborn, formerly of the Foreign Office, a Trinity Church Square resident and the Society's chairman, recalls two proposals which the residents and Trinity House successfully fought off – conversion into a missionary headquarters and into luxury flats. Now the church is Henry Wood Hall, a much-needed permanent rehearsal hall for London's symphony orchestras. This solution preserved and restored both exterior and interior, and makes much greater use also of the crypt and tower for office and other facilities.

The Borough Society, which is represented on Southwark's conservation advisory committee, has fought hard to conserve fine old buildings (including GLC-owned Georgian terraces in Trinity Street, which were decaying and which County Hall has now restored); and for good and suitable designs in redevelopment. One current battle concerns the former Nettlefold & Moser headquarters immediately opposite the parish church. The developers' first proposals here were for a bulky horizontal layer-cake of a building; but the Society successfully argued that the townscape of Borough High Street from here right to London Bridge is essentially one of narrow, vertical frontages, which Southwark council insist should be the pattern even where it permits new office development.

Another successful campaign, which brought tangible benefits to the area, led to installation of a "pinch point" on Trinity Street to keep out traffic-dodging heavy lorries. These made the area unsafe for pedestrians, especially children and the elderly; kept residents awake at night; and threatened to cause collapse of the cellars which run out under the pavements in front of the cream-stuccoed 19th-century terraces.

Unlike the North Southwark Community Development Group, Mr Osborn sees most of his Society's battles as already fought and, in recent years, won. He thinks that hopes of a mass return of industrial jobs are unrealistic; but that limited improvements in the local environment, visually and in relation to traffic, are attainable. The price of conserving and improving the local environment is, however, constant vigilance.

The Society's secretary, Miss Betty North, also a Trinity Square resident, has known Southwark since she came to school there and believes it is an area with many attractions and much underrated. The Borough has lost many pleasant old buildings which could and should have been conserved, she says; but she could also point to successful conservation projects like Trinity Church, and the conversion of warehouses in Union Street into elegant and satisfactory offices and training premises for accountants Price Waterhouse.

Trinity Square residents anxious to stop small children from exploring the railinged gardens have long encouraged the legend that the 14th-century statue, said to be of King Alfred, sometimes leaves its pedestal and walks at dusk through the Borough, then presumably on to Westminster Hall, where it used to be quartered. If Alfred does walk he must be puzzled and depressed by all the Borough's derelict areas and empty buildings. Why, half a mile from the Bank of England and with magnificent views of St Paul's and the Tower, should such splendid riverside sites go unused? Something is rotten in the state of property and planning law. Yet, where buildings are used, the acres bloom brightly enough; a new two- and three-storey GLC housing estate at Scoresby Street shows that families with children can live happily even in the shadow of the great 19th-century railway viaducts; and at last, after twenty-five years of stagnation (thanks to the Jubilee Walkway and that planning bonus from the Lloyds Bank scheme), one stretch of the riverside is now coming alive again. Wren, who lodged on Bankside during the building of St Paul's, would (one likes to think) have approved of 110 more households sharing that view.

13

Putney

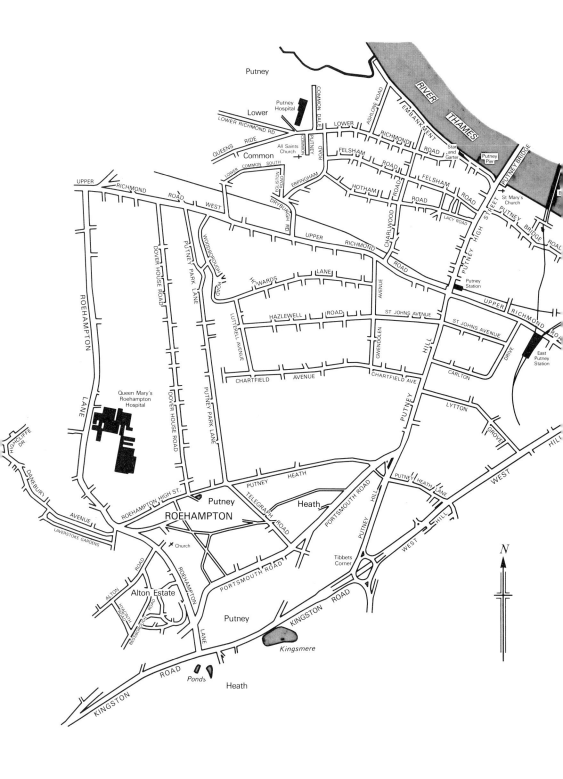

13

Putney

To some people Putney is simply one end of the Oxford and Cambridge Boat Race course – and the end without the brewery, to boot. Yet despite being municipally a part of the monster Wandsworth, Putney more than most inner London districts stands distinct and retains its separate identity. A village has stood at this point on the Thames since Roman times; and recent excavations by the Wandsworth Historical Society under archaeologist and Bank of England official Nicholas Farrant have provided evidence not only of a Romano-British settlement just west of the High Street, but of an apparent pattern of Roman roads converging on a crossing point just upstream of the present Putney Bridge.

The first bridge, opened in 1729, was one of the earliest on the tideway and predated Westminster Bridge by a couple of decades. In the 18th century Putney had fewer than 3,000 inhabitants, and until the 19th century it consisted of little more than its High Street and surrounding cottages, and St Mary's Church with its 15th-century tower by the bridge. Highlights of its past included inter-parish disputes with the residents of Barnes over commoners' rights, which led, in 1859, to *the* common being split into two commons, Barnes and Putney; and a Roundhead council of war, which in 1647 sat coolly round the communion table in St Mary's, wearing black puritan hats, debating the principles of Britain's future constitution.

Putney's golden age came, Sir Nikolaus Pevsner tells us, in the mid-19th century when spacious villas rose on Putney Hill and Putney Heath. The grandest houses of Putney's adjoining hamlet Roehampton (part of Putney parish) dated from a century earlier, and those that survive are generally in institutional use: Roehampton House by Thomas Archer is now Queen Mary's Hospital; Grove House, the Froebel Institute; Manresa House by Chambers, part of the South Bank Polytechnic; Downshire House and the Palladian

135

Mount Clare are now Garnett College for teachers of higher education.

These were jewels in a landscape setting which the LCC architects sought to preserve when building the many-towered Alton Estate in the 1950s and 1960s. In landscape terms they achieved some measure of success; but the recent complaint has been that this was not an environment in which either youngsters or a real community could take root firmly or grow gracefully.

In spite of the grafting on by County Hall of this vast new estate, Putney (including Roehampton) has kept its identity. And the main reason for this is topographical. A green crescent of open spaces separates it from other districts to the west and south: Barn Elms Park, Putney Common, Barnes Common; sports grounds such as those of the Roehampton Club and the Bank of England; Palewell Common; Richmond Park with its 2,400 rustic acres; and the big green wedge of Putney Heath and Wimbledon Common marking off Putney to the south. In the north is the river, so only to the east does Putney merge into Wandsworth town.

St Mary's Church, Putney, where the Roundheads sat in council of war with their hats on, now dwarfed by a computer firm's office block.

Part of the GLC's Alton Estate, Roehampton, conceived as a series of tower-blocks amid green communal spaces. Most people now demand two-storey houses with their own gardens.

This chain of open spaces is one of the great attractions of the area to those who live there. Peter Gerhold, vice-chairman of the Putney Society, was born in the "village" and moved to his present house in Hazlewell Road, built for his grandmother in 1908, when he was four years old. "When I was a child you could walk right out into Surrey; we were on the edge of the country." The impression of being "on the edge of the country" persists: Putney and its neighbour Wimbledon lie out of sight of each other, their separateness maintained by a mile-and-a-half of heath and common.

The other big attraction is the Thames. If Putney is an island surrounded by grass and water, then Roy Plomley of *Desert Island Discs* is not the most surprising person to find living there. His garden runs down to the river, and from his top-floor work-room he has a magnificent view of the tideway. "I take a critical look at every crew that passes," says Plomley who used to row for Kingston Rowing Club. "There are always boats going up and down the river, and they've never yet succeeded in making an ugly boat. Even the dredgers are attractive."

Plomley and his wife moved to Putney in 1950, because they wanted a house with a garden. He previously lived in Dolphin

Square. "I've always lived on the river," he told me. In twenty-seven years Putney has become noisier and more crowded, and though in theory there are plenty of useful bus routes, in practice he finds there is often a dearth of buses. He said he would like to see river buses running on the Thames into central London, but above all wishes some way could be found to make the High Street a pleasanter and more satisfactory place for shoppers. As it is there is a constant tawdry battle between crawling traffic and jostling, frustrated shoppers.

Judge Ian Fife, chairman of the Putney Society and a resident since 1929, believes most recent changes have been for the better. The now vanished great houses on Putney Hill had begun to decline and go into multi-occupation before the Second World War. "I think the redevelopment that has taken place is all to the good," he says. Like Fulham across the river, Putney has had its middle-class invasion, with couples from Kensington, Chelsea and elsewhere buying up family houses at reasonable prices on the modest Victorian terraces near the river. "It has meant that the old Putney residents are no longer able to rent houses; but the houses are better looked after."

Judge Fife agrees that there has been a decline in the shopping centre. He blames "the inability of the local authorities to do anything about parking, at least until this year, when they brought in yellow lines and wardens." Until that happened Putney suffered from solid parking, largely by commuters, in many streets close to the Southern Region station in the High Street, and near East Putney Underground station. The town centre has only one small off-street car park, despite developers' promises.

An environmental improvement close to Judge Fife's heart is the forty-year-old scheme for a footpath link between the river at Leader's Gardens and Richmond Park, the first stage of which – a path along Beverley Brook – is now coming into effect. The Department of the Environment agreed to open a new gate in the wall of Richmond Park as a Jubilee Project, but by the end of Jubilee Year (1977) it was still not open. Judge Fife thought it not unusual or odd for a circuit judge to head a local civic society. "The society is non-political and I stay clear of politics. Sometimes it helps. People are prepared to talk to a judge when they wouldn't to someone else."

Writers, artists and actors particularly abound in Putney – perhaps because, as Roy Plomley puts it, "it's still within taxi range

Putney High Street: traffic jams and a changing shopping centre.

of the West End if you're working late." Swinburne was nursed back to health by his friend Watts-Dunton in the 1880s in a house (then No. 2, The Pines) at the foot of Putney Hill, which still stands and bears a blue plaque; Edward Gibbon (whose parents' home earlier stood on that same site) largely grew up with his aunt in "the house, near Putney bridge and churchyard, of my maternal grandfather [which] appears in the light of my proper and native home". Today's writers, a somewhat different band, include Marjorie Proops of the *Daily Mirror*, Hugh Stephenson, editor of *The Times Business News* (who was also for a time a local councillor) and, from television, David Dimbleby, who lives on Putney Common. Actors include Penelope Keith and Nerys Hughes; among the musicians are harpist Marisa Robles and her flautist husband Christopher Hyde-Smith.

Though most readers of the *Business News* would perhaps be surprised to hear it, Hugh Stephenson was a member, not of the opposition Tory group on Wandsworth council, but of the much criticized then-Labour majority. On the opposite side of the council

Skiffs and skulls: the tideway at Putney.

chamber sits Dennis Mallam, who lives on the Wandsworth-Putney border but who grew up in Putney, where his parents moved when he was four. A quantity surveyor by profession, he deplores the decline of the High Street which he feels is no longer a shopping centre since it lost its department store. The seeming countryside of commons and heaths, on the other hand, is one of the great joys of the area for him. He is critical of the then-Labour Council's policy of continuing to redevelop wherever possible with housing. "Some of us think we should be looking for industry for some sites close to the High Street." In the spring of 1978 the Conservatives gained control of Wandsworth and elected Mallam leader of the council.

Marie Jenkins and her husband Hugh, Labour MP for Putney since winning the seat from the Tories in 1964, came to live in Putney in 1958. Moving from Pimlico they wanted somewhere overlooking the river, and Marie Jenkins told me she delighted in both the place and its lively population of actors, musicians and journalists. Noise from traffic and aircraft and the emergence of a National Front presence on the Wandsworth border were two of the few blots on an attractive scene. Mrs Jenkins, who was a GLC member for seven years, blames living conditions in Wandsworth tower blocks as one reason for the aberration of the Front; but she praised council housing in Putney which, she said, was rightly indistinguishable from the homes of neighbouring owner-occupiers. She cited with pleasure the incredulity of American visitors on hearing that it was public housing.

Sooner or later in Putney you come back to the river. The approach across Putney Bridge, with its pretty, newly repainted lanterns, is, says Peter Gerhold, "the finest approach from London to any inner London suburb". The tideway is a constant delight; and what gives this particular stretch of the Thames the edge over, say, Chelsea or Battersea, is its rowing clubs.

The London Rowing Club, which currently has some 800 members, is among the most illustrious in the world. It established itself on the Putney riverside in 1856, when club rowing outside Oxford and Cambridge was in decline, and set about changing the face of the rowing world, winning both the Grand Challenge Cup and the Stewards' Challenge Cup in the very next year, and recording eighty-five wins at Henley in its 121 years. It pioneered the sliding seat in Britain, and introduced coxless fours on the tideway; it has played a leading part in the development of sectionalized boats for ease of transport; and the indoor rowing tank which it installed in 1928 has been used by many thousands of oarsmen from clubs and schools all over Greater London.

LRC's solid and distinctive Victorian clubhouse, recently modernized at a cost of £70,000, and the bustle of boats and oarsmen in front of it, are a familiar sight not only to Putney folk but to members of the boating fraternity from all over the world. They make the Putney waterside what it is. As Judge Fife puts it, speaking both personally and for the Putney Society, "We are very conscious of the importance of the rowing clubs, and of sailing on the river. This sporting use of the Thames gives it a great deal of colour and makes it unique." This has been recognized by the GLC who, in raising its flood defences against the threat of a surge tide from the North Sea, is running a higher river wall not along the front of the Putney riverside, but behind it. No concrete block wall can be permitted to impede the oarsmen or obscure that hallowed view.

14

Enfield

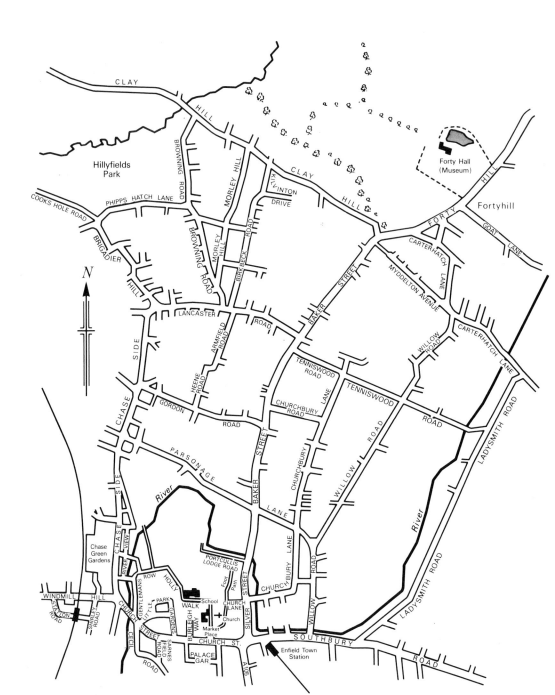

14

Enfield

To many users of the A10 Great Cambridge Road, Enfield must seem one of London's least prepossessing places. Lines of 1930s and 1950s factories, whose names are household words but whose faces lack all charm, are interrupted only by lowlier rows of brick and pebble-dash suburban houses. The scene is urban but devoid of urbanity. The traveller's chief relief comes in place names: Brimsdown, Ponders End and Enfield Lock, Wash or Highway and – most graphically named of these former villages and hamlets strung along the western side of the Lea Valley – Freezywater. The Roman road, Ermine Street, ran this way and the later medieval route to Cambridge. And for centuries these were villages set in a countryside that supplied London with much of its foodstuffs, and had special licence to do so during the Great Plague. Now they are part of a congealed suburban mass – somewhere not for lingering in but to be passed through with as much dispatch as speed limits and traffic lights allow.

But if you divert from the Great Cambridge Road only a mile to the west you find quite a different Enfield – Enfield Town – which is still a town rather than a suburb or a village. "It still remains much more of an entity than most places in London," says local GP Dr Christopher Jephcott. "I think that's because it's on an east-west route, rather than on a radial road out of London." This distinction, this feeling that here is place of consequence in its own right, is one of the factors that make Enfield folk want to live there; another is its remarkable heritage of attractive old buildings.

The name Enfield (Enefelde in the *Domesday Book*) is Saxon in origin and means "the forest clearing belonging to Eana". Indeed by the time that the survey was made in the 11th century this was a settlement in a clearing at the south-eastern fringe of the royal hunting forest, Enfield Chase. The parish church of St Andrew dates in part from the 13th century, though most of its structure is later, and its most notable monument, commemorating a Lord Mayor of London, Sir Nicholas Raynton, dates from the end of the Civil War. By then the parish had some 2,000 inhabitants, and Enfield men were prominent in resisting Charles I's illegal forced taxation – more by pleas that they were too poor to pay than by more direct and hazardous resistance. After the war they found themselves at odds with the Commonwealth government when the sale of Enfield Chase threatened the rights and livelihood of the commoners. So determined was their resistance that the commissioners charged with effecting the new enclosures had to call upon local justices to protect the new proprietors against "the rude multitude from Enfield Town" which had broken down hedges and ditches and threatened to do likewise with the houses.

Local historian David Pam offers two versions of events on 10 July 1656. One describes twenty-five commoners facing fifteen armed soldiers with only axes, cudgels and the like, and defeating them and taking them prisoner despite several deaths among their number from shots fired by the soldiers' muskets; the other (official) version tells of as many as 250 bloodthirsty Enfield men attacking the poor soldiers with pitchforks, scythes and poles, most unsportingly overrunning them while they strove to reload their muskets and "making great shouts and declaring for Charles Stewart".

Enfield Town, some nine to ten miles from the Bishopsgate entrance to the City of London, was long before our 20th-century suburban sprawl closely linked to the metropolis. The gentry like Raynton, who built Forty Hall in the early 1630s, could reside on their country estates yet be no more than a couple of hours' journey from the City or Westminster; and the farms and small holdings hereabouts had a ready market for their produce close enough for fresh, daily delivery.

It is this sense of being at once accessible to London and yet in, or at least on the edge of, real countryside that holds people to Enfield. It is, says Mrs Valerie Carter, chairman of the Enfield Preservation Society, "an ideal compromise. We're on the edge of the green belt and we still have the feel of a country town." Another local conservationist, Don Gresswell, points out that there are twenty-three farms in Enfield and twenty-four miles of public footpaths. This he knows because, with the then deputy borough engineer, he headed a brisk campaign in 1962 which surveyed, cleared and signposted the paths in twelve months. Gresswell, an electrical

Contrary to the impression that may be given to the motorist on the Great Cambridge Road, Enfield, is not all industry. It has no fewer than twenty-three farms and twenty-four miles of footpaths.

engineer by training, came to the district in 1938 as a result of a merger by the firm that employed him. He then opened a little tobacconist's and stationer's shop which on its first day took 7s. ("My wholesaler said that was very good.") With the passing of the 1944 Education Act, however, he expanded into school and library supplies and by 1978, running the business with his sons, had a business with a turnover of around £1 million and customers in 120 countries. At sixty-nine he was still active with the EPS' trees group, which arranges and advises on the planting of new and replacement trees.

The Enfield Preservation Society, founded in the 1930s, took on a new lease of life in the early 1960s when a local resident, Mrs Carinthia Arbuthnot Lane, saw white crosses on trees in Enfield's most attractive backwater, Gentleman's Row. Now a vice-president of the EPS, she recalled how she and fellow students at an art class were all set to chain themselves, like suffragettes, to the tree trunks to avert the threatened felling. The trees were, happily, saved by less drastic means; she became secretary of the revived society; and she and her late husband Tony found themselves involved in a campaign to prevent the old borough council running a relief road through the market square and the heart of the historic town.

"The council used to laugh at us and call us fuddy-duddies," she said. Fuddy-duddies or not, the campaigners fought with determination and resourcefulness: they staked out the route of the road to show their fellow-citizens just how much damage it would do; carried a six-foot-long model of it everywhere to meetings and lobbyings; and collected several thousand pounds to fight the expected public inquiry. The road never came. The council suddenly dropped the scheme and in the years that followed became progressively more conservation-minded. Now a conservation panel and study groups for particular areas examine all development proposals; the borough listens to and usually heeds their advice.

Gentleman's Row is a delight. A small terrace of elegant but idiosyncratic 17th- and 18th-century houses, it is separated by a footpath from its row of front gardens bordering the New River,

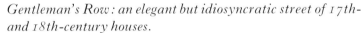

Gentleman's Row: an elegant but idiosyncratic street of 17th- and 18th-century houses.

which is dappled with ducks and crossed by delightful arched iron footbridges. Charles Lamb spent several summer holidays at a house there, and later came to live in Enfield with his mad sister Mary. Also delightful, in a different way, is the town's little market-place, bustling with stalls on Saturdays and Thursdays. The name Gentleman's Row could perhaps these days mislead. Mrs Carter emphasized that Enfield is "a balanced mixed community – not all stockbrokers and solicitors". The drawbacks of Enfield are: its traffic; the relative weakness of its shopping centre; and the lack of places for teenagers to go and amuse themselves. Mrs Carter, who has two boys in their teens, says there is "a crying need for more for youngsters to do in the evening".

Traffic ploughs through the town centre on a one-way system which was put in as temporary and then found too expensive to remove; and though Enfield generally supports the M25 outer orbital road, which promises to remove heavy lorry traffic between the Midlands and Tilbury, it fears the time when an only partially completed motorway pours its load on to the town's inadequate roads in even greater numbers than now.

Enfield Town has suffered from a seventeen-year hiatus over plans to give it a new shopping precinct. Dr Jephcott, chairman of the EPS' architecture and planning group, regrets that while Enfield dallied with schemes too ambitious to be either suitable or viable, neighbouring Wood Green, Edmonton and Waltham Cross built their shopping centres and now exert a pull that is threatening to undermine such shopping facilities as his town has.

Jephcott, born in Enfield, the son of a local GP, regrets both the loss of many fine houses which, with hindsight, most people would have wished to save, and the spread of building society offices where previously there were useful shops. He takes pleasure in the change of mental atmosphere which has followed the designation of conservation areas in the town, and the way in which the borough now consults local opinion not just on major proposed changes but on much smaller (though sometimes crucial) ones. His practice is housed in White Lodge, a spectacular, weatherboarded, 18th-century house in which Joseph Whitaker, compiler of the Almanack, lived during the late 19th century.

Across from White Lodge in Silver Street is a sculptured representation of the Enfield Beast, a mythical amalgam of forest animals once to be found in Enfield Chase; and behind it the steel-encased twelve-storey tower of the London Borough of Enfield's

White Lodge, the 18th-century house which was once the home of Joseph Whitaker, compiler of the famous almanac.

new civic centre. Dr Eric Ridge, then a Liberal member of the Enfield borough council, summed up a widespread local feeling about the tower, designed by architect Eric Broughton. "I think it's a beautiful building," he says, "but regrettably placed." And after three and a half years as a councillor he had come to the conclusion that functionally it was "terrible".

There must be something about Enfield that attracts medical men. Dr Ridge, like his fellow-professional Christopher Jephcott, is the son of a local GP; his grandfather was a GP, and so, he told me, were his brother and that brother's son. He believed that Enfield shopping facilities, and the progressive revitalization of this and other towns generally, could have been encouraged had his party's proposals for site value rating been carried into law; but one hope he expressed when I talked to him in 1977 that a more modest redevelopment of the long-cleared shopping precinct site (plans for which were to be made public early in 1978) might at last begin to reinvigorate the centre of the town, now at last, at the time of writing, seems to be going ahead. For many years almost all that had held

Enfield together as a shopping centre was the admirable and lively family-owned department store, Pearson's. The shop stands on the site of a Tudor palace, built for Elizabeth I by her brother Edward VI, which was demolished as late as 1926. Four brothers named Leggatt saved one room, which they reassembled in a specially built annexe attached to their house in Gentleman's Row – the plaster ceiling reputedly having been transferred there all in one piece on a cart. A later owner of the house, JP and former councillor Godfrey Groves, threw open this fine, panelled room with its great stone fireplace as a meeting place for all manner of local societies; but on his death in June 1978 the room ceased to be available in this way, and indeed the future of the house appeared uncertain.

Enfield's oldest surviving building is the old grammar school, dating from 1590. Its most celebrated headmaster, Robert Uvedale, was a pioneering 17th-century horticulturalist; and even now the centre of the town boasts many exotic trees such as ginkgos. Uvedale's associations with Enfield may be one of the attractions for gardening writers Frances Perry and Roy Hay, who live to the north of the town at Bulls Cross. Another must surely be the arboretum being developed at Waltham Abbey by the Lea Valley Regional Park Authority, who occupy as their headquarters

*Forty Hall, built by Sir Nicholas Raynton between 1629 and
1636, is now a local museum and meeting place.*

Myddelton House, an early-19th-century mansion once occupied by another distinguished horticulturalist, E. A. (Gussie) Bowles, who designed and planted its gardens.

But Enfield's finest house is surely the Jacobean Forty Hall standing on its ridge to the north of the town, which the council bought and restored during the 1960s. Mrs Valerie Carter, who lives at nearby Forty Hill, recalls that many people criticized the borough for spending large sums on the hall's restoration, arguing that it would be a white elephant. But Forty Hall (now a museum) and the exhibition gallery and reception suite in the adjoining stable block have been a resounding success. The preservation society, for instance, wanted to book the gallery for a photographic exhibition to mark European Architectural Heritage Year, 1975. They put in their application only nine months beforehand. The gallery was so heavily in demand that the earliest date they could get was in 1976.

Enfield Town is a lively and attractive place, and much of the credit for it must go to its preservation society. Without their efforts many of the buildings which the townsfolk today admire and enjoy would have vanished; green belt landscapes would have been built over; and footpaths would have vanished. Gentleman's Row (now recognized by the Department of the Environment as an outstanding conservation area) would no doubt have survived; but much else which council and citizens alike now value would have fallen either in the path of road-building or of redevelopment. Some local councillors argue that the preservationists sometimes go too far, demanding retention of buildings too badly decayed and too expensive to renovate. But a decade or two of steady propaganda has won over most of the critics.

Outsiders may think that the factories along the Great Cambridge Road are all there is to Enfield. Those who live there, and those who have chanced to linger there certainly know better.

15

Woolwich

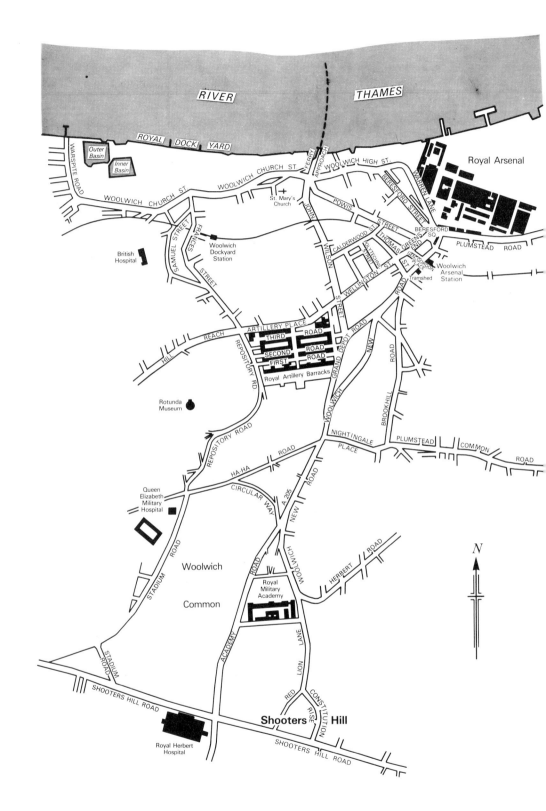

15

Woolwich

Woolwich, it has been said, is not a London suburb at all. It is a northern industrial town set down by accident on the Kentish bank of the Thames. Even today, ninety years after their town was brought within the boundaries of the old London County Council, Woolwich folk still often deny indignantly that they are Londoners. Woolwich, they say, is neither London nor Kent. It is just plain Woolwich.

The name's origins are a matter of dispute. Eckwall's *Concise Oxford Dictionary of English Place-Names* claims that it comes from the Old English Wull-Vic meaning "farm where wool was produced" or "town where wool was exported". Some local historians, however, hold the view that the alternative spelling Wulewic derived from Hulviz, meaning "hill reach", the original riverside town being hemmed in or overhung by hills; and one local road of switchback gradients does indeed bear the name Hillreach to this day.

Woolwich as a riverside fishing village and a ferry appears to go back to Domesday; and certainly state papers of 1308 record a waterman, William de Wicton, as selling the rights of ferry for £10. But what really put the place on the map was the establishment of a royal dockyard there in Tudor times. It built the *Great Harry*, or *Henry-Grace-à-Dieu*, Henry VIII's 1,500-ton warship which, by December 1512, had cost £6,472 8s od excluding timber – a prodigious sum for those times.

Ships needed guns; and that is why, by the time Pepys was visiting the dockyard, the "Gun-Wharf" at Woolwich was well established on what is now the market-place in Beresford Square. The Arsenal was slightly to the east in an area known as the King's Warren. A picturesque story tells how gun manufacture is supposed to have come there. On 10 May 1716, the Master of the King's Ordnance ordered a captured cannon to be recast at a foundry at

Moorfields on the edge of the City of London, and a crowd, including many VIPs, gathered to watch the spectacle. A young Swiss journeyman founder, Andew Schalch, in London on a visit, detected damp in the mould for the gun and warned that pouring in molten metal would cause an explosion. His warning was ignored; he very sensibly departed, the metal was poured and the explosion occurred as predicted, killing seventeen people and doing much damage. The authorities then (the story goes) advertised for the "young foreigner" to call on the Surveyor General "as the interview might be for his advantage". He called and was given the job of master-founder which he held for sixty years.

The truth is rather less romantic. The Moorfields explosion did take place, but Schalch's appointment resulted from a government decision that the King's Ordnance ought to have its own foundry. The authorities invited applications from qualified gun-founders. Schalch was simply the best of the bunch. The Arsenal in which he worked was established at Woolwich because it already had its gun-wharf and munitions stores.

In the same year a Dane, Colonel Borgard, was appointed to found the first fully professional artillery force in England, the Royal Regiment of Artillery, and as gunners already worked along-side foundrymen at Woolwich, it was the obvious location for the first artillery barracks, which were housed in one of the buildings by Vanbrugh inside the Arsenal. In 1741 the Royal Military Academy ("The Shop") started life there, too. Later, when they outgrew those quarters, the Artillery and Academy moved up the hill to Woolwich Common, the one to its magnificent new barracks of 1772 (whose 1,000-foot-long frontage Pevsner compares to St Petersburgh); the other to Wyatt's much castellated and cupola-ed buildings on the eastern side of the common beyond Ha Ha Road.

The Army and the Arsenal spread over the years to occupy about a quarter of the parish, hemming in the town, the one on its river side, the other from its southern uplands. Neither military Woolwich nor the Arsenal are what they were in their Victorian heyday. The Arsenal, though still busily testing munitions behind high walls and strictly guarded gateways, has declined dramatically both in the number of workers employed and acres occupied. Its eastern end now forms part of the GLC new town of Thamesmead; the London Borough of Greenwich (of which the old Woolwich is the greater part) has been offered the section between Beresford Square and the river; and indeed the Arsenal's ultimate closure is only a matter

The Rotunda, an artillery museum housing a range of guns from 15th-century mortars to modern ballastic missiles.

of time. Its gates are closed to all but official visitors and only the favoured few at present get a look at Vanbrugh's fine buildings round Dial Square or his Royal Brass Foundry, built to house Master Schalch's activities. This may soon change, however, if plans the council has published for opening up the area go ahead.

The Army, despite its sentries and guarded gateways, has a much more welcoming attitude to the public. Every year or two it holds an open day to thank the people of Woolwich for their hospitality and friendship; its artillery museums – the national collection in the Rotunda and the smaller regimental museum at the old Royal Military Academy – are regularly open to the public and a great attraction; its new Queen Elizabeth Military Hospital uses any spare capacity to take civil as well as military patients; and during the 1977 firemen's strike its Green Goddesses, often manned by young recruits, had answered more than 200 fire calls.

The Rotunda, which houses a range of artillery from mortars used at Crécy to modern ballistic missiles, was originally one of six stylish canvas tents designed by John Nash for the Prince Regent's meeting with the allied sovereigns in Carlton House Gardens (now St James's Park) in 1814. Colonel Sir William Congreve, second Superintendent of Military Machines, begged it from the Prince to house a growing collection of historic artillery exhibits, and Nash converted it into a permanent building with lead roof and supporting central pillar. Romantic stories attach to many of the guns, and the collection appeals to both veterans and children. The curator, ex-gunner Stanley Walter, exerts a mellower discipline than one might expect over the young visitors. Seeing some ten-year-olds climbing on one of the more venerable outdoor exhibits, he shooed them towards the more robust 20th-century ordnance which can stand up to any amount of punishment.

Twenty-eight military units are stationed in Woolwich; the biggest is the Training Regiment, which can handle up to 450 recruits at a time on fourteen-week training courses, and organizes thrice yearly courses for potential officers. Colonel David Evans, its commander, remembered coming to a rather different Woolwich as a young officer in 1956. "There was no heating, I don't think there was mains electricity, and in the morning a batman brought me an enamel pail of tepid water to wash and shave with." Whereas today, he said, the rank-and-file gunner lives in a centrally heated room with all mod cons; and facilities at Woolwich include a swimming-pool and an artificial ski slope. Behind the grand façade of "the

Depot" certain features – like the Mess, with its bewigged and liveried waiters – continue as ever; but the barracks have been substantially rebuilt to provide acceptable modern accommodation for recruits and regulars alike.

The most impressive new army building at Woolwich is the 460-bed Queen Elizabeth Military Hospital, which replaced the nearby Royal Herbert Military Hospital, the Queen Alexandra at Millbank and three other military hospitals in south-east England. The actual hospital, forming part of a larger complex of buildings all designed by architects Powell, Moya & Partners, is a low-key, two-storey building with a most unmilitary and unhospital-like atmosphere, but its 800 staff are all soldiers, from the man in charge, Brigadier Roger Freeman, down to nurses and receptionists.

As the QEMH came gradually into full operation a nearby civilian hospital, the British Hospital for Mothers and Babies, fought for survival at the hands of Health Service rationalization. "The British" began life in 1905 under its earlier name, "Wood Street Home", as a pioneer in the improved training of professional midwives to take over from the "handy women", the tragic results of whose deliveries the three founders – Mrs Parnell, Miss Gregory and Miss Cashmore – had seen at first hand.

Just down Grand Depot Road from the Artillery lie Woolwich town centre and Thames Polytechnic – an amalgam of the old Woolwich Poly, founded by Quintin Hogg in 1890 on the initiative of one of his Regent Street Polytechnic students, and the departments of architecture and surveying from Hammersmith Polytechnic. Thames Polytechnic was to have occupied new buildings at Thamesmead, but by the late 1970s there was no money for this, and the combined polytechnic has been consolidated in Woolwich.

Joe Stanyer, senior lecturer in materials sciences at the polytechnic and also deputy leader of Greenwich Council, came to Woolwich in 1968 from Stoke-on-Trent. It seemed to him from the first that this wasn't London but "a northern industrial town set on the south bank of the Thames". Though for many of his colleagues it is, he knows, a town to get out of into the Kentish countryside, he told me he likes working in Woolwich and feels at home there.

The town centre, as Stanyer (a former planning committee chairman) readily concedes, is full of "holes" – empty sites awaiting redevelopment, which "hasn't gone according to the plans drawn up for it in 1955. The property development bubble burst and there is no impetus for redevelopment at the moment." Some did take place, however. The publishing firm Morgan-Grampian moved from central London to a new office block which sits between Sainsbury's and a multi-storey car park on one side, Littlewood's and the main shopping street on the other. The borough built itself a new, quite pleasant looking, red-brick office building, and the Government put up a thoroughly nasty Crown Building alongside it. In and around the town centre can be seen the results of two decades of slum clearance, including a number of tower and slab blocks of flats. They have, most local people agree, vastly improved living conditions; but Stanyer personally accepts that "environmentally the result is not very happy". Now the council, like others that went in for high-rise housing in the 1960s, is belatedly trying to give its citizens the little houses with gardens most of them want.

The biggest shock the town has had in recent years was the closure in 1968 of AEI's huge engineering works, which threw more than 5,000 people out of work. Howard Blackman, who later became personnel controller for the 800 employees of Morgan-

Francis Street, Woolwich: on the right, the 19th-century barrack wall; on the left, council tower-blocks; ahead down the hill the river and heavy industry.

Grampian, was then running a three-generation family tobacconist's business. He was acutely aware of the impact on retail trade
of 5,000 pay packets disappearing. One solution seemed to be to
bring in office employment and Blackman, at that time also
secretary of the town's chamber of commerce, quite by accident
discovered that one of his visiting speakers, Peter Dew, then
chairman of Morgan-Grampian, had been unsuccessfully seeking a
suburban office location for his publishing group. "If Woolwich
can show me that it can support a large-scale publishing operation
and accommodate 120,000 square feet of offices, you're on," said
Dew. Woolwich could and did, and in 1972 the firm moved there.
Blackman, going to a thank-you lunch some time before the move,
heard Dew say out of the blue: "You started this. What about
seeing the job through, as personnel director?" Blackman took the
job.

Another big employer, but of much longer standing in the town,
is the Woolwich Equitable Building Society, whose origins go back
to 1842 and a gathering at the Castle Inn, Woolwich, presided over
by the landlord, a Mr Thunder. This was a "terminating" building
society – once it had financed houses for all its subscribers it would
wind itself up – as was the "improved" society formed by seceding
members the following year; but from this second group in 1847
emerged the "permanent" building society later known as the
Woolwich Equitable. The Society now has assets of £1,772 million
and more than 1,400,000 borrowers and investors. Though, thanks
to television advertising, "the Woolwich" is well known wherever
people tune to ITV, it still, says Donald Kirkham, one of its four
general managers, inspires a special loyalty in south London.

His colleague, chief general manager Alan Cumming, admits that
the Society had considered moving away from Woolwich in the
early 1960s. It was outgrowing its impressive white stone-faced
1930s headquarters. Two reasons apart from sentiment kept it in
the town: the large area of purpose-built underground strong
rooms which few prospective purchasers of the building would
have wanted; and the availability of high quality locally recruited
staff drawn largely from the adjoining Bexleyheath and Dartford
areas. In the event, the Woolwich kept its headquarters in Woolwich
but housed its computer and accounts staff at Bexleyheath.

Cumming is at one with local opinion in regretting the demolition
of solid family houses in the town during the borough's all-
embracing, clean-sweep redevelopment programme. Other changes

"We're with the Woolwich." The headquarters, in General Gordon Place, of the famous building society.

long-standing Woolwich citizens regret include the way in which multiple retailers have displaced the old family firms, so that no one lives above the shop and the town centre goes dead after 6 p.m.; and the loss of almost all live entertainment. The one exception is there on sufferance, in a building owned by the council and scheduled for demolition.

The Tramshed, once an LCC tramways electricity transformer station, has been turned into a lively and popular theatre for local people as an offshoot of the nearby Greenwich Theatre. A Greenwich architect, Ian Morton Wright, designed a cheap conversion of the empty shell – it had to be cheap because the theatre company has legally no more than a weekly tenancy from the council. One half of its 90 feet by 45 feet space was converted into an auditorium, the other half into a bar/café. The Tramshed's general manager, Australian Margaret Prior, and her four colleagues, offer local people varied fare ranging from rock, jazz and folk to old-time music hall, Saturday morning children's theatre and the Tramshed's own brand of cabaret which, says Miss Prior, is "what we almost think Tramshed is about". It has drawn, and held, audiences in a way that early, ill-fated attempts to stage straight plays failed to do. Woolwich, as an outside observer remarked, "is proletarian and proud of it". It knows what it likes, and it likes Tramshed cabaret.

One element that is not, happily, under threat is the Beresford Square open-air market. A market has existed in Woolwich since medieval times, but the present ninety-pitch affair under the gates of the Arsenal began in the 19th century. Mrs Grace Ellis married the great-grandson of one of five sisters called Hicks who set up a

street market near the ferry; the related families of Ellis and Manchester, together with the Delieus and the Edwardses, for many
years dominated the market. But now, Mrs Ellis complains that
unless a stallholder has a son or daughter who has worked on the
stall for a period of years, the family stand to lose all the good-will in
the business when the holder retires or dies. The council, which
allots licences, refuses to recognize a stallholder's right to nominate
a successor. The borough's reply is that the long-standing market
families have had too tight a hold, and it is in the public interest to
let in outsiders.

Whatever the rights and wrongs of the case, Beresford Square
market remains one of the most attractive and popular features of
the town, bringing in trade just as surely as Sainsbury's and the
town's department store, Cuff's, do. The big drawback to shopping
in Beresford Square and the main shopping street, Powis Street, is
traffic. The borough has plans for restricting access to buses and
off-peak delivery vehicles and for paving over more of the street for
the benefit of pedestrians, and also supports the more controversial
GLC proposals for running a widened Plumstead Road, the through
traffic route, behind the gateway of the Arsenal, in the hope of
taking most traffic out of the square, but turning the gateway – a
listed building and perhaps the town's best known feature – into a
sort of local Marble Arch.

Just round the corner from Beresford Square is a covered market,
and next door to it a thriving Indian grocery business. Woolwich
has something like 7,000 people of Asian origin, many of them
Sikhs who attend the Ramgarhia Association's Temple and community centre in Mason's Hill just behind Woolwich Arsenal
station. Piara Singh Rahi, for some time its secretary and now full
time community worker, recalls that the building which is now the
Sikh Temple was empty and officially labelled as a dangerous structure when his association bought it. But the community had among
its members not only bricklayers and carpenters but architects and
engineers. The association repaired and converted it, largely with
its own labour. "Before, it was so dilapidated that no one would
touch it. Now it's probably one of the best buildings in Woolwich,"
Rahi says. Besides Sikhs, Woolwich also has its Hindu and Moslem
communities.

Woolwich attracted many people from India and Bangladesh
because its polytechnic had a good name for engineering courses.
The main problems, thinks Rahi, are language and xenophobia. But

the latter, he considers, is an instinctive rather than deep-seated reaction. "Once one makes contact, people are very friendly here." He told me that his association was busy organizing language courses – English for the older people, particularly the women, and, increasingly, Punjabi for the children, who have become so integrated that English is their natural language. Currently 150 youngsters turn up each evening to learn the language which was their fathers' and mothers' native tongue.

Woolwich Ferry runs from 6 a.m. to 10 p.m. approximately each day, and carries around 5,500 cars or their equivalent daily. The present three boats are the third generation of ferries and came into operation in 1963, replacing four paddle steamers built in the 1920s when container lorries were not dreamt of. David Page, one of five skippers who command the ferries, first served on them as a boy sailor in 1930 and returned to stay in 1946. The present boats, with their variable pitch Voith-Schneider propellers, are much more efficient and carry twice the tonnage, "but as far as character's concerned, we preferred the old ones". Then the passengers were visible above deck and you got to know your customers, he says. Mothers used to bring their children with sandwiches and lemonade for an outing, and small boys used to slide down the boilers ("I used to do it myself!"). Now the awkward members of a different generation let rip more destructively below deck, so that saloons have to be locked at night to prevent vandalism. Whenever Blackwall Tunnel or Dartford is blocked by an accident queues build up for the ferry; day-in and day-out it carries vehicles not permitted in the tunnels and on Sundays the one-boat service is clearly still a treat for many family outings. Fog sometimes stops the ferry, though not as often as in the past; but the man in charge, Captain Tom Hooper, believes that, with extra navigational aids, the ferry could do better.

Across from where the ferry stops is its Italian namesake, *Il Traghetto*, an Italian restaurant run by Mario and Paula Pescatore from Avellino near Salerno. Mario told me he had been twenty-one years in the restaurant business in Britain, but in Woolwich only nine years, most of the time catering for what he called the "daily trade". More recently he had geared a new restaurant to more elaborate menus and price brackets, and in spite of Woolwich's "proletarian" character it is doing well. He values businessmen who bring their potential customers to lunch, but his best clients and spenders are, he said, working-class. Woolwich is changing,

The "Free Ferry": fog and sunlight on the river.

says Pescatore: there are more offices; the riverside has been opened up and there is talk of a recreational complex near the ferry; and local people, who ten years ago would not have looked at Italian food, are proud to come and spend an evening here and eat his scallopine in marsala. Yet they remain also proud of being Woolwich folk – for though their town may be *in* Greater London, it is still distinct and separate for all that.

16

Islington

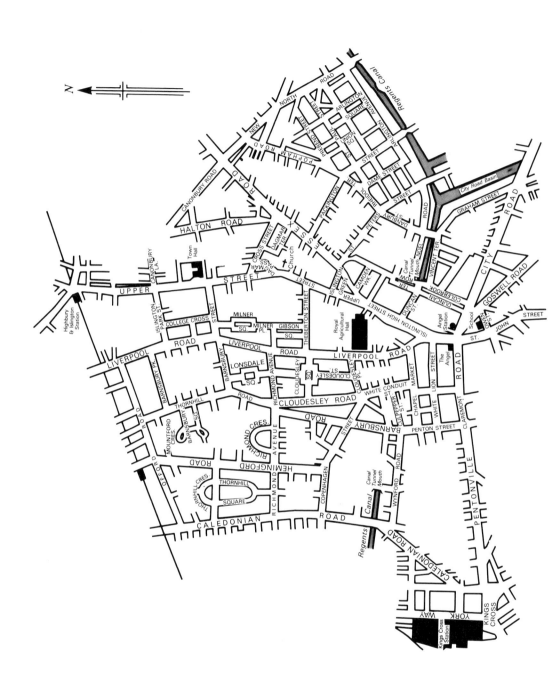

16

Islington

If profusion of restaurants, taxis and passing references in the Press were the hallmark of fashion, then Islington became fashionable in the late 1960s. Whether that is to its credit or benefit is a matter for disagreement among those who live there. Mary Cosh, architectural historian and former secretary of the Islington Society, takes a dim view of the whole process. "That 'fashionable' tag made Islington almost a dirty word for a time. Fleet Street think they discovered Islington. They didn't; all they did was exploit it."

Miss Cosh, who lives in an 1830s house facing Gibson Square, moved to Islington in 1959. She came, she told me, because it was the only district where she could find the sort of house she wanted at a price she could afford. She had never heard of the place until Duncan Grant asked her to come and model for him there earlier in the 1950s. In the ensuing twenty years she became hooked on her adopted London village, both for its architecture and its atmosphere. But, she said, many of the newcomers who followed the "gentrification" wave of the 1950s had not coalesced with the other Islingtonians. "When I first came there was a very strong community feeling. I don't feel there is so much now."

Islington means different things to different people. At one extreme it is the London Borough of Islington which stretches from Highgate Archway to the borders of the City of London; at the other it is that tight little shopping centre round the Angel. For the purposes of this article my definition is an arbitrary and in some senses a personal one. I include Barnsbury, where my mother grew up and where her father owned and ran a small back-garden factory – and where, in Barry's Holy Trinity, Cloudesley Square, my parents married; Pentonville, whose Chapel Market fascinated and delighted me as a child; and St Peter's Ward, west of Upper Street, in whose now truncated Union Square my father's family lived before moving to the then more fashionable heights of Muswell

Hill. I exclude Clerkenwell, Canonbury and Highbury, each of which merits separate treatment.

This "Middle Islington", as I shall call it, was certainly not fashionable when I first came to know it as a boy. Second World War bombs and lack of maintenance, as well as some barrack-like blocks of LCC flats, had reinforced a steady social decline which began when the great noisome and polluted corridor of railways was cut through to the west of Pentonville in the 1830s and 1840s to reach Euston and King's Cross. It was not so much that the railways made the distant prospect from the heights of Barnsbury less pleasing, as that they put into the heads of the Victorian lower-middle classes the notion of an easily accessible place in the country. They left Islington and became commuters. Even so, until the turn of the century Islington kept some of its cachet; shops in Upper Street still lived off the "carriage trade" and only the opening of the Metropolitan Line to Bayswater seems to have tipped the scale so that the up-and-coming Mr Whiteley established his new emporium there instead of in Upper Street.

The name Islington is said to derive from a 12th-century form *Iseldon*, which can be traced through documents in Corpus Christi College, Cambridge, back to a 10th- or 11th-century form

Gibson Square: suitably housed Victoria Line ventilator shaft.

Gislandun, the hill or down belonging to Gisla. By Tudor times it had strongly commercial and recreational links with the City of London: its dairy farmers supplied milk to the capital, whose citizens sought fresh air and entertainment in its byways and fields, at its taverns and archery butts. Owen's School, which my father attended sixty years ago, owes its origin to the lucky escape of young Miss Alice Wilkes from a stray arrow. In 1613 as Dame Alice Owen she built almshouses and a free school for thirty local lads on that spot "in commemoration of the great mercy shown by the Almighty in that astonishing deliverance". Some fifty years later Pepys, in his diary, was to speak of childhood trips with his father to Islington, but by then it had become a country town of some size and prosperity.

Though in the 18th century Islington's tea-gardens and cheese-cakes grew famous and the building of the New Road (now Penton-ville and City Roads) encouraged Mr Henry Penton, MP, to lay out the quarter that bears his name, it was really only in the 1820s that the great march of bricks and mortar hit the fields of Islington and Barnsbury. The Cloudesley and Milner Gibson estates were among the first to be developed in Barnsbury. They followed the pattern already set in Canonbury and Clerkenwell of spacious squares and orderly terraces which the district's devotees today find so appeal-ing. Islington's squares are indeed its chief architectural glory: Gibson and Milner, Lonsdale, Barnsbury, Cloudesley and Thorn-hill, Malvern Terrace (a square in all but name); and, to the east of Upper Street, Arlington and Union Squares and Duncan Terrace/Colebrooke Row. They are all different in shape and character, and indeed scarcely one of them is actually square.

Gibson Square looks smart and well cared for these days. It was not always so; indeed its recovery from post-war doldrums was almost wrecked by an ugly Victoria Line ventilator shaft. Deter-mined local protest secured instead the disguise of a classical, stone-faced gazebo, so restrained and right that it convinces most be-holders that it is Georgian. Milner Square used to be considered the ugliest of Barnsbury squares. Pieter Zwart in his book on Islington suggested that the thinness and verticality of its façades gave it its dark, oppressive quality; but since he left Islington to live in Oxford the borough council have bought, converted and splendidly re-stored the square. With cleaned yellow stock-brick and freshly painted stucco, it is amazingly elegant and unoppressive.

Barnsbury Square stands out as probably the most idiosyncratic of them all, not only for the two little closes which attach ear-like to its western end, but because it is industrial and commercial as well as socially mixed residential. Lonsdale is, with its 1830s gothic gables and glazing, like a square full of Trollope vicarages, Miss Cosh says. To its north stands one of the most lovingly restored streets in the area – Barnsbury Street – which a local architect, Kenneth Pring, refurbished and converted into flats and maisonettes for the Barnsbury Housing Association. His nearby new housing for the association at Lofting Road and Lonsdale Place manages to catch the spirit, scale and materials of the area, without resorting to pastiche and while staying within cost limits. It also gives people good homes in an attractive environment.

Another local architect who has something of the same feel for his adopted village is Harley Sherlock. His firm's infill housing at Popham Street in St Peter's Ward underlines his own preference for small-scale, low-key, architecture. The buildings are all two- or three-storey yet, he points out, accommodate as many people an acre as the ill-fated Ronan Point tower-block did; what is more each household has a patio or small outdoor space.

Islington has come a long way since the early 1960s when the borough's policy was to clear large areas of substandard housing and rebuild on new lines, all at odds with the urbane Victorian street pattern as well as unsympathetic in scale and materials. Now the council is spending £20 million a year on repairing and converting old houses. Whereas in 1973–74 it completed only forty-one homes by rehabilitation as against 1,395 by new building, in 1976–77 the figures were 1,378 for "rehab" as against 1,261 for "new build". These borough-wide figures disguise the fact that in "Islington Proper" rehabilitation and conservation are now the norm. What brought about that change of policy? Partly it is to be attributed to the influence of new Islingtonians – middle-class immigrants from other parts of London – drawn by attractive houses at prices they could afford. Not a few worked their way into positions of influence and power on the council and, in particular, in the ruling Labour group. Mrs Margaret Watson, chairman of the housing committee, is one of these. She came from Kennington in 1968, and her concern about growing sub-Rachman "winkling" and its effect on less well off and less articulate tenants led her to stand for the council. Later, with the collapse of the property boom, Islington bought up Victorian houses at bargain prices and modernized and converted them. When council tenants are getting

flats in the elegant restored terraces of the Scott, New River and
other 19th-century estates, somehow the stigma that once attached
to "conservation", because it was synonymous with "gentrification", simply dissolves. Mrs Watson talks enthusiastically of mixed
communities in which council-owned houses and those of owner-
occupiers exist side by side in the same street and are indistinguishable from one another; and scathingly of the anti-middle-
class, Islington-for-the-Islingtonians propaganda which made
some headway a year or two back. "We did a survey and found that
only about two per cent of heads of households were actually born
here," she says. She would probably agree with Mary Cosh's
dictum. "Some people see everything in class terms. But
Islington's divisions are not class ones, but those of haves and have-
nots."

One place where any class antagonism certainly disappears is
among children at play by, in or on the water. The Regent's Canal,
linking the Grand Union with the Thames at Limehouse, was built
in 1820; it tunnels underground for 960 yards beneath Islington – a

*The New March of Bricks
and Mortar : housing rehab.
in Cloudesley Square.*

reminder that Islington is Gisla's hill. At the eastern, St Peter's
Ward end it emerges into a cutting below Noel Road, one of several
Islington addresses where Sickert lived and painted (now much
smarter than in his day, with the canalside turned into attractive
public gardens), continuing on to the City Basin, a large stretch of
commercially redundant water on which a lively children's boat
club has operated for several years, helping to redress a shortage of
open space.

But strong disagreement has blown up between Islington
Council and a residents' group called Crobac (City Road Basin
Action Group) as to the future of the surrounding wharves. Tony
Howell, who lives in the adjoining Graham Street, vigorously
supports the Crobac view that the existing warehouse buildings on
the western side of the basin should be turned into flatted factories
or small workshops. Margaret Watson defends the council view
that the site would be more fruitfully used for housing. Howell
counters this by pointing to the presence of adjoining industry and
the large amount of traffic caused by a new electricity board depot at
the southern end of the basin. The council's decision will not go
unchallenged, he says; there will be a fight at any public inquiry on
compulsory purchase orders, and Crobac is considering going to
the Ombudsman. Islington Council, it should be said, are planning
to build flatted factories on the eastern side of the basin, and the
borough architect is working on plans that would enliven the
waterside with a pub, shops and quarters for the boat club together
with housing.

A rather different attraction for children from Islington and
farther afield is tucked away through an arch in the Dickensian
streetscape of busy Cross Street, in the heart of Islington. John
Wright and his wife Lyndie founded the Little Angel Marionette
Theatre in 1960 in a previously derelict hall in the shadow of the
spire of St Mary's, Upper Street, the parish church. South Africans
who preferred to live in England, they had toured abroad as
puppeteers for several years before deciding that they needed
permanent headquarters to develop their art. Islington at the time
was cheap; and when they bought the hall they also got a cottage
alongside, where they and their two children live, and the services
of a carpenter who had his workshop there. The Little Angel has
prospered, and now has a repertoire of some twenty-seven productions of which the most popular are Hans Andersen's *The Little
Mermaid* and *Rapunzel*. Grants from a charitable trust founded by

*Islington is short of open space. Newly opened canal towpaths
and canalside parks help to make up for this deficiency, as here,
on the Regent's Canal near Noel Road.*

Lord Marks of Marks and Spencer, the Arts Council and more recently Islington Council have helped the Wrights to maintain an ambitious standard of puppetry, and to build on a back-stage extension; though part of the Little Angel's attractiveness is that its former church hall auditorium seats only a hundred people. Wright told me he and his neighbours in Dagmar Passage hoped soon to be living on Islington's newest square. They had persuaded the council that the site of a recently demolished late Victorian building should not be built on but instead paved and planted as a piazza in front of the theatre.

Despite its divisions and feuds, its suspicion of newcomers (though most Islington people are in some sense newcomers) and the periodic ritual waving of the banners of class warfare, Islington is a friendly and lively place. The borough boasts some 500 local societies of one kind or another (a high proportion of them in "Middle Islington"); and one vehicle for bringing some of them together has been InterSoc – a loose federation founded by the present chairman of the Islington Society, James Ogilvy-Webb. It came into being in 1973 or 1974 with the first signs of government concern about the "inner city", arguing that housing and certain kinds of job-creating industry could (and in Islington *should*) live side by side. "The council said then it couldn't understand what we were talking about," Ogilvy-Webb recalled. Now the idea has become widely accepted.

A retired civil servant, he came to Islington in 1964 from St John's Wood, where his lease had run out. He and his wife settled in Islington because their two daughters were attending the North London Collegiate School at Canons Park and could continue to reach it by train. But Islington quickly became his love and obsession. Since he came one change has been in house prices. (His first house, a five-storey 1780s terrace house round the corner from the Little Angel, cost him £6,750!) Another is the deterioration of public transport: they will soon, he suggested, have to put up memorial tablets to "citizens of Islington who died waiting for the No. 30 bus". But like Margaret Watson he finds his adopted village a friendly place: people are ready to chat and there is a feeling of camaraderie, especially in Chapel Market. For while Camden Passage on the east side of Upper Street draws the tourists with the bait of antiques and *filet mignon*, if you are looking for the natives or for good, cheap, fresh vegetables, then the other side of Upper

The city Basin, headquarters of a very successful children's boat club started by Crystal Hale. Her father, the late A. P. Herbert, wrote a book called The Water Gypsies.

Street – Chapel market in Pentonville – is the place to go.

Between these two lies the heart of Islington, the Angel crossroads and its immediate surroundings. Here the future is uncertain. To save the "Aggie" – the Royal Agricultural Hall – in Liverpool Road the borough council sought a gigantic grant from the Sports Council to provide a skating rink. But it was competing with three or four other local authorities; and in 1978 Manchester got the money. While in principle welcoming other uses, the borough did all too little by way of going out and looking for them, and at the time of writing there seemed an all too real danger that this great

The Angel's threatened townscape. The building just to the right of the lamp standard is The Angel, former pub and later Lyons Corner House.

covered open space would be demolished for want of cash to repair and convert it for useful present-day purposes. The redevelopment of the large empty site bordered by Islington High Street, Upper Street, Duncan Street and the backs of houses in Duncan Terrace is also still in doubt. "It has been blighted for getting on for thirty years by the GLC and the borough council while they talked about what to do with it," complains Tony Howell. Doubts about road-widening schemes delayed development decisions; then the mirage of a profitable office development lured councillors. "We have a saying here 'Eldorado lies in Duncan Street'," says Howell. The council turned down a scheme it commissioned from Frederick Gibberd & Partners for mixed office and housing development. Quite rightly, say Howell and other conservationists, because it would have replaced a varied street scene with one long, relentless monolithic frontage. Oddly, the council resolved to drop the housing and go for a smaller, offices-only scheme. But, argues Howell, although the borough's development consultants advised that such offices would be be lettable, they have not produced convincing evidence of prospective tenants for such a location or of any developer willing to put his money into the scheme.

However, the council's rejection of it led the borough architect, Alfred Head, an Islington native and a prime mover of the council's policies of conservation and rehabilitation, to draw up sketch schemes for a much more attractive rebuilding of the area – keeping some of the more interesting existing buildings, linking Upper Street to the Angel Underground station by courtyards and arcades, and even demonstrating that a small number of homes could be acceptably fitted in on the Duncan Street side of the site, which has always been residential. It is to be hoped that councillors will listen to the arguments for a more modest mixed development that keeps the character and liveliness of the High Street.

Finally, the Angel building itself – the 1899 pub-turned-Lyons corner house – which, even by the choosier standards of 1952, Sir Nikolaus Pevsner described approvingly as "jolly commercial vulgarity". The building, while in the hands of the GLC, became so rickety that it was the subject of a dangerous structures notice. County Hall acquired it for a road "improvement" which has since been drastically reduced, and it has recently sold it to a developer who, apparently, means to refurbish it. Let us hope he holds to that intention. The Angel, on its dominant corner site, with its great bulbous cupola and turn-of-the-century oriental-looking skyline, forms part of a marvellous hotchpotch townscape stretching from Pentonville Road to White Lion Street – a motley collection of quaint and curious buildings that give this place its identity and make it unlike any other. Yet none of the buildings is protected. The owners would need no permission to demolish them. They fall just outside and between the Barnsbury and St Peter's conservation areas, and the Department of the Environment say that the Angel itself is not architecturally important enough to list. Yet in townscape terms it is crucial. Eastwards for three-quarters of a mile down City Road it dominates the skyline. For that reason it is more important than most listed historic buildings. Without it the Angel would no longer be the Angel.

17

Dockland Hamlets

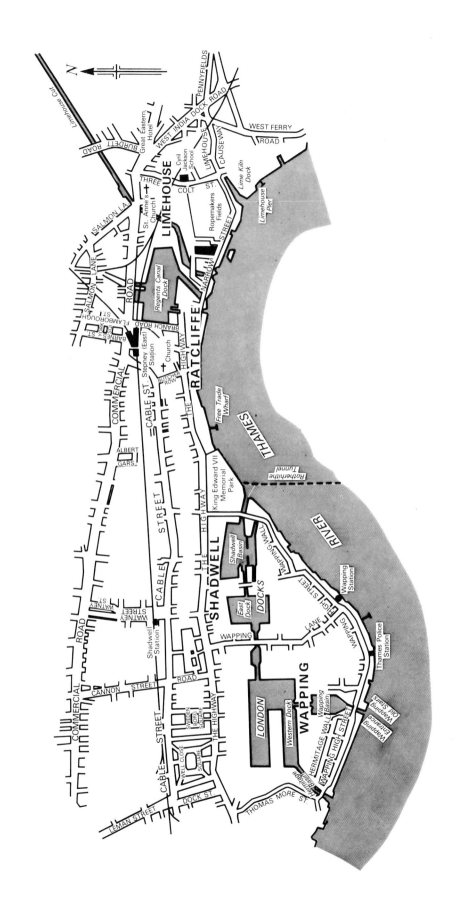

17

Dockland Hamlets

The modern borough of Tower Hamlets takes its name from a group of settlements in that stretch of the old county of Middlesex which lay east and north-east of the City of London. Their inhabitants belonged to parishes which owed a special duty to muster, on the call of the Constable of the Tower, as a militia if invasion or some other emergency threatened. This chapter covers four of these, Wapping, Shadwell, Ratcliff and Limehouse: the four riverside hamlets which spread downstream to the beginning of the great loop of the Thames round the Isle of Dogs. All are of medieval or earlier origin and their names partly tell their story. Wapping meant mud or marsh; Shadwell, shallow well or stream; Ratcliff, the red cliff of higher, gravelly ground which made this stretch of Thames-side attractive for loading and unloading cargoes; Limehouse derives from the 14th-century lymostes – lime oasts – whose remains could until comparatively recently be seen at Limekiln Dock.

Traditionally associated with sailors and dockers and with all the trades and skills connected with the river, these riverside hamlets perhaps reached the peak of their prosperity in the 18th century. Then each district had its streets or squares of well-to-do houses, such as those of the Scandinavian timber merchants in Wellclose Square and Swedenborg Square. The late 18th century saw the start of the system of enclosed docks which made the Port of London the envy of the world; but paradoxically that advance in efficiency held the seeds of the area's present sad decay. Victorian dock promoters built too ambitiously, so that supply soon exceeded demand; and in the 1850s and 1860s bigger docks of deeper draught soon stole trade from earlier ones such as St Katharine (1828) and the London Docks (1805) in Wapping. The enclosed or "wet" docks had another and debilitating effect on this area. They pushed out poor inhabitants and compressed them more tightly and more

183

miserably into the overcrowded streets that remained – streets narrowly hemmed in by the high walls of wharf, warehouse and dock alike. Twenty-foot-high brick walls built to stop pilfering (which by the 1890s was costing importers £500,000 a year) also shut off these tight-packed communities from the river which gave them life and from their East End hinterland. They are a physical cause of the traditional insularity of these dockland villages.

The 19th century also brought another change to the detriment of the dockland area. Better urban transport – trains, trams, horse-buses – facilitated social polarization. The West End was smart, other suburbs to north and south were acceptable, the East End was neither. Merchants who no longer needed to live above the shop commuted to and from dockland. Cable Street, once lined with prosperous and attractive houses, and the parallel Ratcliff Highway made it their function, as East End historian Millicent Rose puts it, "to provide sailors with the means of losing a voyage's earnings in three days' dissipation".

Today the slums and stews of Cable Street have gone, replaced by antiseptic, tawdry blocks of flats; the Highway is a fast, four-lane lorry route; but the riverside districts from Wapping to Limehouse are still in many ways squalid and deprived, partly, say local people, because Town Hall and County Hall have been too quick to use the bulldozer and too slow and clumsy in their replacements; partly because they ignored the organic nature of local communities and thought people would transplant and blossom – whereas the fruits of such transplants have often been among successive generations, rootlessness and persistent petty crime.

The Highway: four fast-moving lanes of traffic, homes stacked up in "human filing-cabinets", and much tawdriness, disused land, and lack of employment around them.

Few local people have observed these changes more closely than social worker Bob Gilding. Born in Limehouse, son of a dock crane-driver, he trained as a cooper and worked at that trade for twenty-seven years, much of the time in the bonded wine and spirit vaults of London Docks. Save for two years at Ruskin College, Oxford, he has lived all his life in these riverside parishes. Ships' hooters and a skyline of cranes have been for him what birdsong and clumps of elms were to the rural village lad. His crane-driver father, he said, could tell you exactly what each ship on the river was doing just by listening to distant hooters. Now the cranes are disappearing from up-river dockland, as are dockers and seamen; and the hooters only sing out in chorus now to usher in each New Year.

As a social worker especially concerned with adolescents, Gilding has seen all too clearly the unhappy results of sweeping and ill-digested clearance and redevelopment schemes: fragmented communities, youngsters bored, without prospects, out of control. When he was a lad, he said, "If I took a liberty in another street, someone would come out and belt me; then they'd tell my mother and she'd belt me." Everyone knew everyone else; acceptable standards of behaviour were clearly understood; and kids knew where they were; now, with more "permissive" attitudes "children get confused". And there is no longer the closeness of community which made his wife (a Poplar lass, now a hospital administrator) regard marrying a Limehouse boy as going ever so slightly beyond the pale.

A much more recent Limehouse resident, publisher John Chesshyre, is, with Gilding, a leading light in the small but influential Tower Hamlets Society. He lives in and has been gradually restoring an attractive 18th-century terrace house in Newell Street, whose back windows look out on Hawksmoor's splendid St Anne's Church. This strip of Thameside was once full of pleasing, modest houses like these, and the even more beautiful ones of the Scandinavian timber merchants in Wellclose Square. LCC, GLC and borough tore them down as unfit for occupation, applying criteria that made no concessions to architectural worth or neighbourhood roots. In their place they threw up slabs and towers, better in internal amenities than the barrack-like blocks of the inter-war years, yet ugly and impersonal from the outside and with only an apology for open space – too often becoming a litter-strewn mud-bath – where the kids could play. More recently the local authorities have done rather better. Although someone in the GLC architects' department has ruined one of dockland's prettiest squares, Albert Gardens, with a totally unsympathetic new block at its north-east corner, new mansarded, stock-brick houses put up by the borough alongside St Anne's are at least roughly of the right scale and materials; and someone more perceptive at County Hall managed to get the GLC to keep and restore the little brick houses of the Mercers' Company Estate round York Square, which originally it bought for demolition.

One of the best runners from the County Hall architectural stable is an ILEA primary school, the Cyril Jackson School, just south of St Anne's beyond the viaduct of the disused Blackwall Railway line. Faced in brown brick and timber with distinctive "inverted arch" windows, the building won a Civic Trust Award in 1973 and (which does not always follow) is popular with both the children and the teachers who use it. Mrs Marion Selwyn-Smith, a Hackney woman who is its head, comments that, lack of storage space apart, she finds it a good building to work in. Her 400-odd pupils certainly need the bright, stimulating environment the school offers, with even the adjacent railway arches turned to good account as play space; for in general their lives are drab and oppressive. A trip to Crisp Street market in Poplar is about as far as most of them go on an outing, unless they go with the school to the Tower; a depressingly high proportion of them come from families on the social service department's lists as unable to cope, violent or persistently criminal; and even the river is barred to them – because of high walls. "They can't get at it unless they're delinquent," says Mrs Selwyn-Smith. Her conviction that even the newer blocks of flats are unsuitable for families with children is underlined by the frequently expressed ambition of her pupils to "have a back and front" – a front door, a back door and their own garden.

Limehouse used to be associated with the London Chinese community until council redevelopment scattered them and the Gerrard Street area of Soho stole the title Chinatown. The Limehouse Chinatown was traditionally quite a small area, a few streets and alleys round Pennyfields and Limehouse Causeway, close to the gates of the West India Docks; and indeed its founders were mostly Chinese seamen who married local girls, such as the father of Mrs Gladys Farmer, who owns one of the newest but best of local Chinese restaurants, the Chinatown in Commercial Road, almost opposite St Anne's parish church. Her father came from Shanghai, her mother was a Scot; they lived in a row of houses off

Pennyfields and kept a restaurant which, during the Second World War, was reduced to serving very un-Chinese dockers' breakfasts and lunches to survive. Until three or four years ago she was associated with perhaps the most famous of Limehouse restaurants, the Old, New and Good Friends, owned by her friend Charlie Cheung. Then she opened the Chinatown and her three daughters all take a hand in running it. They scarcely look Chinese at all (her husband, Cyril, was a hundred per cent, roast-lamb-and-mint-sauce Englishman from the world of chartered accountancy); but her grandchildren look more oriental, since her eldest daughter Jean married a Chinese, who is also in the firm. Her restaurant, in an early-19th-century former wine merchant's house with tunnels leading under Commercial Road, provides well prepared Chinese peasant food served in a leisurely way, authentic and with few concessions to those who cannot handle chopsticks. She has two great assets: a good chief cook and a betting shop virtually next door. Chinese kitchen staff are inveterate gamblers, and if a restaurant is too far from the nearest bookmaker you may not be able to find them when you need them!

There is in these riverside hamlets considerable suspicion of middle-class newcomers from the West End, particularly those who have acquired and restored houses with riverside views. A whole colony of them lives in a row of tall old merchants' houses backing on to the river at Narrow Street, Limehouse, running eastward from The Grapes, one of the less tourist-ridden riverside pubs. These houses are largely 18th century, but the oldest of them survived the great Ratcliff fire of 1794 and their leases run back to Elizabethan times. In one of these live Lady Rozelle Raynes and her doctor husband. Mrs Raynes, as she is generally known, by no

York Square: pleasant, modest 19th-century houses which Tower Hamlets nearly demolished, but has now restored and upgraded into high-standard "council houses".

means fits the stereotype of the aloof, middle-class interloper who shuts her front door on the traffic and her neighbours. Rozelle Raynes (Lady Raynes in her own right) turned out to be a governor of three local schools and a hard-working voluntary school visitor for one of them, the Cyril Jackson. A former Wren, she worked for two years as a purser on a cross-Channel ferry; helped out one night a week in The Grapes when her neighbours, the landlord and his wife, were hard-pressed; and teaches local boys seamanship and navigation on the boat she and her husband have at North Woolwich. She lives where she does, not so much for the views of the river as out of affection for the place and its people.

The Rayneses first came to Narrow Street in the 1960s, renting a flat in one of the Narrow Street houses which a lorry driver friend had spotted was being restored; then they moved to Blackheath, to rather more modish quarters in the 18th-century Paragon; but she was homesick for Limehouse, and when one of the Narrow Street houses came on the market they returned there with alacrity. She admits that a barrier of shyness long separated the "nobs" of Narrow Street from the council tenants of Brightlingsea Buildings opposite – until the Silver Jubilee. Then the publishers, MPs and doctors from the fashionable side and their neighbours from The Buildings got together for a street party. It was a great success, and has been followed by a Guy Fawkes party and generally a much greater feeling of togetherness, especially among the children.

Rozelle Raynes' most celebrated neighbour is the former Foreign Secretary, David Owen, who has lived there since the mid 1960s. His wife Debbie, who hails from the United States and runs her own business as a literary agent, told me she loved her views of the river in its endlessly changing moods and lights, and the lopsidedness and idiosyncrasy of the different houses in the row. She believes that as an American she has an instinctive feeling for Cockney humour. Her husband, she says, had previously lived on a houseboat up-river at Chelsea. They have two small sons, for whom this tall, drunken, riverside house (derelict when Owen took it, and restored floor by floor whenever he, then a poor, fledgling politician, had the money to do it) is a fine place to grow up in. Despite the initial disapproval of government security advisers, to some of whom Limehouse seemed not at all the place for a Foreign Secretary to live, the Owens have no plans to move away from Narrow Street. Whatever odd looks the name produces at diplomatic parties, Limehouse for them is home.

Slightly farther west, beyond the empty Regent's Canal Dock, Narrow Street runs into Ratcliff, a hamlet which bombs and bulldozers have almost turned into a non-place. One of its newer residents is Mrs Ray Hoffenburg who, with her husband Leon, rescued a derelict Georgian tea warehouse and turned it into four luxurious, river-facing homes. Aware of criticism from some politically conscious Tower Hamlets people of such conversions, she argues that basically sound and attractive buildings which give the area its character would otherwise have gone beyond repair; that the £50,000–£60,000 a-piece price tag on her three surplus units, though out of reach of most East Enders, is beyond all comparison better value than bijou residences in Hampstead or Chelsea; and that, bluntly, the area will benefit from the leavening of professional, middle-class outsiders. The three who have taken flats in her converted house are a musician, an interior designer and an art dealer. Her Narrow Street conversion is an undoubted success, but on a more ambitious project Mrs Hoffenburg has been thwarted. She engaged a group of young architects to design the conversion of a much larger group of warehouses bordering The Highway into a "village community" including flats, studios, workshops and light industry, as well as offices. It would, she argued, provide the kind of employment opportunities and mixed community needed for the regeneration of Dockland. Tower Hamlets Council did not agree. It preferred to give the go-ahead to a very different project: a new complex for ILEA's City of London Polytechnic. Mrs Hoffenburg's devotion to the dockland's riverside and the rescue of fine old warehouse buildings is compelling; but scepticism about her proposals for this group of sixteen warehouses between Narrow Street and King Edward VII Memorial Park goes wider than Tower Hamlets Council.

What enraged conservationists and planners alike, however, was ILEA's action in starting on demolitions before producing any clear or detailed plans as to how they proposed to redevelop. Even those who held that a polytechnic with recreational facilities to be shared with local people was the better use of the site, nonetheless bitterly complained that ILEA was repeating the mistakes of the past by blighting the area with premature demolition. One building, the Grade II listed Free Trade Wharf, it had in any case to keep. The argument that one neighbouring building, Hubbock's Wharf, has floors impregnated with highly inflammable paint resins is seen as a poor excuse for bulldozery on the scale now proceeding. The best hope is perhaps that the Poly can begin their new complex quickly, using more of the surviving buildings than originally intended, including some for student housing, and producing something attractive and in character.

Just north across The Highway, in a group of buildings centred on a Georgian former vicarage, is the Royal Foundation of St Katharine, founded in 1148 by Queen Matilda for prayers and practical charity in the area east of the Tower. Remarkable right from the start for equality between the brothers and sisters under vows there, this religious community began life where St Katherine Dock now is, but moved in 1825, when the dock was built, to more salubrious surroundings at Regent's Park. There, according to the Master, Father George Sidebotham of the Community of the Resurrection, the brothers and sisters lived a life of gentle ease: scarlet cassocks and lace trimmings crept in, and the East End grew remote. After the Second World War, however, the foundation returned to dockland, providing a venue for all manner of conferences and retreats: "dockers and Rotarians, the maladjusted and the well-adjusted, monks and nuns, social workers and nursery school-children". Though so-called road improvements mean that the community, already sitting above the chasm of the entrance to the Rotherhithe Tunnel, now also suffers a constant battering from the noise of heavy traffic in a widened Butcher Row, it remains a place of calm.

Father Sidebotham, John Chesshyre and Bob Gilding have all been involved in a recently founded Limehouse and Ratcliff Road Action Group, very concerned about GLC-Borough-Docklands Joint Committee plans for a relief road to run through the area. The two options apparently most favoured by the politicians would respectively slice grass and trees off the Commercial Road edge of St Anne's churchyard, and rise out of a cutting, to cross Limehouse Cut, at a point appallingly close to both the church and Cyril Jackson primary school, not to speak of a whole complex of new GLC homes now nearing completion. John Chesshyre thinks the scheme might be acceptable if a modest new road were completely boxed in, but wants to know why Tower Hamlets asked the GLC to withdraw a more southerly option which would have taken the road through derelict land between the canal basin and Narrow Street. Father Sidebotham worries that road building schemes, designed to revive the area, would break up communities and spread blight.

Indeed, dissatisfaction with the ways of planning committees and

The up-river docks have steadily lost trade to more modern port facilities at Tilbury and elsewhere, and most now face closure.

councillors is deep-rooted in the area, which has its share of fairly militant community workers and advocate planners. Notable among these are J-DAC, the Joint Docks Action Committee, which has a resource centre (officially financed but vociferously independent) at Watney Street, Shadwell; and community groups operating from St George's Town Hall in Cable Street, where Dan Jones, social worker son of Sir Elwyn Jones, is an active lobbyist for the needs of a chronically deprived community living amid publicly created blight. Dan Jones, his wife and their three small children live in Cable Street; and he and another social worker, Mike Thomas, are much involved in a project called the East London Marine Venture, which is developing the $5\frac{1}{2}$-acre Shadwell Basin for water recreation for youngsters.

One of the project's strongest exponents has been Tower Hamlets councillor Charlie Mudd, who has lived in the area all his fifty-two years, and knows all too well the vicious circle of lack of opportunities, lack of skills, boredom, petty crime and vandalism which goes with fourteen per cent unemployment. With hindsight, he told me, he believed the authorities' biggest mistake was that, in trying to replace the slums, they smashed up cohesive, stable communities. But he has great hopes of the new style of redevelopment represented by the recently published Wapping Local Plan. This, based on a report by a team of consultants, including architects Shepheard, Epstein & Hunter, envisages redevelopment of the redundant London Docks area with two- and three-storey housing; the retention of the dock basins – Shadwell and Hermitage – for recreation; and the creation of a well-treed open space, Wapping Wood, in one of the basins already filled in by the former owners, the Port of London Authority. Architect Gabriel Epstein explained that the plan provides for tree-lined wedges giving people in the new houses views of the river – something of which the old dock walls largely deprived Wapping residents. Along the river itself there would be a continuous river walk – but not a broad, uniform and boring promenade; rather a route that runs in and out, sometimes behind existing buildings, sometimes widening into squares, gardens or parks.

Present-day Wapping, still almost an island, shut off by the 19th-century dock basins, contains a depressing degree of decay and

Low tide at Wapping. Many of the warehouses hereabouts have been converted to new uses, like Ahmed Poachee's Great Wapping Wine Company.

dereliction. Along the riverside you find one or two areas of life and prosperity: Oliver's Wharf, a well established warehouse conversion into studios and flats; Wapping Pier Head, two elegant rows of beautifully restored Georgian houses grouped round a garden that was once the dock entrance; Wapping river police station, head-quarters of a marine police force established there in 1798 to curb rampant pilfering on the river; and the Great Wapping Wine Company, founded four and a half years ago in a riverside ware-house by Ahmed Poachee, and now boasting an annual turnover of more than £1 million. Mr Poachee, born in Britain of Iranian parents, earlier founded Odd-Bins, which also has premises at Wapping and which he sold before starting the new firm. Though he originally planned to unload wine direct into the warehouse from the Thames, the Dock Labour Board levy system made it, he said, quite uneconomic for him to do this. He chose Wapping because it is near the centre of London but much cheaper than any comparable premises to the west. His office window looks out on the river, and he said he liked the water and the sense of space – but not the level of Tower Hamlets rates.

Businesses like Wapping Wine and the office blocks now planned nearer the Tower certainly help Tower Hamlets' rate revenue, and do something to remedy the area's unemployment. But community workers argue that they do little to correct the dearth of skilled, reasonably well-paid job opportunities for the young men of these decaying riverside hamlets. The area, complains youth worker Alan Smith, who grew up in Whitechapel, has become "a human dustbin"; and "toffee-nosed" folk from Wapping High Street (significantly now without a single shop) are, he argues, no help to the community at all.

What can bring salvation to these benighted dockland villages? The planned new houses, on the first stage of which work has now started, will help to upgrade the area. But it desperately needs new jobs, especially industrial jobs. A range of listed warehouse build-ings along the northern edge of the main dock basins is earmarked for such a use; but so far little seems to be happening. Decay still characterizes this whole stretch of Thamesside. Perhaps new policies and a more buoyant national economy will shortly begin to reverse the spiral.

18

Highgate

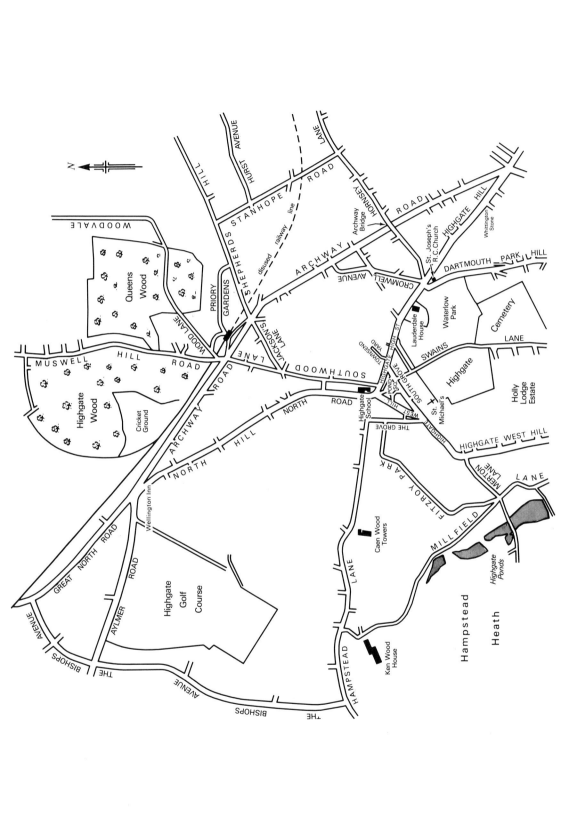

18

Highgate

In the time of Elizabeth I Highgate was still no more than a small hamlet almost hidden in the great Forest of Middlesex, a royal hunting preserve. But the Manor of Hornsey or Haringey had belonged to the Bishop of London at least since the Conquest; and it was the bishop's toll gate, high on the hill, which gave the place its name. The gate controlled access to the road through the bishop's park; its guardians were the inhabitants of Highgate Hermitage – "hermits" in the older meaning of individuals who devoted themselves to the service of the community. Some of the hermits, for instance, repaired the steep and eroded track up Highgate Hill. The Hermitage, as a religious foundation, was dissolved by Henry VIII, but the estate of which it formed part became the property of Sir Roger Cholmeley, Lord Chief Baron of the Exchequer and later Chief Justice of the King's Bench, who in 1562 established a free grammar school on its site – the origins of the now by-no-means-free Highgate School.

An earlier name with which Highgate is associated is Richard Whittington, a prosperous and philanthropic City merchant who served three terms as Lord Mayor during the late 13th and early 14th centuries. The Whittington stone, encircled with a protective iron cage, stands near the foot of Highgate Hill marking the spot where supposedly, in default of gold-paved streets making dejectedly for home, he heard Bow bells bid him turn again. Presumably Whittington's commercial and political acumen exceeded his grasp of geography. Aiming for his home in Gloucestershire he had taken the A1 in mistake for the A40.

By the late 18th century Highgate, like its better known neighbour on the Northern Heights, Hampstead, was already becoming an extension of the fashionable West End. From this period date the many large houses standing in spacious gardens from which men of commerce commuted and in which men of letters and the arts communed with their muses. At least one still does: Yehudi Menuhin, who lives in The Grove in one of the relatively few remaining houses of even earlier date. He is president of the Highgate Society and a most enthusiastic admirer of his chosen village. His front windows look through greenery towards The Flask inn; his back windows through more extensive greenery towards Kenwood.

Menuhin and his wife, formerly Diana Gould the dancer, have lived in their elegant 1680s house for more than seventeen years; he loves it for its peacefulness and (despite traffic jams) its proximity to central London; and the two of them savour their occasional Sunday walks through Waterlow Park, where Mrs Menuhin (as her husband once put it) "blows her ritual kiss to Sir Sidney, splendid in his stone frock-coat, donor of that beautifully kept small park, who gave it as 'a garden for the gardenless'". Menuhin is by no means a mere figurehead or letterhead president. When the Highgate Society celebrated its tenth anniversary in 1977, he demanded

The Flask, one of Highgate's original coaching inns. Its patrons today, arriving in Vauxhalls and Volvos, pack rather more horsepower.

to know what he could *do* to help – and with another musician gave a concert in St Michael's Church.

Highgate's present active social organization must be attributed in considerable measure to the 1,700-member Highgate Society. (Not so many years ago business Highgate talked only to business Highgate, literary Highgate only to literary Highgate, and neither of them talked much to the rest.) It runs a playgroup, mother-and-baby afternoons, a drama workshop, children's craft sessions and art exhibitions as well as the more usual activities of a local amenity society such as talks from visiting speakers and committees watching eagle-eyed for unsuitable planning applications. It also runs Saturday coffee mornings which are always packed and bursting with local gossip and intrigue. "I don't call it a coffee morning; I call it a parish pump," commented Dame Geraldine Aves, who told me she has lived in Highgate for more than forty years but had really only begun to get involved in its activities when she retired from the Civil Service in 1963.

The society occupies premises looking out over Pond Square, in the heart of the village, and has as its neighbour and landlord the much older Highgate Literary and Scientific Institution founded in 1839. This body, too, is these days remarkably lively and enterprising, thanks in no small measure to a new generation of enthusiasts such as Ion Trewin, literary editor of *The Times*, himself a native of Hampstead but with a wife, Sue, who grew up in Highgate. The Institution, remarked Dame Geraldine with approval, still boasts an extensive library and a comfortable reading room with a coal fire.

Highgate also boasts a profusion of pubs, such as The Flask in Highgate West Hill, which spills drinkers and atmosphere convivially out into another little square, and Ye Olde Wrestlers in North Road. There occasionally the supposedly ancient ceremony of Swearing on the Horns, the Highgate Oath, still offers swearers a spurious "Freedom of Highgate" in return for donations to charity. Highgate also has the heath, which belongs as much to it as to Hampstead, and many other green open spaces. And, despite its long-standing balkanization between three or even four different boroughs, it retains a sense of village community.

Certainly as compared with its sister village, Highgate has long been the Cinderella – traditionally less talked of, less thought of, less artistic and Bohemian, and probably rather relishing a degree of sedateness and reserve. But of late Highgate has taken the centre of the stage with its notorious series of public inquiries into the controversial Archway Road widening and diversion scheme. Trouble over traffic and roads is not, however, new to the place. The first bypass for the village was proposed in 1809 – a new road and tunnel along the line of the present A1. The part-completed tunnel fell in on 15 April 1812, with a crash said to have been heard in Kentish Town.

Opponents of the scheme, which was backed by John Nash, had a whale of a time. John Tyme, who played a leading part in bringing recent inquiry proceedings to a grinding halt, might nonetheless have learnt a thing or two from the author of one pamphlet, who in a fine frenzy of satire wrote: "The Highgate Archway having fallen in, it is intended to remove the whole of the hill entire by a mechanical slide, including the chapel and bowling ground. It is intended to remove it into the Valley behind Kenwood where the seven ponds now are, thereby forming a junction with Hampstead and inviting the approach of the two hamlets in a more social manner. On the spot where Highgate now stands it is intended to form a large lake of salt water and to supply the said lake with sea water from the Essex coast by means of earthen pipes, iron pipes being injurious to sprats. It is intended to stock the said lake with all kinds of sea fish except sharks, there being plenty of land sharks to be had in the neighbourhood, to supply the metropolis with live sea-water fish at reduced prices. It is intended to have a hundred bathing machines to accommodate the metropolis with sea bathing, and to erect a large building on the north side of the lake, which building is intended for insane surveyors and attorneys who have lately infested the neighbourhood . . ."

That Georgian bypass to Highgate Village was eventually, with Telford's help and with a bridge over rather than a tunnel under, satisfactorily completed. In the 1870s it was made toll-free; in 1944 as a child growing up in Highgate, I remember it jammed with D-day invasion convoys. By the 1950s the road, lined with tall Victorian and Edwardian terraces, could no longer cope with A1 trunk road traffic and was fast becoming what we now call "an environmental problem". In the heyday of road-building, therefore, Ministry of Transport engineers laid plans to turn it into something close to an urban motorway: a six-lane carriageway with limited access and egress. A quarter of a mile of it, from Archway tube station to a pub known as The Winchester, actually got built at vast expense. It is Whitehall's plan for relieving the bottleneck to the north that, like the road itself, has divided Highgate; has been the subject of three inquiries (two of them abandoned); and thereafter has been the subject of further consultations between the Transport Secretary and local authorities. The issue is sometimes presented as a straight conflict between Highgate-on-the-Hill (the Village), which would be glad to divert its excess traffic on to an improved A1, and folk who live on or near the Archway Road and oppose the destruction and disruption involved.

The divisions are in fact more complex. They separate those who bought houses in the expectation that a widened and diverted road would come, and those whom the road would deprive of their present homes; people who suffer noise and vibration now, and those who fear they would suffer it if the road were built; those who think some modest-scale improvement is needed, and that

The City from Archway Bridge – St Paul's lost among the office towers.

uncertainty and blight are worse than the disruption of road building, and those who hold, like John Tyme, that large new roads
are almost never justified.

Among this last group we may count playwright Simon Gray
who, with his wife Beryl, lives in a street called Priory Gardens on
the other, eastern side of Archway Road from the Village, in one of
the same terrace of tall, crazily planned, turn-of-the-century houses
in which I spent most of my first nineteen years. They bought it
freehold in 1968 for £8,000, moving from a top floor flat behind
John Barnes in Finchley Road to the kind of suburban environment
"we said we could never stand". But with Queens Wood ten
seconds away beyond their back fence, and the Underground two
minutes away at the end of the road, they developed a great
affection and loyalty for their bit of Highgate. Foxes, kestrels;
neighbours who include policemen, postmen, car mechanics and
immigrants as well as Anglo-Saxon, middle-class university lec-
turers; dogs and cats and children (of which the Grays have two,
five and two respectively) – all these, he says, help to make it an
agreeable, friendly and interesting place to live. When not writing
plays, he lectures in English at Queen Mary College, mostly
commuting by tube.

Though Gray admits to getting ideas for his characters from his
bit of Highgate, he says he usually moves them over to the other
side of the Archway Road, which he regards as the great social
divide. "People in the Village see themselves as privileged," he
says. "Traffic doesn't go through the Village – it has been kept out –
and people there have the attitude that the Village is sacrosanct. But
I don't care for the atmosphere there. I find it very precious." He
gave evidence at the third and latest Archway Road inquiry against
the new road, basically because he believes a larger highway would
simply generate more traffic. "I'm not a Luddite. I accept that we
can't go back," he says; but nonetheless sees the steady encroach-
ment of cars and other vehicles as being antisocial and a threat to a
good and agreeable life. Two characteristics stand out in his own
street in spring: blossom and cars. The cars, parked along kerbs,
eating into gardens with their carports and hard standings, are
gaining ground. He prefers the blossom.

Architect Patrick Lawlor, Chairman of the Highgate Society's
environment committee, would agree with much that Simon Gray
says about people, cars and environment, but disagrees about the
road and about the character of Highgate Village. He told me he

favoured a limited widening as a means of "reconciling improving the environment with keeping the city alive". He thinks Gray's view unrealistic. "Whether we like it or not, Highgate happens to straddle a major road in and out of London." Though much can be done to divert heavy traffic round London, "we don't think it's realistic to believe that all the traffic will go away".

Lawlor lives close to Archway Road rather than up in Highgate Village, and fears that the Minister's abandonment of his latest proposals will simply prolong the blight and misery of many of his neighbours. He favours a four-lane road, partly using the line of a disused railway to the east of the existing road. Gray's assertion that Priory Gardens is "the wrong side of the tracks" and not really part of the Highgate Society's Highgate, he bluntly calls nonsense. Many active members live east of the road, he points out, and all manner of social organizations cover much wider areas than just Highgate-on-the-Hill – notably the very lively Jackson's Lane Community Centre which functions from a former Methodist church on Archway Road.

His fellow architect Lord Cunliffe, who lives on Gray's side of the road, is not so sure. He thinks Highgate east of Archway Road is in many ways "on the wrong side of the tracks", or at least separate and looking to different shopping and social focuses – though he and his wife Clemency now have strong links with the Highgate Society and the Village. She is the very much full-time chairman of the Hill Homes, set up after the Second World War to provide residential accommodation for the elderly. The Hill Homes Trust now provides a home for 190 old people in six houses in the lusher residential roads of Highgate towards Kenwood; it boasts that however frail or infirm they become, if a hospital discharges them it will always have a place (and skilled care) waiting for residents to come back to; and it has lately set about raising funds for a £400,000 housing scheme to meet the wishes of an increasing number of old people to have their own small flats yet the assurance of a warden on the premises.

Roger and Clemency Cunliffe came to Highgate in 1964 on their return from a spell in America; and almost immediately he found himself, with no great enthusiasm, inheriting the title Third Baron Cunliffe (his grandfather was made a lord after being governor of the Bank of England). From their "blue collar tenement" in the States, they moved to a 1912 house which he dubs "poor man's Voysey", but which had the advantage, with three children about,

of $13\frac{1}{2}$-inch-thick walls and a large garden. Highgate suited them because architects tend to commute along the Northern Line and not a little work is picked up through the architectural grapevine on the tube. The Cunliffes were drawn to the Village by excellent children's services at St Michael's parish church and the activities of the young and virile Highgate Society. Their own local shops include an ironmonger's where Heath Robinson bought wheels and pulleys. They feel relieved not to need to car-crawl to the country at weekends, because now they have woods and open spaces all about them; mallards and foxes occasionally visit their garden; and inquiries of a neighbour when they were buying the house produced only one serious snag: "The noise of the hedgehogs when they're mating is quite maddening!"

Michael Wright, editor of *Country Life*, also lives in Highgate, in a roomy Edwardian house, high up by the Archway Bridge, which is no less Highgate for being municipally Islington and postally upper Holloway. He cites good air, views over London, proximity to work and to central London, and a "strong village atmosphere" as being reasons why he likes it. He and his wife moved there because they had many friends in that part of north London, particularly in Hampstead – but Highgate turned out to be "a more attractive proposition. Our family had grown too big for a flat and there were more properties here we could afford to buy." The centre of the village, he says, gives a "very definite physical focus for local activities. It approximates to a village green – the really strong focus that perhaps Hampstead doesn't have." Grouped together are pubs, St Michael's parish church, and the premises of the Highgate Society and the Institute. Pond Square is the scene of the Society's annual carol singing, and sometimes village fêtes "when we can persuade Camden Council to give us the necessary licence". A keen singer, Wright, when I talked to him, was just back from rehearsing *The Dream of Gerontius* with the Highgate Choral Society. A real village, Highgate? "I'm not sure that they exist. But some of the more attractive country villages are basically commuter villages." In terms of community and identity, his village ranks as "real".

Is it also inward-looking and selfish, as Simon Gray had suggested? Patrick Lawlor argues not. He points to the part the Highgate Society has played in a thirteen-strong group of residents' and amenity organizations seeking to change Haringey Council's plans for its Parkland Walk along the disused railway line from

St Michael's Church, on its hilltop above the famous cemetery.

Highgate to Finsbury Park. Some councillors want housing at all costs, whereas (argue the residents' groups) it is precisely in the areas of poor housing towards Finsbury Park that the chain of open space would be most valuable. Lawlor characterizes the council's plans as "knocking down houses to provide open space, and building houses where the open space already, potentially, exists". He would like this section of the Parkland Walk to follow the pattern of the very successful northern stretch between Highgate and Alexandra Palace which serves both as linear open space and wildlife habitat.

But, though critical of Haringey on this issue, he says that generally relations with local authorities have moved from hostility and suspicion to respect and co-operation. The Highgate Society has persuaded Camden that it ought to extend its part of Highgate's conservation area; and Lawlor sees purely negative development control being superseded by positive design policies for development. Several local organizations have lent a hand in restoring the 16th- to 18th-century Lauderdale House in Waterlow Park for community use; a trust presided over by Dame Geraldine Aves and including local and national interests has a statutory say in the way Camden Council manages Highgate Cemetery (which it has a right to buy, not yet exercised); and likewise Camden has been con-

Waterlow Park with, behind it, part of St Joseph's Roman Catholic Church, known to locals as "Holy Joe's".

Kenwood House, which now houses the Iveagh Bequest of pictures and furniture, and is the venue for regular concerts and recitals.

sulting local interests on how to use the house in rustic Fitzroy Park left to them by the architect Vincent Harris. Lawlor argues that it could well serve several different functions, including a visitors' centre to tell people more about the heath and a much-needed place of refreshment for those who walked over from Hampstead.

Fitzroy Park, still a private road leafily running down from The Grove to Highgate Ponds, has many illustrious residents, including engineer and designer Ove Arup, Lincoln's Inn solicitor Ambrose Appelbe, one of the Pink Floyd pop group, and – most recently – King Khalid of Saudi Arabia, who ruffled local sensibilities by making alterations to his house, Beechwood, without planning permission (local rumour has it, to install a separate female entrance), and by having helicopters land in his grounds.

Ambrose Appelbe (accent on the "pel") lives at The Elms just below Beechwood. When he first moved in 1947 he found he had enough land to get a Ministry of Agriculture ploughing grant, and what he found in ploughing up his acres convinced him that his house stands on the site of a Roman villa. He said he glories in its location, so near the centre of Highgate Village and yet so tranquilly rural. Some people say that it was in this lane that Keats began to compose his *Ode to a Nightingale*; and indeed, says Appelbe, there were nightingales in plenty to be heard until a few years back. When he first lived there he kept geese, and in his first year shot seven foxes. "They made me Master of Foxhounds on the strength of it," he laughs. He notes that Witanhurst, the mansion at the top of West Hill which had been the subject of a planning inquiry and of innumerable development proposals, now had an Arab owner who has done some restoration but had lately put it on the market again.

Across the heath in what is just Highgate stands Kenwood House, whose curator John Jacob lives in a flat in the 18th-century mansion, above the stupendous Iveagh Bequest art collection which he administers for the GLC along with Twickenham's Marble Hill House and Blackheath's Ranger's House. His own favourite in the collection is, he told me, Rembrandt's self-portrait; the best known is Vermeer's *The Guitar Player*, which was stolen in 1974 for political reasons connected with the IRA but after three nerve-racking months recovered. Jacob lamented that he nowadays had too few staff and too little money to run the three houses as they ought to be run, but takes pride in detective work with sandpaper and microscope which made possible the restoration of Kenwood interiors to their Adam colour schemes; also in selecting for chamber music and poetry recitals portraits which have some connection with the evening's programme. He is also proud of having to some extent reversed the fine art tide, by buying cheaply in the United States items of furniture for Kenwood which in Britain would have commanded prohibitive prices. Jacob, living where he does, can take a detached view of neighbouring villages. "Shop in Highgate Village? Can anyone afford to do that these days, at 52p for a quarter of a pound of tea? We do our food shopping in Kilburn High Road." He admits to buying an occasional antique in Highgate, but drinks in Hampstead, where the supply of "real ale" is better.

Most Highgate folk, even if they patronize supermarkets in Holloway or Muswell Hill, are on nodding or naming terms with their local shopkeepers; a surprisingly high proportion of them are active in the wide range of local societies and organizations; and they have a sense of belonging to their village. They enjoy a feeling of identity with the place and its people which makes the name "village", in Highgate's case, much more than just a quaint survival.

19

Camberwell

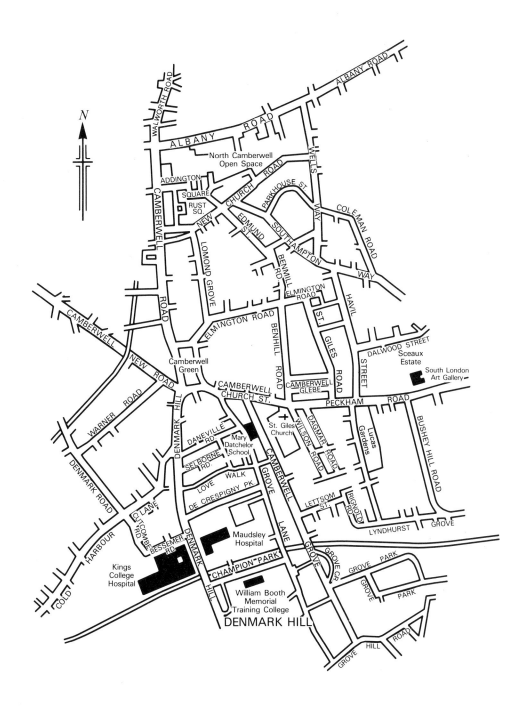

19

Camberwell

Most Londoners, in so far as they think about Camberwell at all, probably regard it as a rather desolate, traffic-racked sector of the Victorian inner city. Yet in reality it is one of London's oldest villages. By the 11th century, certainly, it had its own church; and Domesday Book presents it as quite a substantial and thriving place. It had ploughland, cornland, sixty-three acres of meadow for cows, and woods with nuts enough for sixty pigs. Its name seems to have meant either "crooked well or pond" or "the stream or lake of the cranes". Opinions differ.

The place did not alter much in the next five or six centuries, except perhaps for the building in Elizabethan and Stuart times of several great houses. When Parliament under Charles II levied a hearth tax the returns for Camberwell parish showed at least six establishments with ten or more fireplaces. The village benefited from its position on the main road from the south coast to London's only bridge across the Thames, but it was in the 18th and 19th centuries that Camberwell really began to prosper. Its market gardens and farms supplied the needs of a rapidly growing capital; and the district attracted City merchants who, to establish their position as gentlemen, sought convenient country seats. It was on a local farm, Tenpenny's, that in 1748 an attractively coloured red, yellow, blue and black butterfly was first spotted and dubbed Camberwell Beauty.

The man who more than anyone made Camberwell fashionable was a certain Doctor John Lettsom, on the site of whose house and gardens up a hill to the south of the old village centre now stands Southwark's Lettsom housing estate, impinging rather unsympathetically into Camberwell Grove, one of the two or three tree-lined streets where the architectural delights of Georgian and Victorian Camberwell still remain almost intact.

Lettsom, son of a West Indies planter, was an extremely successful physician, his income at one stage reaching £12,000 a year, which in the 18th century was a prodigious sum. But he was also a philanthropist and something of an eccentric. He founded dispensaries for the poor and contributed generously to these and other charities; and (as Camberwell's 19th-century historian Blanch tells us) when a poor woman who had seen better days begged him for a prescription he sent her with a note to the parish overseers. "A shilling a day for Mrs Moreton," it read. "Money, not physic, will cure her." Once the victim of a highway robbery, he detected that the young man who cocked the pistol was a novice at the game, pushed to it by necessity rather than habitual lawlessness, and later got him a commission in the army. His best known prescription reads:

"When patients comes to I,
I physics, bleeds and sweats 'em.
Then – if they choose to die,
What's that to I – I lets 'em."

Even in Dr Lettsom's time, incidentally, the descendants of those sixty Domesday swine were still about and causing some local concern. In 1797 Camberwell residents were "much troubled by hogs being suffered to range at large in the roads"; a committee was formed "to inquire what steps could be taken" to deal with the menace; and eventually parishioners were offered 5s reward for information leading to the indictment of the owners of these wayward and threatening animals! Fifteen years earlier Camberwell had suffered from a rather different kind of plague. "Caterpillars," Blanch tells us, "so abounded in the parish that the overseers spent £10 in 'apprehending' them at the rate of 6d per bushel. The caterpillars were described as being 'dangerous to the public in general'."

The building of more Thames bridges in the late 18th and early 19th centuries, expansion of horse omnibus services on the lines pioneered by Shillibeer, and finally the burgeoning shoots of rival railways pushing out into south London – these turned Camberwell from village into suburb. Two notable 19th-century residents were Robert Browning (born there in 1812) and Joseph Chamberlain, whose birthplace at 188 Camberwell Grove bears a plaque to that effect. Browning first heard the tale of the Pied Piper of Hamelin as a boy in Camberwell, and at the Elmington community centre near Camberwell Green a sculpture by Willi Soukop recaptures a scene from that tale. Mendelssohn stayed with relations on Denmark Hill in 1842, and wrote the piece known today as "Spring Song" in honour of the tranquil, rustic scene. Originally he called it "Camberwell Green".

But Camberwell was growing into something more than just a village. In the century from 1801 to 1901 its population increased from some 7,000 to 259,000. Unlike the elegant, spacious Georgian houses of the Grove (originally a tree-lined avenue), this later development consisted largely of narrow streets and mean houses. The squalor and poverty of Victorian London engulfed large areas of Camberwell.

But from the late 19th century dates what is perhaps the district's best-known institution: the Camberwell School of Art and Crafts. It started, its principal Ian Jenkin told me, from a growing concern after the Great Exhibition that British industry was suffering from a lack of good design. A group of leading artists including John Passmore Edwards, Walter Crane and Edward Burne-Jones offered £5,000 to establish a school alongside the recently opened South London Art Gallery, doing so in memory of their colleague Frederick Leighton who had died in 1896. The school, whose aim was to encourage craftsmen to become also designers, opened its doors in January, 1898, and two years later was able to boast that its premises were "lighted throughout by electric light".

Today the school has some 800 students, 600 of them full-time, including some from Japan, Nigeria, Brazil, Australia and North

Camberwell Grove, the well-preserved residential parkland of this village. Residents include a high proportion of architects and doctors – and lately, also, diplomats.

America. Its specialities include textile design and paper conservation, its students in the latter field going on to do crucial restoration work in such establishments as the British Library and the Fitzwilliam Museum at Cambridge. Jenkin, who was himself a Camberwell student in the late 1940s, returned there from the Slade as principal in 1975. Two of his aims were to establish closer links with the local community and to make it possible for more students to live in Camberwell.

This second objective was, he said, beginning to be realized. Housing societies have allowed the school temporary use of houses waiting to be converted and upgraded (an arrangement which gives students cheap lodgings and safeguards otherwise empty premises against vandalism); Southwark Council has recently made available some council flats which it finds hard to let to families; and a row of 19th-century terrace houses in Jephson Street reprieved from Southwark's Selborne redevelopment scheme are being repaired and converted for use by some of Jenkin's students – partly as a result of the Camberwell Society's efforts.

As to involvement in the community, Jenkin recalls how in his own student days artists like Victor Pasmore and Edward Ardizzone taught large numbers of part-time students, many of them local people. He said he dreams of a community arts centre (an empty church just north of Camberwell Green would in many ways be ideal), with the student houses at nearby Jephson Street also accommodating visiting artists or "fellows" from abroad. In return for free lodging and studio space they would teach and help to stimulate community art.

Another way in which the Camberwell School of Arts and Crafts renewed and found fresh relevance in its founding doctrines is in

Selborne: demolished by Southwark council despite the protests of residents and High Court writs, and still, five years later, standing empty.

fabric design. Though it and other schools have been training fabric designers of quality, British manufacturers have nonetheless tended to go abroad for their designs. The link between the textile industry and design education was somehow missing. To provide it, the School and the industry recently got together to launch a British Fabric Design Studio. Art and Crafts may sound old-fashioned, but what the Camberwell School does now is as relevant to Britain's needs today as its policies were eighty years ago.

Camberwell's great *cause célèbre* of recent years has been over the borough's disastrous Selborne redevelopment plan, which made national newspaper headlines when residents took action in the High Court to try to avert demolition of their homes. The area's seven acres contained 170-odd modest 19th-century terrace houses, which residents – backed by the Camberwell Society – demonstrated were capable of effective and economical improvement. South-wark's Labour-controlled council would not listen. At that time most of its members regarded the Camberwell Society as a clique of selfish middle-class owner-occupiers intent on preventing the building of much needed council homes. Though the society had done a thorough survey of Selborne's residents' needs and wishes involving computer analysis by a social psychologist, the majority of councillors were not then open to argument.

Stephen Marks, an architect now employed by the Department of the Environment, notes the irony of the date on which the Minister confirmed Southwark's compulsory purchase orders. It was the day a new provision of the 1974 Housing Act came into force allowing councils to rehabilitate homes they had already received permission to demolish. Yet, in November 1975, the bulldozers moved in, flattening houses that people cared for and which could have been brought up to acceptable standard more cheaply than even a prompt rebuilding. Prompt? Selborne's seven acres still stood empty behind corrugated iron fences at the time of writing, three years after demolition.

Yet the public outcry and obloquy it was subjected to did make the council pause. It strengthened the hand of members like Ron Watts, sometime secretary of the Camberwell Society, more recently chairman of Southwark's planning committee, and a resident of Addington Square, which only a fierce battle prevented from demolition at the hands of the GLC Parks Department. It also led to the setting up of a joint council-developer-GLC-Camberwell Society working party to consider the future of the long-blighted

Camberwell Green site, a block of property supposedly ripe for redevelopment to the south of the green. The working party considered six options for road improvements at the bottleneck which is the Camberwell Green, but eventually adopted a seventh option, put forward by the society, as least damaging and likely to be most effective. But the authorities were slow to act; and by the autumn of 1978 the Camberwell Society found it necessary to campaign again, pressing for the working party's proposals to be implemented so as to bring new life to the languishing Green.

Southwark Council's fiercest critics certainly include Camberwell Grove resident Charles McKean, whose book *Fight Blight* amounted to an indictment of the clumsiness and unresponsiveness of local authorities in environmental matters and a championing of community self-help. McKean, a Glaswegian who works for the Royal Institute of British Architects, came to Camberwell in 1968. He and Margaret, his Welsh, careers adviser wife, live in a tall, 19th-century terrace house, split into flats, at the top of Camberwell Grove. To those who complain that the Grove and its surroundings are a middle-class ghetto (architects and doctors abound, and as for the arts, within a hundred yards or so live Albert Finney, Terry Jones of *Monty Python* fame and pianist Jeremy Menuhin), McKean replies that he lives in the middle of a council estate. The rest of his terrace of stately Victorian houses Southwark Council bought and converted into local authority flats.

Architects perhaps flocked here because they discovered houses of a character and beauty which provided spaciousness at a reasonable price in a way that modern houses cannot. Jim Tanner, when I met him chairman of the Camberwell Society, and his wife Shirley – both architects, both from Australia, and originally intending to return there – bought a house in Camberwell Grove in 1959 and soon became hooked on the place. "Houses were much more run-down then," he recalled. They realized the place had "come up" when a policeman knocked on their door to say that £50,000 woth of jewellery had been stolen from a house opposite. But such households were still, added Tanner, a very small minority.

The reason why doctors are fairly thick on the ground seems perhaps more obvious. Grouped about Camberwell and Denmark Hill are King's College Hospital, the Maudsley Hospital and their various offshoots. Dr Gwyn Williams is a King's man who returned to practise near the hospital where he studied. From south Wales,

A few yards from the heavily trafficked main road we find the tranquillity of this path through Camberwell church yard.

he is now one of the longest-serving of local GPs. He and his wife Mary, who is Camberwell born and bred, live in an attractive porticoed house of 1824 at the top of Grove Lane in which she grew up. The stable building alongside still has the hay racks from which some Georgian coachman must have fed his master's horses. Mrs Williams, who acts as her husband's receptionist in the surgery below their living room, remembers her husband sticking up his first brass plate to practise in Camberwell. "We had no patients. We just put up the plate and waited." By the end of the first week they had twenty-seven Welshmen. Mrs Williams told me she thought the area round about, at the top of Grove Lane and Camberwell Grove, still retained something of its village-like sense of community, but regrets (as do most local people) that the Green and its once flourishing shopping centre have been ruined – curtailed by demolition and emasculated by long-standing blight.

Mrs Williams regrets not only the destruction of the physical fabric of the place – big houses and fine gardens, little houses and lovingly tended backyards – and the hostile quality of much that the local authority has substituted for it, but also the loss of a sense of belonging among ordinary Camberwell folk. "They no longer have any love of the place," she says. "They all seem to want to get out."

Not far away in Champion Park is a group of buildings devoted to

Camberwell Green. Seats and lawns and chestnut trees – but in the centre of a busy traffic roundabout.

curing social sickness with a combination of practical help and good old-fashioned blood-and-fire evangelism: the William Booth Memorial Training College for Salvation Army Officers. Currently it trains about a hundred officers every year for the full-time ministry, putting them through a two-year course which generally involves working in its south London citadels and other establishments. In 1978 the college's complement of students included seventy-seven single women, thirty-four single men and forty-eight married couples. At its peak in the 1930s it had twice as many. Like other Camberwell residents many of them find the erratic nature of local bus services makes life difficult, but like other student populations the "Sallies" now attain to a fair degree of personal mobility. "A lot of them have cars," the college's administrative officer, Brigadier Gordon Knapman, told me. "They may be old ones, but they do mean they can get about." Blood and fire assisted by bangers.

The Salvationists' local citadel in Lomond Grove suffers, he said, like its surroundings, from chronic vandalism; and students tend to see the more desolate side of Camberwell when they leave their great brown castle on the hill and penetrate the proletarian neighbourhoods of the flat flood plain beyond the Green – potentially a flood plain in earnest these days until the Thames barrier is completed. From the spacious 18th- and 19th-century houses of Camberwell Grove, the view is altogether greener and brighter.

Dr Philip Hugh-Jones, who lives in Grove Crescent, is a consultant physician at King's and director of its chest unit. He told me that it was his delight to be able to walk to work in a few minutes by green and relatively traffic-free routes while his colleagues sat in traffic jams on their way in from Beckenham and Bromley – places which he and his wife regard as dull, one-class suburbs, not nearly as interesting or sociable as Camberwell, and lacking such advantages as being able to drive to the National Theatre in seven minutes.

The Hugh-Joneses have two boys aged, when I met them, eight and ten, but that did not stop Hilary Hugh-Jones from going to an auction seven years ago and buying, for £2,000, a tumbledown building in the mews between the Grove and Grove Lane which had been used for sorting rags. "One lunchtime she announced that she'd just bought this place – and we had nothing to pay for it with!" recalled Hugh-Jones. Now it houses her thriving Passage

Bookshop, in which she employs two assistants, and whose opening seems to have coincided with a prodigious growth in the area's book-buying population. Hilary Hugh-Jones argues that the Grove/Grove Park area is a kind of "ivory tower" insulated from the pressures and environmental nastiness that the rest of Camberwell has to live with. Her husband partly agrees but urges that the social mixture, which still for one reason or another still exists in these streets, makes for a much healthier and more interesting community than can be found in most commuter suburbs. He regards heavy traffic at Camberwell Green as one of the area's worst problems, not least because it helped to destroy the social focus of the Green.

The Mary Datchelor School in Camberwell Grove was by 1978 doomed to go out of existence, its governors having resolved to close rather than submit to what they quaintly believed was a fate worse than death – going comprehensive. Dr Hugh-Jones said he dreamed a dream of far-sighted city fathers demolishing it and re-creating there a much needed open space – a new Camberwell Green with shops and pubs about it but freed from the crippling weight of incessant streams of cars and lorries. As a former chairman of the Camberwell Society he knows that the odds are against that ever happening. Yet if town planning really were concerned with conserving communities, and equipped to do so, then that – rather than demolishing people's homes and then leaving the sites empty for years – is the kind of thing it should be attempting.

20

Chelsea

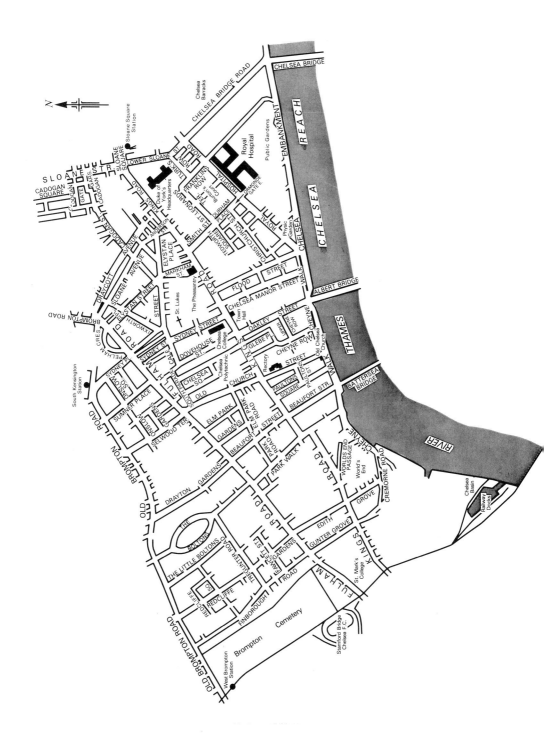

20

Chelsea

To many tourists Chelsea still means "swinging" King's Road. That, says John Yeoman, local councillor, conservationist and thirty-odd years a Chelsea resident, is an increasingly common misconception. It grates, because to most Chelsea-ites King's Road as it has now become is the very reverse of the essence of Chelsea and is altogether an alien and irritating presence; brash, noisy, sometimes violent, it seems to constitute a crude commercial cancer on this still attractive and agreeably unconventional quarter.

The name Chelsea means, according to Ekwall's *Concise Oxford Dictionary of English Place-Names*, a landing place for chalk or limestone. And indeed until the building of the Chelsea Embankment just over a century ago Chelsea still was a riverside village, which Carlyle described in 1834 on moving to a house in Cheyne Row as "a singular heterogeneous kind of spot, very dirty and confused in some places, quite beautiful in others, abounding in antiquities and the traces of great men. Our road runs out on a parade running along the shore of the river, a broad highway with shady trees, boats lying moored, and a smell of shipping and tar."

Chelsea still is a "heterogeneous kind of spot" – that accounts for much of its charm. It is still "dirty and confused in some places, quite beautiful in others". The shipping has largely been replaced by a well-nigh insupportable weight of road traffic, the smell of tar by petrol and diesel fumes.

In Carlyle's time Chelsea was just about to become a part of London. The westward march of the metropolis had until then been held back by the open, marshy, desolate and highwaymen-ridden Five Fields, the land that was to become Belgravia. Its riverside situation had made it attractive as a commuting area for the noble and wealthy: in Tudor times it became known as the village of palaces. Sir Thomas More, whose statue adorns a small garden near the ancient parish church in Cheyne Walk, found it a

223

Chelsea Embankment and Albert Suspension Bridge – still arguably London's prettiest Thames bridge despite the temporary central pier made necessary by the weight of modern traffic.

convenient place to escape to by river when Henry VIII and the cares of state allowed. Erasmus described how "More hath built near London on the Thamesside a commodious house, neither mean nor subject to envy, yet magnificent enough; there he converseth with his family, his wife, his son, and daughter-in-law, his three daughters and their husbands, with eleven grandchildren. There is not any man so loving to his children as he; and he loveth his old wife as well as if she were a young maid."

A further landmark in Chelsea's development came with the building in the 1680s of the Royal Hospital, following the example of Louis XIV's Hôtel des Invalides, as a solution to the problem of what to do with old and disabled soldiers from the nation's new standing army. Wren's splendid group of buildings facing out over lawns towards the river has its naval equivalent down-river at Greenwich, which he also had a hand in. The Chelsea Royal Hospital continues to this day to accommodate pensioners, but Greenwich was found by a 19th-century board of inquiry to be not only corrupt in its administration but to have rather more women in residence than pensioners. Chelsea apparently avoided such excesses, though it has had two women inmates, one a redoubtable lady who was wounded in the siege of Mafeking and received an army pension – which is still a condition of residence.

Nowadays there are some 420 in-pensioners, and Major-General Gordon Morrison, then physician and surgeon at the Royal Hospital, told me they were "an extremely healthy body of men. They're not allowed to die before they're eighty. We get very cross with them if they do!" General Morrison, assisted by three other medical officers, was responsible for the Royal Hospital's infirmary, to all intents and purposes a hospital within the Hospital with its own X-ray department and large and well-equipped chiropody and physiotherapy departments. Wren, he says, was remarkably thoughtful for the welfare of the inhabitants when he designed the buildings, stipulating, for instance, that the treads of stairs should be not more than three inches high. "He had tremendous insight into what old men would need." The pensioners, who are entitled to a pint of ale a day, wear their familiar scarlet coats and tricorn hats – their 17th-century walking-out uniform – only on more formal occasions. Everyday wear is a less flamboyant and more practical blue. "They are great old boys," says General Morrison, "with a tremendous sense of their own history."

Another venerable local institution, the Chelsea Physic Garden, the general public know less well because it is not open to them. It was first leased in 1673 by the Society of Apothecaries for research into medicinal plants. In 1722 Sir Hans Sloane, in his time president of both the Royal College of Physicians and the Royal Society, made them a gift of the freehold on condition that they used it "for the manifestation of the glory, power and wisdom of God in the works of creation." His statue by Rysbrack stands in the garden.

Ten years after Sloane made his gift a plant successfully imported into and propagated in the Physic Garden was sent to America. It was cotton, from which sprang the whole development of the southern United States. Rather earlier, in the 1680s, the Physic Garden grew and demonstrated the uses of quinine. In the present century two important lines of research have been under-taken there: photoperiodism, the study and manipulation of plant hormones which, for instance, allows us to produce chrysanthemums all the year round; and vernalization, the study of the resting periods needed by cereals, which now enables farmers to optimize their yields.

The Physic Garden's present curator, Allen Paterson, learnt his stuff at Kew and Cambridge and, before taking up the Chelsea post in 1973, lectured at a college of education. He emphasizes that although the public as such are not admitted to the garden except on occasional open days, serious students do visit it by arrangement in fairly large numbers. University of London extra-mural classes, for instance, account for more than 3,000 visits a year.

Paterson, who with his wife and two children lives on the premises, says he regards his home as "one of the best tied cottages in London". The family have their own little vegetable garden within the Garden, in which the children are beginning to take an intelligent interest. He dislikes the present day King's Road ("Where you can buy the same pair of jeans in twenty-seven different shops") and traffic and aircraft noise, which in certain weather conditions fracture the Physic Garden's tranquillity. But the real Chelsea of elegant squares and charming, small-scale streets he has discovered to be delightful. He sometimes wishes that the Garden went right down to the river without the rush and roar of the Embankment supervening; he wishes also that some latter-day Hans Sloane would come along, secure the future for the Physic Garden (now an independent and not particularly well endowed charity) and in particular pay for a range of new greenhouses to replace the outworn Victorian ones. His big regret is that more school parties do not visit the Physic Garden. The Inner London Education Authority's magazine for teachers, *Contact*, has featured the garden, and some enterprising primary schools have paid it a visit and been delighted and informed.

Better known than the Physic Garden but of more recent foundation is the Chelsea Flower Show, which dates from only 1913. The Royal Horticultural Society, which runs it, had previously held shows at Chiswick and in Temple Gardens on the Victoria Embankment, sites which it outgrew. An international horticultural exhibition held in the grounds of the Royal Hospital in 1912 opened the eyes of the society to the large crowds prepared to flock to Chelsea, and regularly since then they have rented garden room from the Royal Hospital. At the end of the four public days everything goes: flowers and plants are sold off; set-piece gardens are removed and often re-established elsewhere – like the formal English rose garden at the 1978 show, designed by Telford Development Corporation and destined after its brief sojourn in Chelsea to become a feature in that Shropshire new town's developing Town Park. Attendances in recent years have hovered around the 200,000 mark, but in 1962 and 1963 they reached a quarter of a million and the RHS had to close the gates. Chelsea pensioners have free unrestricted access and "bring some extra colour to the occasion".

Chelsea College, with premises virtually on the King's Road, is one of the progeny of specialist colleges spawned by a Victorian polytechnic founded on the site; Chelsea School of Art is another chip off the same block. Formerly Chelsea College of Science and Technology, the college was at one time to move to St Albans or some nearby site and become the University of Hertfordshire. Instead it became a constituent part of London University and developed a strong line in the medical, social and behavioural sciences as well as its traditional physical sciences base. John Head, who started his teaching career as a chemist, joined the college in 1974, having already been involved in projects concerned with the behaviour of teenagers. He told me he was now one of eight researchers seeking to understand more closely the behaviour and motivation of adolescents, and the mismatch between the language of secondary school textbooks, teaching material and methods and the understanding and perceptions of the typical adolescent in a comprehensive school.

Head, who now lives just across the border in Fulham, for three years occupied what in value per square foot of floor area must be one of the costliest pads in London – a bungalow owned by the college just behind King's Road. One of the qualities he liked about Chelsea was the way in which the famous and the man in the street rubbed shoulders. It was not just the aura of Carlyle, Whistler and

Smart residential Chelsea: modest back-street houses bought by affluent entertainers and others, now go for prices well into six figures.

King's Road: the Chelsea the world knows and visits.

Wilde, Isherwood and Noël Coward, but the possibility of finding yourself drinking in a local pub alongside Edna O'Brien, John Osborne or Laurie Lee. "World famous film directors and market porters playing bar billiards or shove-halfpenny in the same Victorian pub; in the back-streets of Chelsea you have an incredible mixture."

As one who lived close to King's Road, he thinks it hit its worst patch from several points of view in 1977 when gangs of punks and teds erupted into violence with bottle throwing and senseless violence that at times made residents apprehensive of going near it. Also, when the property boom reached its peak boutiques crowded out the necessary, everyday shops. "I had to walk half a mile to get a pint of milk or a newspaper. Now a newsagent, a greengrocer and a general purpose food store have all re-opened within the last two years." The property bubble burst, and Chelsea residents heaved a sigh of relief.

Chelsea College then wanted to move out of Chelsea just as soon as it could persuade Whitehall to thaw a frozen building budget. It owns a former hospital site at Wandsworth Common on which it has already built one hall of residence; there it would be able to expand in a way that high Chelsea land values could never allow. Meanwhile occasional lettings of student bedrooms almost on the King's Road, through the London Tourist Board, to visitors from abroad help in a small way to balance its budget. But if and when Chelsea College goes that will not mean the end of students in Chelsea. The Art School will surely stay in a district whose name for so long has been associated with artists; and the Victorian gothic buildings of the College of St Mark and St John, on Chelsea's western boundary, empty since the college moved to Plymouth, recently received a visit from the United States ambassador. The idea is that some American university or consortium of universities should take them over as their London campus.*

Residents of Chelsea use local knowledge to avoid King's Road traffic jams; avert their eyes as far as possible from what John Yeoman calls "an extraordinary street which has little to do with the district around it, and which is full of so-called Chelsea-ites who come from Battersea"; and regard with tolerant resignation the slow moving strings of No. 11 buses. "The policy of running them in convoys has evidently paid off," remarked one wag. "They haven't lost one yet!"

Since Chelsea reluctantly found itself merged into the Royal Borough of Kensington and Chelsea in 1963, its separate interests have depended for their defence upon Chelsea-minded local councillors like John Yeoman and, to an increasing extent, upon its long established amenity group, the Chelsea Society, which was founded in 1927. In its early days the society fought in vain on many issues like the demolition of cottages round the church and proposals to erect a "super power station" across the river at Battersea where the prevailing winds came from. On some issues these days it can expect more success – the council is conservation-conscious and has powers to prevent demolition and ill-judged development. Had such powers existed a century ago it is doubtful whether architects like Norman Shaw and C. R. Ashbee could ever have put up what are now judged some of Chelsea's most characteristic buildings – either in Cheyne Walk or in the heartland of "Pont Street Dutch" towards Sloane Street. In one of the district's most charming oases, Paultons Square, a new owner added an unauthorized storey to one house, throwing it out of scale with the rest of the group. A Chelsea Society stalwart who lived a few doors away fought him in the courts and forced him to remove it. A salutary lesson, but one that

*Chelsea College has since bought this site from the GLC.

would have greater force if local authorities acted more firmly and quickly with their own planning enforcement powers.

One continuing preoccupation of Chelsea conservationists has been traffic – not the congestion of the King's Road, which can be shrugged off as a bad joke, but the continuous pounding the district gets from heavy through traffic along the Embankment and up and down the deplorable one-way system of Edith Grove and Gunter Grove. In the early 1970s, while urban motorways were still regarded as feasible and on the whole benevolent projects, the GLC proposed at a cost of something like £30 million a mile to bypass that one-way system with the West Cross Motorway. The Chelsea Society had nothing against that scheme as such, provided it was extended over the river. The likely alternative of unleashing an extra burden of traffic on to their Embankment they opposed tooth and nail. In the event the electoral unpopularity of urban motorways killed the scheme, with a Ministry inspector pronouncing its final epitaph by judging that the benefits it would have provided did not justify spending that kind of money, and by suggesting more modest relief. Such solutions have been studied by joint working parties, but actual implementation seems as remote as ever. The attractive houses that Whistler and Turner painted are now, in some cases, visibly disintegrating as the heavy lorries grind past.

Another long-standing issue has been the fate of the Pheasantry in King's Road, a 17th-century building once used as a club, the most important elements of which have been salvaged for incorporation in an oft-promised but long-delayed redevelopment. The summer of 1977 saw confident statements in the local Press that work would shortly begin. "We've heard that before," commented Mrs Lesley Lewis, sometime secretary and acting chairman of the Chelsea Society. "I shall believe it when it actually happens."

One piece of significant development that did happen, despite a long strike and soaring costs, is at World's End where two groups of nobbly, attractively sculptured orange brick towers rise high above Cheyne Walk and Whistler's Reach. Ironically the man who designed these, among the last and arguably the best of high-rise council housing, is Eric Lyons, an architect more generally associated with low-rise, owner-occupied Span housing in the boskier suburbs. The new World's End has a quality and humanity that most high-rise housing has conspicuously lacked. The estate has been plagued with vandalism, but from without not within. Indications are that, this apart, the tenants really rather like it.

The World's End: Victorian pub with, background right,
Kensington and Chelsea council World's End tower-blocks.

Mrs Lewis and her medical entomologist husband Dr David
Lewis came to Chelsea rather by chance in 1955. It was convenient
for the Natural History Museum, where he was going to work after
many years in The Sudan; and they found an agreeable flat there.
The things she likes include, she said, its greenness – Chelsea is well
endowed with trees, including the planes in Royal Avenue, which
was originally intended to run from Chelsea Royal Hospital to
Kensington Palace; its rich historical and artistic associations; and
the interesting mixture of people of different backgrounds and
classes it still contains. Dislikes include traffic; the buying up of
houses by foreigners who then leave them empty for much of the
year, laying a dead hand on the life of the neighbourhood; and
burglar alarms ringing spuriously in the night with no one willing
or able to silence them. She cites as one of the Chelsea Society's

notable positive achievements the laying out of the Old Burial Ground, almost opposite the Old Town Hall, as a public garden.

One significant thing about the Lewises is that they do not regard Chelsea as a place to escape from at weekends. Away from the Embankment and King's Road there is much that is surprisingly tranquil, attractive and well cared for, lively in a less raucous way than the "swinging" Chelsea the world knows and talks of. Swift walked to the riverside village of Chelsea in 1711 through flowery meads where the air was sweet, but commented that "the haymaking nymphs are perfect drabs, nothing so clean and pretty as further out in the country. There is a mighty increase in dirty wenches in straw hats since I was last in London." Given some poetic licence that could be today's King's Road, but then King's Road is not the real Chelsea.

21

Soho

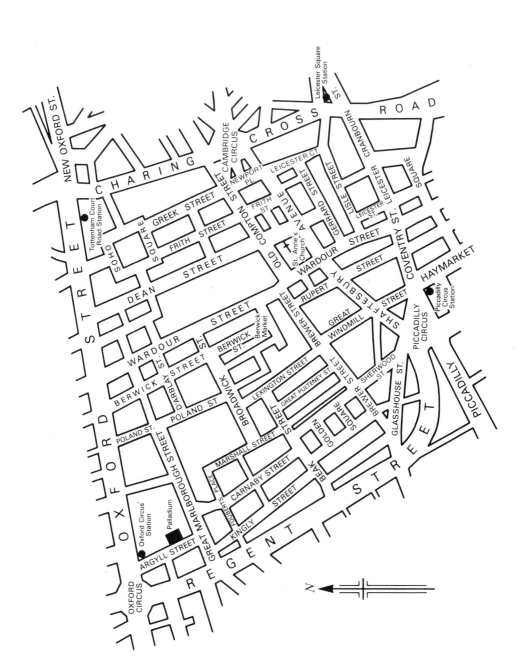

21

Soho

Soho has some claim to be regarded as the most misunderstood of London villages. Behind its most widely known but superficial face of commercialized sex – blue cinemas, strip clubs and what the local people loosely and disparagingly refer to as "sex shops" – lies the longer-established quarter of culinary delight and exotic eating houses. Look deeper and you find a living and working community: not just shopkeepers and restaurateurs, but theatrical costumiers, clock repairers, tailors, film-makers and a score of ancillary trades that support them. Some 3,500 people also reside in the area, have flats and lodgings in 18th- and 19th-century houses, live above their shops or round the corner from their workshops, take a pride in their homes and pleasure in their neighbours, and lovingly cultivate shrubs and geraniums in minute backyards or on balconies and roofs. These are the real Soho villagers, and lately they have been fighting back.

Soho's reputation for vice is not a new one. The *Survey of London's* volume on the Parish of St Anne's, Soho, begins with a reference (the earliest recorded mention of the name) to the binding over in 1641 of one Anna Clerke, described as "a lewd woman", for "thretening to burne the houses at So:ho". These were apparently an isolated group of wayside houses east of where present-day Wardour Street stands. Hunting took place to the west in what was then open country and the name Soho probably derives from the hunting cry "So-ho".

In the 1670s sporadic ribbon development along the highways through the area now known as Soho gave way to building on the land behind them – some of it mean and ill-constructed, some quite grand and for a time fashionable.

Soho was from the first a cosmopolitan area. Even before Henry IV of France revoked the Edict of Nantes in 1685, discrimination against Protestants, including the *dragonnade* – forcible quartering of dragoons in Huguenot homes – led the English King Charles II to declare that he felt himself "obliged in Honour and Conscience to comfort and support all such afflicted Protestants who by reason of ye rigours and severitys, which are used towards them upon ye account of their Religion". About the same time Greek refugees came to Soho (perhaps the origin of Greek Street); but the French came in the greatest numbers, so that by 1711 of a total population of 8,133 in the parish of St Anne's about 3,400 were French. This French colony included goldsmiths and silversmiths, clock and watchmakers and tapestry workers, for whom it was important to be near the fashionable clientele of the Court.

As well as the craftsmen and shopkeepers, gentry and noblemen, both English and foreign, found their way there. Arthur Onslow, Speaker of the House of Commons from 1728 to 1761, was among twenty-seven Members of Parliament with Soho addresses in 1733; but by the 1790s their number had declined to four and titled persons had likewise dwindled in number. Presumably the newly fashionable suburbs farther west attracted them, and their departure accelerated the tendency to multi-occupation. But others came in their place – artists like Hogarth and Reynolds, writers such as Hazlitt, musicians, theatre people, and a multitude of craftsmen associated with them, like (jumping a century) Willy Clarkson,

Charles II in Soho Square, where Oxford Street shopping, Greek Street restaurant-land, and the film world of Wardour Street all come together.

theatrical wigmaker (1861–1934), whom a GLC blue plaque cele-
brates at 41 Wardour Street. In the 1860s and 1870s came considerable numbers of Germans and Italians, cooks and waiters who
later prospered and opened their own restaurants, and also Swiss;
in the 1890s Polish and Russian Jews, a high proportion of whom
were tailors.

Today much of this still lives on and colours the character of the
place. Take the Polish tailors. Lou Walters' father came from
Warsaw in about 1910. He is a journeyman tailor making jackets for
the tailors of Savile Row and Sackville Street; he told me he had
lived in Soho all his fifty-eight years. He works with his wife Lily –
his "kipper" or assistant – in a basement workshop off Wardour
Street. Where once there were several thousand journeymen tailors
in Soho now only a few hundred remain, he said. They have been
forced out by high rents, by the creeping growth of offices in place
of workshops and, more recently, by the rank and ugly growth of
"dirty" bookshops, so-called saunas, massage parlours and the like.
In the early 1970s demolition and redevelopment seemed to him
and his neighbours the big threat to Soho as a community, now it is
this change of use.

Lou has never seriously thought of living or working anywhere
else but Soho; his wife, who came from Ilford, says it is the
friendliest and most conveniently situated place in London; and
there are signs that journeyman-tailoring, for long a poorly paid
trade, is now looking up. The Walters' workshop is in a tall, mid
18th-century terrace house, which is otherwise completely residential; and in the yard behind it one green-fingered tenant has created
a garden which could be in Mayfair or Chelsea. Round the corner,
too, in the Wardour Street flats where the Walters have their home,
tenants have made backyards and window-boxes bloom extraordinarily. This is the Soho most visitors never suspect exists: a
Soho where families live. Lou and Lily have two sons: one reading
chemistry at King's College, the other at Marylebone Grammar
School. They will not become journeymen tailors, says Lou. But it
will be interesting to see whether they wish to stay in the London
village where they grew up.

One important factor in deciding which way Soho goes is the
active Soho Society, founded in 1972 by one of the Westminster
City councillors for the Soho/Mayfair ward, Mrs Thelma Seear.
Property was booming then and demoliton was in the air. One of
the factors that provoked her into starting the Society was walking

into Soho Square and seeing 18th-century houses on the north side being torn apart. "I've never lived in Soho, but have known it ever since I came down from Cambridge; always gone there; always shopped there, even when we lived in Colchester." Since then, the Society – now with over 1,000 members – has gone from strength to strength: it has successfully fought redevelopment and change-of-use applications which would have destroyed the community and its vitality, and has persuaded Westminster Council to include the whole of Soho in a conservation area, which brings all demoliton within planning control. It holds an annual festival; runs a football team, a youth club, a local history group, a community newspaper; and has just sprouted a housing association which, with help from the Council, is renovating and converting several blocks of property which a year or two ago seemed doomed to demolition.

But as Soho began to exert its strength and fight back against outsiders many of its residents became more and more impatient with the City Council, whose members and officers sometimes did not seem to realize anybody actually lived in the place. Ironically, at the last borough elections, Tory Mrs Seear found herself, with her running-mate, housing chairman John Wells, voted out. Two independents got in, breaking the Conservatives' hold on the ward for the first time in seventy years. One of them, Mrs Lois Peltz, wife of a Soho GP, campaigned strongly on the basis that the City Council was betraying Soho by turning it into "a mini Manhattan" instead of encouraging families to stay or settle. That accusation clearly rang true with many Soho people, and subsequent events, notably the City Council's vote in favour of demolishing Sandringham Buildings West on the Soho side of Charing Cross Road, have not reassured them.

Sandringham Buildings – one of two blocks of tenements above bookshops facing each other across Charing Cross Road – may be regarded as a test case of the city's attitude towards Soho. The GLC has rehabilitated and upgraded the eastern block. Westminster carried out work on one staircase in its block and was advised on the strength of it that rehabilitation was both feasible and economic. Mrs Seear, though a Conservative, calls the decision of the planning committee's Tory majority to demolish and rebuild "utterly deplorable". It will, she says, provide less accommodation at greater cost and impose the hiatus of demolition and rebuilding, damaging the community and depriving people of good, low-cost homes in the centre of London.

Ennio Camisa came from Parma at the age of thirteen to work for an uncle in an Italian grocery business in Soho. Now he is seventy and he and his wife Inez still live above their shop in Berwick Street where they make their own spaghetti and ravioli, though much of the work is now done by their son Alberto, who also lives in Soho. He runs the business during the long holidays his parents can now allow themselves in Italy. Mr Camisa senior had been eighteen years in Britain when the Second World War broke out; he found himself interned on the Isle of Man and, Alberto told me, the family business in Old Compton Street was confiscated as alien property. Hence they had to start from fresh in Berwick Street in 1944. Alberto Camisa explained that the business has changed from being strictly Italian to being international. Their range of 150 cheeses now includes more English than Italian varieties, and they import direct from as far afield as Australia and Argentina. Like the Walters, the Camisas have one of the younger generation at university: Alberto's younger brother is studying surveying at Keele.

Alberto Camisa told me he likes to live in Soho because "it is more of a village than many country villages. We know everybody and everybody knows us. Even if you don't know all by name you know them to nod to; and if you fell down in the street they'd help you up. Besides, there's everything here in Soho, all the amenities." The aspect he dislikes is the growth of the sex shops with their obtrusively explicit window displays. "I'm not prudish. Sex has always been here. It's just that it's now so blatant, it's scaring people away, forcing families out and pushing rents up." He suggests that if sex shops are going to be there they should be required to turn blank shop-fronts to the street with modest lettering instead of advertising their wares so unrestrainedly. He cites the case of a Hungarian restaurant that recently moved into Fitzrovia because customers would not come through Soho any more.

Architect Douglas Stephen set up his practice in Soho because "I'd lived for a great part of my life abroad, in Shanghai, and believed a great city must be cosmopolitan. Otherwise it's rather provincial and parochial like Edinburgh. London was my first choice, and having decided on London, I picked the most cosmopolitan part of it." His first office, seventeen years ago, was in Foubert's Place, just off Carnaby Street. In those days there was only one small tailor in the neighbourhood, which was slightly seedy and housed a mixture of businesses, including a saddler and various other small craftsmen. "They catered mostly for the people who lived round about," he recalls and regrets that offices and Carnaby Street boutiques have steadily pushed them out.

Some years back Stephen moved his own office a couple of blocks south to Beak Street. He tried to include there a small flat, but it ended up with a desk and filing cabinet in what was meant to be the shower-room. "I've always wanted to live in Soho, but somehow never quite managed to get the right kind of place. The life of Soho is so marvellous – there's every kind of eating and entertainment. Within a few yards of my office there's a little nosherie where you can eat for £1 a head and another where you can eat for £10 a head. We do all our shopping in Soho, which has the best butchers' in London, Slater & Cooke Bisney & Jones in Brewer Street, where you can buy every kind of French cut; they take out the bone for you, prepare it however you want it." He also delights in Berwick Market. "You can get everything there. For the weekly shop you go either to Sainsburys or Berwick Market, which is much more enjoyable. You have to watch yourself or you can be sold a pup. You need to understand the rules of the game. That's what living in Soho is about."

He, too, had watched the growth of commercialized sex with distaste and apprehension. "It's always been sleazy, but now there's more organized violence." He had seen, while sitting in a restaurant, a fire-bomb thrown into a shop opposite, and knew of one case of youngsters opening up a porn shop and suffering the same fate. "It's getting worse," he says, and thinks the police have not acted firmly enough.

Douglas Stephen's other dislike is "the incredible effrontery of the City Council and its architects" in replacing one side of Berwick Market with an alien style of building topped by two tower blocks. "They destroyed Soho overnight. It was small-scale and should have been kept that way, they didn't understand the importance of the street." He called the plan to demolish Sandringham Buildings "ridiculous".

Henry Joelson was born in Soho and keeps a delicatessen shop just off Berwick Market. His grandparents came from Poland via the East End of London and the business has existed in Soho for more than seventy years. He has seen the market dwindle and lose the variety given it by trades like furriers and milliners; and he would agree strongly with Douglas Stephen about the effects of that

Berwick Market: shopping here is always fun . . .

official redevelopment. Certainly, he says, the little houses and
shops on the west side of the market were sub-standard, but in
rehousing people the authorities destroyed a vital community. He
remembers a time when Soho boasted eight primary schools; now it
has one. His own business, however, thrives, though its nature and
its clientele have changed. So has the competition. "I'm the only
Jewish delicatessen shop in central London. My nearest competitor
is Selfridges." Among his best selling lines are salt herrings and
kosher packet soups; and Arabs are valued customers because "for a
Muslim only kosher salami carries a written guarantee that it
doesn't contain pork". He sees much of the village atmosphere
going, pushed out by the spread of porn. "The trouble is anyone
under thirty-five at City Hall tends to assume that Soho has always
been a den of vice."

It was in an upstairs room in Frith Street in 1926 that John Logie
Baird demonstrated television to forty distinguished guests; but the
film industry came to Soho in force during the 1920s and 1930s.
Carl Gover, producer at Richard Williams Animation, explains

The spread of porn. Soho residents oppose it because it brings high rents and insecurity.

why his firm is there. Film laboratories, recording studios, everything they need is at hand. Also their clients, including the advertising men, have their offices close by or, if they come from outside, "enjoy the environment. It's exciting, it has a certain atmosphere, and there's such a range of restaurants and entertainment." But Gover, too, says if he could he would banish the porn shops. "I'm not a prude, but they just dominate the scene now."

One man who thinks commercialized sex in Soho is less bad than it was is Welsh dairyman Islwyn Pugh, whose Oxford Express Dairies shop stands in Frith Street. "A lot of people think Soho's gone down but I disagree with that. During the mid 1950s it was terrible. There were prostitutes so thick on the streets that as a kid coming home from school I had to say 'Excuse me' to get to my own front door." Today's rash of commercialized sex is less objectionable than that and he suspects that some of it is investment by "rich folk down in Sussex". Its most harmful effect, he says, has been to raise property owners' expectations on rents to absurd levels, so that even Boots, International Stores and the big brewers have been jibbing at recent asking prices.

The dairy business run by him and his seventy-six-year-old father was started by a dairyman called Townsend in 1850. It was called Express because milk was rushed by train from farms in Oxfordshire and then raced by horse and cart from Paddington.

Islwyn Pugh thinks things in Soho are now improving; he believes the porn shop bubble has burst; and that when the new planning committee settles down it will begin to see the sense of what the Soho Society is telling them. "With housing, the Society's virtually doing their job for them," he says. "For the first time flats are actually being built or renovated in Soho instead of being demolished." He points to a 1940s bomb site south of Shaftesbury Avenue which is still empty, and the nearby Newport Buildings site which the council demolished in 1973 and which has still not been redeveloped. "They were like little palaces, those flats. And the people who lived in them were employed in restaurants and cafés. The Council didn't seem to realize they had to have somewhere to live, they can't commute from Uxbridge or somewhere like that."

Much later than the French, Italians, Poles, Welsh milkmen or even Wardour Street film men the Chinese invaded Soho, particularly south of Shaftesbury Avenue, in the Gerrard Street area. Eric Wee, who himself came rather earlier, for the Festival of Britain in 1951, dates the main influx at about 1959 or 1960. They came from Hong Kong and, laundries being in decline, went into the only other business that most of them understood – restaurants. The Gerrard Street area was at that time threatened with demolition, so rents were low, and being gamblers the Chinese took the risk. When the threat of demolition lifted that gamble paid off. The Chinese restaurateurs thrived, and into the same area moved Chinese hairdressers, tailors, accountants and a whole host of ancillary services.

Wee says that the community originally, for reasons of language and culture, kept very much to itself, but lately has been integrating more. At the last Soho Festival 400 to 500 Chinese took part; and he, as contact man between the Soho Society and the Chinese, has offered them the use of space at the proposed community centre which it is hoped to build on a site near St Anne's church tower.

Wee hails from Singapore, where he was prominent in youth work, for which he was awarded the MBE. His wife, who is Korean, persuaded him to open London's first Korean restaurant in Poland Street two years ago, and now they have a second in Knightsbridge. He opposes the spread of porn shops not on moral grounds but because they are pushing out light industry and residential use.

Bryan Burrough, Soho Society vice-chairman, works at the Foreign Office and lives in Wardour Street. He came there first to stay with friends of the family in his student days, and after duty tours abroad always gravitated back to familiar territory. He likes his London village not only because he can walk to work, but because it is a friendly, close community with vitality and colour. He stresses the importance of the district's hidden industrial base, not only the film industry, but tailoring, costume-making, silver and goldsmiths, clockmakers and all manner of other, often interdependent crafts. The young clockmaker who is repairing the clock of St Anne's tower also repairs antique time-pieces for Sotheby's; without the specialist services of a couple called Hands, Soho's only remaining gold-lace embroiderers, theatrical costumiers Gus and Harry of Carlisle Street would not have landed a recent valuable export order for Renaissance costumes for a waxworks exhibition in Tokyo. The export trade of this hidden craft industry in basements, attics and first-floor backs is, reasons Burrough, worth many times the turnover of either the porn shops or, for that matter, the restaurants. And yet, he adds, most Westminster City councillors just do not know it exists.

Carnaby Street: relic of 1960s' Swinging London, but still trading briskly.

In 1974 the Soho Society invited the newly elected planning committee to come and look at the area. "We split them into groups of four, and took them round. The group I was with we took to Kettners' basement, then into the kitchen of a Chinese restaurant, then to a drum maker's and a flute maker's, and finally gave them all dinner in a 1730s house in Great Pulteney Street with a coal fire burning in the grate. They were amazed to learn there were such places, and quite staggered to be told that every single place they'd been to that night was due for demolition."

The threat of demolition has now largely been lifted – but Burrough considers that most City councillors (and some of the top planning officials) still do not understand or respond to Soho's needs. An example of how out of touch they are was shown in a recent planning decision. A café proprietor asked for planning permission for a simple, non-illuminated shop sign saying "Café" and "Coca-Cola". The planners refused him on the grounds that it would be "out of character with the conservation area", apparently oblivious to the fact that all round that café porn shop and strip club proprietors had put up unauthorized, brightly lit signs and shop-fronts a thousandfold more garish and objectionable – without the planning authority lifting a finger. The scorn and anger that local people felt about that decision were maybe one reason why they voted out their sitting Tory councillors and voted in the indepen-dents – just to show City Hall how disgusted they were at official lack of understanding.

The City plan, which at first seemed to be saying most of the right things, has, complains Burrough, now been watered down, by the insertion of adjectives like "normally" and "reasonably", into an anodyne document which provides no real support at public inquiries. He contrasts Camden's helpful attitude in Covent Garden with the battle the Soho Society has had to get public notice-boards in the area. Perhaps, he suggests, the cure for City Hall remoteness would be for each such London village to have its own urban parish council, able to get on with the job itself within certain limits and able to speak with authority for local people about the needs and wants of its area. Perhaps one day urban parish or village councils will come. Until then the Soho Society and its community group and housing association offshoots are doing a remarkably good job with fairly meagre resources. One can only hope the new batch of City councillors will come to recognize that fact and take the advice of the people who know what Soho is all about.

22

Blackheath

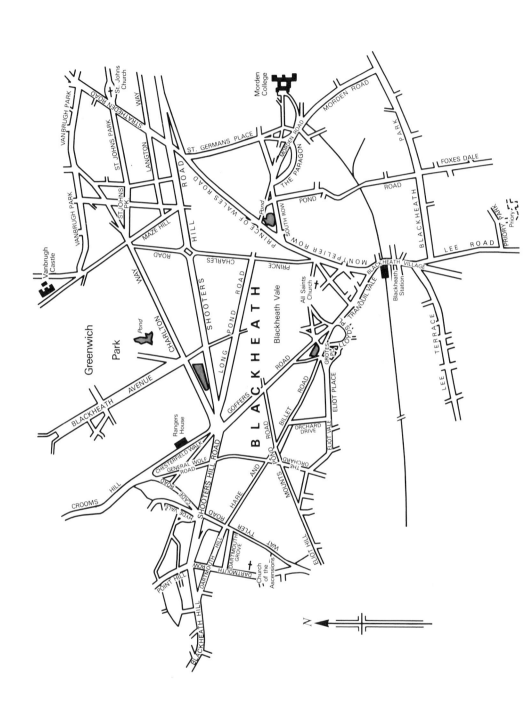

22

Blackheath

If you head out of London along the A2 towards Dover, tight-packed, grimy inner London hems you in all along the Old Kent Road and through New Cross and Deptford. Then comes a steep hill, and suddenly all is changed: the buildings draw back, you find yourself on a wide expanse of green, an irregular fringe of houses, many of them elegantly Georgian or early Victorian, as its backcloth, and wooded hills beyond. This is Blackheath: 270 acres of football-playing, kite-flying, bicycle-riding, tadpole-netting, picnicking, sunbathing and just plain strolling.

Blackheath has four ponds, five public houses on or near its edges, the tall, brown wall of Greenwich Park on its northern edge, and a constant, noisy, impatient stream of traffic battering its way from east to west. But there is more to Blackheath than you can see from a car. What lies behind those peripheral clumps of trees, down in the dips of old gravel pits, or behind the little enclaves of houses that crept on to the heath in the wake of now vanished windmills? There are orderly streets of charming and now much sought-after Victorian villas and terraces marching down steep slopes into Lee or Greenwich, vistas, statues and eccentric architectural set-pieces.

Reaching Blackheath via the A2 today marks a change from grey to green, from urban to urbane. It was not always so. For Wat Tyler, Jack Cade, Sir Thomas Wyatt and other rebels against an uncaring or oppressive state, it was a place to camp before marching on London; for the Petitioners of Kent, provoked beyond endurance by Parliament's Civil War exactions and extortions, the place where Fairfax's horse drove them firmly and without much bloodshed back in a rout towards Rochester. It was a grim, wild place then, of highwaymen and gravel pits, called Blackheath either because of the colour of the soil among the gorse and scrub, or, it has sometimes been suggested, because it was bleak.

The heath itself was also the scene of many royal meetings: between Henry VIII and Anne of Cleves, when "from the tentes to

Mounts Pond, Blackheath: water, sky, trees, and the fringe of pretty houses.

the Parke gate were all bushes and tyrres cutte down, and a large and ample way made for the shew of all persones"; between Charles II on his restoration and the welcoming citizens of London. On Blackheath, George II reviewed his troops, among whom was a young ensign named James Wolfe; and in 1687 John Evelyn watched a trial of "those develish, murdering, mischief-doing engines called bombs, shot out of a mortar-piece on Blackheath".

The same century saw the founding of perhaps Blackheath's grandest and most beautiful building, Morden College. Sir John Morden, born in the City of London in 1623, became a merchant and a member of the Turkey Company. The story runs that he put all his capital into three ships trading in the Levant. The ships went missing, causing him acute financial difficulty; and he made a vow that if ever he became rich again, he would found a "college", or charitable institution, to help other merchants whose fortunes had similarly foundered. Eventually the ships turned up again and Sir John, no longer a "decayed merchant", engaged Wren or one of his associates to build him the pretty red-brick quadrangle – with clock-tower, cupola and effigies of Morden and his wife above its entrance – which forms the nucleus of the present college and so elegantly adorns the south-east corner of the heath.

Nowadays the Morden College trustees apply Sir John's benevolent intentions more widely than simply to decayed merchants. The college has about 200 residents, of whom forty – "the members" – live in rooms in the original quadrangle; but the resident beneficiaries also include wives, widows and daughters of those who are or have been members; and though predominantly elderly folk who have held positions of responsibility in commerce, they currently include a retired architect and a bishop.

Off the north-east corner of the heath, in Maze Hill, stands the Roan School – an Inner London Education Authority grammar school now quietly becoming comprehensive, and whose foundation goes back even earlier than Morden College. Sir John Roan was another philanthropic merchant who wished to do good for his fellow men – in this case "to bring upp soe many poore towne-borne children of East Greenwich aforesaid at schoole, that is to reading, writing and cyphering", with "fortie shillings per annum towards their clothing until each of them shall accomplish the age of fifteene yeares".

The Paragon: seven pairs of Georgian houses in an arc and linked by colonnades. Converted into flats after Second World War bomb damage.

The school's headmaster, Dr A. J. Taylor, told me that he believed that in some respects Roan as a comprehensive would be meeting its founder's intentions better than it had as a grammar school; for it was becoming once more very much a school for the Blackheath/Greenwich neighbourhood.

A century after the benevolent foundations of the two Sir John's, Blackheath first began to appeal to the City's rising middle classes. The Paragon, a curving row of three-and-a-half-storeyed pairs of houses linked by stuccoed colonnades, dates from 1794 and stands close to Morden College gates on its own carriage drive behind an expanse of lawn. It marked one boundary of the estate of Sir Gregory Page, on which for sixty-four years stood his splendid mansion in extensive landscaped grounds; but in 1783 Page's heir, who lived comfortably in Oxfordshire, sold the estate to the Cator family, who had a country seat at Beckenham. So the house was demolished, and the Cators over the next century and a half let the estate out in building leases.

Development went on by fits and starts throughout the Georgian and early Victorian eras, fringing the heath on lands owned not only by Page and Cator, but by the Earls of Dartmouth and St Germans and Morden College Estate, all reflected in local place-names. City bankers and merchants who had tired of living in cramped quarters over warehouse or counting-house commuted first by horse-bus then, from 1849 onwards, by rail. From the 1860s on the area found favour with the new professional classes and a Civil Service reformed and expanded to administer the Empire, and the development really got into its stride – not only in terms of bricks and mortar, but as a community. The Blackheath Proprietory School (found in 1833, and in which parents were shareholders), a conservatoire of music (which still exists), an art school, a concert hall, and the Royal Blackheath Golf Club on the heath were some of the amenities. The local chemist, William Butcher, was a pioneer of the popular cinema, demonstrating as early as 1897 "animated pictures" of railway stations, a German cavalry charge and a minuet (hand coloured) on a machine called a Motophotoscope. His great-grandson John Butcher still runs a thriving chemist's and photographic business there.

But it was a later wave of development, in the 1930s, that led to the establishment of two influential local bodies, the Blackheath Society and the Blackheath Preservation Trust. Preservation, conservation and "amenity" are subjects that sometimes seem to outsiders to obsess Blackheath residents – though the interpretations they put on them vary greatly. Thus Neil Rhind, leading member of the society, part-time secretary of the Trust, local historian and journalist, has lived virtually all his life in the area, and views with regret fine houses lost to the demolition men before official conservation policies and legislation became strong enough to protect them. In particular he sighs for a row of 17th-century gothic houses by Vanbrugh, including one called Mince Pie House, and for several fine houses demolished in Blackheath Park to make way for the widely admired Span development of the 1950s and 1960s. Span, he argues, could have built in the huge back gardens and satisfactorily converted the houses into flats.

In contrast to Rhind is Leslie Bilsby, founder of Span Developments, whose well-landscaped, relatively tightly packed estates of terrace houses and flats for young professionals by the architects Eric Lyons and Partners won a steady stream of awards. A second-generation builder from Lincolnshire with an irrepressible enthusiasm for high-quality modern design, Bilsby came to Blackheath in the late 1940s to help an architect friend, C. Bernard Brown, to restore the Paragon, and has lived there ever since, exploiting with the Cator estate the falling in of old leases to build the hundreds of little houses that gave so many present (and conservation-minded) Blackheathans their first foothold in the district.

Blackheath's best modern house, No. 10 Blackheath Park: built by Span entrepreneur Leslie Bilsby for his own use but since sold to a businessman from the Middle East.

The first Span flats, the Priory, originally sold in 1954 at around £2,250 apiece. The smallest now go for £20,000 upwards, and Span's latest houses, being built to a very much more "traditional" design than Eric Lyons offered in the 1950s, went on the market in 1978 at between £25,000 and £35,000. In the early 1960s Span had to fight the LCC at appeal to build new flats on the heath's edge at South Row; now one local planning authority, Greenwich, has placed two Span estates on its local list of buildings of special architectural importance. Unlike Rhind, Bilsby told me he took pleasure not only in the spaciousness of Blackheath Park but in the way in which, as he sees it, Span's and other people's good modern designs fit in with existing buildings. He has given Blackheath one modern house of real distinction – 10 Blackheath Park, a series of connecting three-storey pentagons faced in black glass, designed for his own use by architect Patrick Gwynne and tucked between two existing houses. Bilsby said he believed he had been proved right in redeveloping. His enthusiasm for good modern design and what he would call creative redevelopment make him assert flatly: "The band-waggon of conservation is totally misguided." Effort and imagination which ought to go into creating something new, he argues, now goes only into preserving buildings of "poor quality, physically and aesthetically".

Blackheath in general disagrees. It sees him almost as its amiable neighbourhood Jekyll-and-Hyde – on the one hand, civilized, likable, the creator of excellent new environments; on the other, proclaiming openly that he would like to tear down the picturesque jumble of shops and houses at the centre of the village which most of the residents regard as a key piece of cherished townscape; saying also that he regrets the ministerial about-turn by Richard Crossman · which saved the Regency terraces on the edge of the heath at Montpelier Row, and that it would have benefited the community more to build an hotel and filling station.

Incomprehensible sacrilege to the conservationists this – for the Montpelier terraces were a *cause célèbre* that local residents and the Blackheath Society fought for long and hard, briefing counsel, writing letters to *The Times* and lobbying Ministers and civil servants. One of the fighters then, in 1966, was a newly elected Labour MP, Roland Moyle, at that time happily living in a Span house. Lately Minister of State at the Department of Health, Moyle lives in an 1830 house just along the row from the terrace he helped to save. Though detectably Welsh in origin, he told me he

Tranquil Vale. A sad misnomer because of traffic noise, but nonetheless part of an attractive and bustling village centre.

had grown up mostly in south-east London, his father working for the National Union of Public Employees, whose headquarters still occupies a 19th-century terrace in the south-west corner of the heath.

In the last twenty years, says Moyle, Blackheath and Blackheath opinion has changed. He instances greater acceptance of good modern architecture ("Then anything modern was bad, nothing but Regency or Georgian would do"); there was, he says, an embattled feeling, as if the Huns and Goths were about to close in and destroy a threatened civilization. Now virtually all Blackheath ranks as an "outstanding" conservation area, which the two local planning authorities are dedicated to defending.

Behind the western fringe of the heath lies Dartmouth Row, a gracious, spacious street of houses including every period from William and Mary to Edwardian, and containing also the Church of the Ascension, first built on that site in the 1680s as a proprietary chapel. Its vicar is Canon Paul Oestreicher, chairman of Amnesty International's British section, East West Relations Secretary of the British Council of Churches and sometime its international affairs secretary, and a member of the BBC's religious broadcasting staff. Oestreicher grew up partly in Germany, mostly in New Zealand, and is a quiet, likable man whose informality and sense of humour may at first disguise his passionate determination to fight injustice wherever he finds it.

Halfway through his first ten years at the Ascension, injustice in an ugly form hit his parish, with a "bent" policeman (as it was afterwards proved) taking it out on a mixed-race family by getting them all falsely charged with theft or connected offences. Another Blackheath fighter of tough causes, criminal lawyer Ben Birnberg, secured their acquittal; and this so enraged the National Front that they heckled Oestreicher's next Sunday morning service. It is typical of him that, despite urgings from parishioners and his bishop, he refused to prosecute the NF for disrupting a church service. "My view is, you have got to try to have a dialogue with them, not victimize them." His parishioners, not all of whom share his political views or pastoral style, to their credit rallied behind their vicar in the face of the Front's assault. "There was total solidarity," he recalls. "The right-wingers were as disgusted as anyone else." Oestreicher regards Blackheath as an attractive, agreeable place to live, but adds that it is still very much a "middle-class enclave in working-class south London".

Moyle does not agree. He sees it as a mixed community, where his youngest child and Oestreicher's went to the same school as the children of postmen, dustmen and shop assistants, but whose more numerous middle class provide more than their share of councillors, teachers, social workers and volunteers for worth-while causes. If a social divide remains, if they fail to get involved as much as they should, then at least they do better than more conventional suburbs such as Beckenham and Bexley. Rhind, too, takes issue with the

Hare & Billet pond: great for mucking about in while Mum and Dad sit with a pint on a bench.

committed canon. The Blackheath Society has succeeded in beating back threats like the Motorway Box and ill-judged redevelopment, he argues, precisely because it has concentrated on environmental issues and has not been led into divisive or dissipatory concern with other matters.

The label "Blackheath" – rather like Highgate on the other side of London – is applied to a number of different residential areas whose only real link with each other is the great green billiard table of the heath. Roy Fuller, the poet, for instance, lives in a leafy mews in an oblong of tall Victorian houses that encroached 140 years ago into the north-east corner of the heath. A Lancastrian in origin, he came to Blackheath when he joined the Woolwich Equitable as a young solicitor in 1938 because "I'd heard of Blackheath Rugby Club and thought it must be a salubrious suburb." He had learnt, he told me, to enjoy it both for itself and for the people he encountered; some, like the late Cecil Day Lewis down the hill in Greenwich, became friends; others – "there was a witch-like figure, and a woman with a very large head" – he put in his poems. The change he most regretted was the growth of heavy traffic on the A2.

Living in a Span flat in Blackheath Park, landscape architect Geoffrey Collens told me his chosen village had, as a pleasant place to live in, turned out to be all he thought it might be when he first moved there fourteen years ago. Collens, as a director of the residents' consortium that bought roads and verges from John Cator in the early 1960s, had a hand in conserving and upgrading this corner of the district. With funds extracted from developers as the price of access, Blackheath Cator Estate Ltd planted trees, resurfaced roads, and threw up symbolic (because they are always open) white gates and speed-restricting bumps to keep through traffic out of its patch.

Living right in the heart of Blackheath village, as tenants of the Blackheath Preservation Trust, are two of its longest-established shopkeepers, Barbara and Keith Mackenzie. Mrs Mackenzie opened a toyshop called Raggity Ann's elsewhere in the village in 1945. At first trade was so quiet that she and her husband sat on the heath opposite their shop and popped back across the road if a customer appeared. Now they have three shops which sell respectively toys, children's clothes and lingerie.

Near Raggity's stands another building owned by the Trust, Martin House. Originally the Blackheath Literary Institution, it dates from 1845, but was substantially rebuilt and restored to something close to its original appearance in 1975, its interior designed to house two hand-picked tenants; graphic designers Banks & Miles, and the Mary Evans Picture Library. Colin Banks and John Miles moved from Mayfair because of soaring rents, and they consider the change has been a great success. They use colour laboratories in the village, share a dispatch service with other designers in the area, and, said Miles: "If something is really urgent, we're right next to the railway station, and it's only twenty minutes to London." The Mary Evans Picture Library began, recalls Hilary Evans, a former advertising man, as a sideline for his wife, run from their tiny, three-bedroomed Span house. Now it "dominates our lives", employs seven people, has something over two million prints, photographs and other illustrations and does a thriving business with publishers, editors, designers and others concerned with visual documentation of the past. Their landlord is one of the longer-established "revolving fund" preservation bodies, having in its forty years restored about thirty properties, normally reselling domestic buildings but keeping commerical ones as an investment. But for the Trust, substantial key sections of the Georgian and Victorian townscape would have fallen to ball and chain and been unsympathetically redeveloped.

Until lately Blackheathants have bemoaned the demise of "real" shops in the village in the face of the steady advance of "useless" ones – which in some people's view include twelve restaurants, almost all of which have sprung up in the last fifteen years. Suddenly now the tide seems to have turned. The village has one of the best stocked small bookshops in London; a new self-service grocery has started up, supplementing a thriving health food shop; Ferns, the coffee and tea merchants, have opened a branch; and in the summer of 1978 two bakers, Ron Stevens from nearby Lewisham and Peter Squire, a Scot from Oban, realized an ambition of many years' standing by opening their own bakery in what had previously been a restaurant – though before that, as they discovered from hidden Victorian ovens, a baker's. They reckoned Blackheath might respond to bread baked by traditonal methods, but even so the response took them by surprise. "It's been fantastic," says Stevens happily. "We've been working eighteen hours a day, and still we can't cope." Evidently Blackheath appreciates quality and the personal touch.

23

Covent Garden

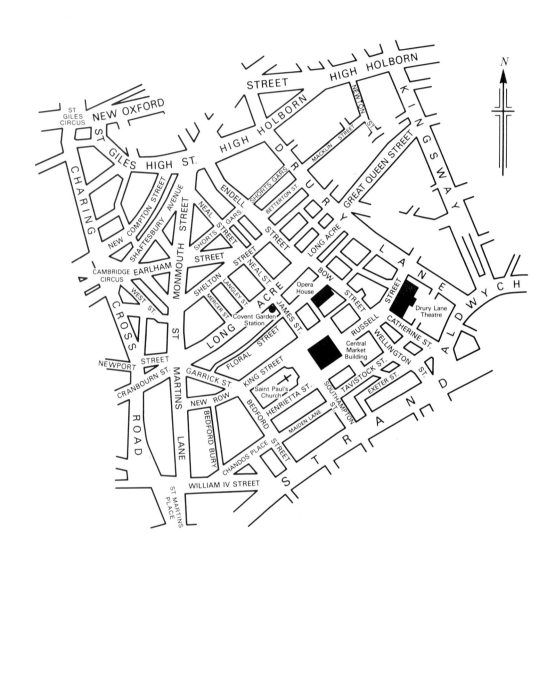

23

Covent Garden

Covent Garden is beginning to bloom again. No one passing, after an absence of two years, along King Street towards the market piazza, or through the more workaday streets of former warehouses farther north round Neal Street and Shelton Street, could be in any doubt about that. It is blooming not with chrysanthemums or cabbages, but with fresh paint, new shops and restaurants and, though much more slowly, new front doors, and new homes behind old front doors. The withdrawal symptoms, experienced in 1974 when after more than 300 years the market moved to its shiny, new, hygienic, food-handling depot at Nine Elms, were acute. For several years Covent Garden seemed to be dying – a ghost town of shuttered wholesalers' shops, with the silent spectre of ten generations of market porters lingering about barrows made redundant by fork-lift trucks. About two years ago the corpse began to quicken; and its recovery is now such that concern with how to contain and guide it along acceptable lines is beginning to preoccupy both the official planners and local representative bodies.

Covent Garden (traditionally a corruption of "convent garden") belonged until the 16th century to the Abbey of Westminster which, being on stony land by the Thames, could not have its market garden or supporting farm immediately outside its walls like most other monastic houses. After the Dissolution of the Monasteries the Crown granted the site to Sir John Russell, whose family became first Earls and then Dukes of Bedford; and in 1630 the Fourth Earl laid out London's first real square, the Piazza, designed by Inigo Jones whose St Paul's Church (although subsequently rebuilt after a fire) still graces the western side. Forty years later the fifth Earl decided he must get some income from the square and obtained a licence for a fruit, flower and vegetable market there; all the original houses disappeared; the market grew and in the 1820s and 1830s came Charles Fowler's four ranges of

261

colonnaded buildings in the centre of the Piazza to accommodate it; so that, to the Victorian cockney (who called the surrounding arcades "piazzas") Covent Garden came to mean, in Sir Nikolaus Pevsner's words, "oranges rather than Inigo".

Public complaints about the congestion, inefficiency and untidiness of the great vegetable market operating over the pavements and in the roadways in and around the Piazza did not begin in the 1950s or 1960s. Dr Francis Sheppard in his admirable *London 1808–1870: The Infernal Wen* tells us that public demand for their complete removal began in the 1860s. By that time the nature and management of the market had already changed greatly. In the early 1800s, Sheppard tells us, there were still some 15,000 acres of market garden within ten miles, and every midnight growers loaded their carts and set out for "the Garden"; seasonal crops like strawberries were carried in baskets by women, who came regularly to London for the season from as far as Wales or Shropshire. By the time Shaw's Eliza Doolittle encountered Dr Higgins under the portico of Inigo's St Paul's the march of bricks and mortar had pushed out many of the market gardens; and steam-ships and cold stores allowed exotic produce to extend the range of merchandise clogging the pavements of the ever widening market district. Nonetheless, right up to the market's move in 1974, it's operation continued to depend on hand-barrows and market porters, skilfully balancing on their heads incredible piles of baskets or trays.

The decision to move the market, taken in the early 1960s, led to the setting up of a joint GLC/Westminster/Camden consortium charged with planning for the redevelopment of the area along the "comprehensive" lines then fashionable. Politicians and planners saw the removal of the market as a great opportunity to tear down and rebuild anew, with high capacity roads and car parks, tower and slab blocks accommodating offices, homes and conference or exhibition buildings, and the retention only of a "line of character" running east-west across the area from Great Queen Street through Broad Court, the Piazza and King Street to the 17th- and 18th-century lanes and alleys of New Row and Goodwin's Court in the west.

Mr John Wood, proprietor of Rules restaurant in Maiden Lane, became all too keenly aware that a three-lane, one-way highway duplicating the Strand would slice twenty-eight feet off the front of his building and that, if the GLC built the road, his restaurant would disappear. He and quite a few others thought that would be a

The Central Market Buildings in course of restoration, 1978. Interest from would-be lessees of the intended shops, restaurants and pubs was intense and boded well for this bid to put the heart back into The Garden.

pity. Thomas Rule started an oyster bar in Maiden Lane in 1798; it blossomed into a fashionable eating house in the 1800s and the Rule family ran it until 1880. Its patrons have included Dickens, Thackeray, Galsworthy, H. G. Wells, and in more recent years both Graham Greene and his brother Sir Hugh. Edward Prince of Wales and the celebrated Lily Langtry used to dine there in a curtained-off portion of the first-floor restaurant. Such was the affection and loyalty Rules commanded that its petition against the GLC's intended demolition won 9,600 signatures, a high proportion of them from overseas. "It became a peg to hand the anti-demolition ticket on," says John Wood who adds that he has run the restaurant since 1964 in succession to his father-in-law Thomas Bell.

Despite the petition and his and other objectors' evidence, the inspector who heard the 1971 inquiry approved the GLC's plans in all but one or two minor details; but by that time two things were happening which undermined his conclusions. Disillusioned by the results of 1960s comprehensive redevelopment, public opinion was swinging quite suddenly and violently towards conservation; and the buoyant economy of the 1960s, on which both public and private sectors depended to fund such large-scale schemes, began to take a dive. Geoffrey Rippon, the Secretary of State for the Environment, saw which way the wind was blowing. He realized, thinks Wood, that not only would the proposed redevelopment prove politically unpopular, but that "financially it was going to be a dead duck. I was regarded as eccentric then for forecasting the end of the property boom; but I think Rippon also saw it coming."

So while nominally endorsing his inspector's approval for the scheme, the Environment Secretary required amendments which made it unworkable; and in announcing this decision he simultaneously added 200 premises (from suggestions submitted by the Joint Committee of National Amenity Societies) to the hitherto slim list of buildings of historic and architectural importance in the area, scattering them so widely – "like confetti," recalled Wood – that scarcely a block remained where a developer, public or private, could go ahead on a large scale without seeking the Minister's consent. Explaining the new list to the Press, Rippon quoted four examples: the late-Victorian Holborn Town Hall: Bow Street Magistrates Court, (Pevsner's description of which consists of two words only: "gravely Palladian"): the market's glass and iron Floral Hall of 1858; and Rules. The haunt of Dickens, Thackeray and the brothers Greene was saved: and so, too, was the fabric, physical character and idiosyncratic street pattern of "the Garden", which outside the Piazza generally follows the line of country lanes and field boundaries rather than an imposed rectilinearity.

But if anyone thought that was the end of argument about Covent Garden, they were mistaken. The Skeffington Report of 1969 had

One of the better and less expensive of the wave of new restaurants opened in the area during the 1970s.

confirmed and encouraged a growing trend among local communities to "participate" in planning decisions which concerned them. The GLC's Covent Garden team, to be sure, had in the 1960s formally "consulted" people who lived, worked or owned property in the area; but local people were now determined to "participate". Plans to clear and rebuild the area comprehensively had no doubt given way to repair and conversion of the existing fabric, with redevelopment only on a relatively modest scale; but all the more reason for Covent Garden folk to have an active say on how, where and when it happened. John Wood found himself chairing a working party, from which in 1973 sprang a remarkable consultative body, the Covent Garden Forum, elected by the community from among such interest-groups as residents, employees, shopkeepers, restaurant proprietors and the Royal Opera House, to examine and influence proposals affecting the area put forward by the GLC's Covent Garden Committee and other public authorities.

How successful has the Forum been? Simon Pembroke, its secretary since it started, told me he believed it had worked very well. "It's rather like a jury," he said. "A collection of people from different walks of life have been successful in reaching a consensus." The Forum, set up by the GLC, has a full-time paid secretary paid for by that body, but depends essentially for its effectiveness on the sharp eyes and unpaid effort of its members in spotting and persuading the planning authorities to stop harmful developments and in hammering out acceptable alternative solutions. Pembroke, a lecturer in Greek at Bedford College, came to live in Garrick Street in 1969 because he had friends there and it was convenient for work and the British Museum. At that time, he said, he felt little incentive to explore the hinterland of Covent Garden – "after all, I knew what vegetables looked like". Now he takes pleasure in buildings that are being looked after more carefully, even if that long overdue care and attention is sometimes accompanied by an unwelcome "trendiness"; in new trades such as Bertram Rota's recently established antiquarian bookshop in Long Acre; and in the fact that "we have all got to know far more about each other than we would have done if the ants' nest hadn't been disturbed."

Jim Monahan of the Covent Garden Community Association is considerably less sanguine about the area's future. He became involved as an Architectural Association student during his practical "year out", came to the conclusion that GLC planners were talking gobbledy-gook and were not really interested in what local people wanted or needed; helped in 1971 to found the Association and fight the redevelopment plans; and then stayed on as architect – one of two now employed by the CGCA to design and oversee housing schemes, their salaries funded by the Monument Trust. The Association in practice shows two different faces: that of the militant neighbourhood ginger group, constantly attacking the GLC for being too preoccupied with saving money and too little concerned with people's needs for homes, jobs and social facilities; and the intensely practical organization which is, through a housing association subsidiary, converting old properties into new flats. It has provided a community centre with bar, café, toddlers' play group, and space for all manner of events from committee meetings to bingo sessions; has turned the spacious upper floor of an empty market building, the Jubilee Hall, into a much needed sports centre and runs tenants' rights and legal advice services for the neighbourhood.

Most recently it played a leading role in providing the most ambitious of five or six community gardens, created on temporarily dormant redevelopment sites in an effort to redress the area's acute lack of public open space; and in this garden, known to local children as "The Pit", the Fifth Covent Garden Neighbourhood Festival was held in September. More than 10,000 people took part in the two-day event. It is characteristic of the CGCA that when they got permission to use part of the old Odhams site for this garden, they cheekily pasted over the word offices in the developer's sign so that it read "200,000 sq ft of air-conditioned gardens"; but characteristic, too, that having thus badly upset the developer's architect Richard Seifert, they repaired relations sufficiently to extract from him a £25 donation towards the garden's cost.

In a profounder way the Community Association showed its characteristic opportunism and nimbleness by securing from the Labour GLC in the last days before it was ousted in 1977 a short-term lease of the Jubilee Hall. Then, with very little money in the bank, they began the £70,000 repair and conversion exercise which gave central London an excellent and much needed sports hall, raising money to pay for it as they went along. The incoming Conservative administration made no bones about its intention to demolish the converted building in four to five years' time. The Association proclaimed in its usual strident style that this was an economy- and profits-obsessed Tory council sabotaging a well used

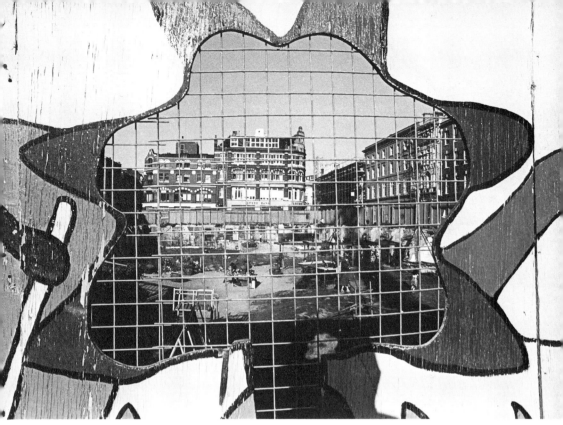

Sites cleared for development which then hangs fire need not be deserts of desolation. "The pit", part of the former Odhams site, is the latest and most ambitious of five "community gardens".

facility the community had struggled to create for itself. GLC officials retorted that the CGCA knew all along that the building was to be demolished; that the GLC let them have it for a nominal rent for a temporary use; and that only by redeveloping the site could they justify the original purchase price, complete a colonnaded south side to the Piazza, and provide the housing which would be one ingredient of the scheme. Monahan retorted that the CGCA could demonstrate how everything the GLC wanted except car parking could be accommodated on the site without demolishing the Jubilee Hall.

Geoff Holland, the GLC's development team leader, joined the original team of three in 1966 as its architect-planner, when the market was expected to move in 1968 or 1969. He argues that in producing the original "clear and build" plan the team were only doing what 1960s' planning orthodoxy and their political masters required. The inquiry inspector, he points out, gave their effort "99 out of 100"; and indeed, he said, some of the team's present critics

"criticized us in 1968 for keeping 'too much old rubbish'". In 1971, as he saw it, two things happened. First, there was a "national nervous breakdown", and instead of assuming that London, the World City, must rebuild its centre, people began to perceive the attractions of those few old districts that had escaped redevelopment and to clamour for their preservation. This coincided with economic recession and the collapse of the property market. Now the team has produced an "Action Area" plan in which, he considers, conservation, social need and economic realism, and the means of regeneration are suitably balanced. When the Strand-Maiden Lane super-highway fell to Rippon's axe, that took Covent Garden out of the London roads' system and turned it into an environmental island, he says.

From his office at the corner of King Street and the Piazza, Holland views the area's progress in a much more cheerful light than he did three or four years ago. King Street itself has only a handful of properties that have not been renovated; in the centre of the Piazza, Fowler's market buildings with roofs added by Cubitt would soon be emerging from their protective hoardings splendidly renovated by the GLC, which is currently entertaining proposals from firms and individuals interested in taking shop and restaurant units. The surrounding areas are to be to all intents and purposes traffic-free; the space between the west end of the market buildings and the porch of St Paul's, repaved in stone, will be the nearest thing London has to that well used *place* in front of Paris's Pompidou Centre, full of jugglers, conjurors, fire-swallowers, illusionists and musicians. London could do with such a centre for street entertainers.

Away in the south-east corner of the Piazza, the 1870s Flower Market is also being restored and converted to hold London Transport's Museum, now in temporary exile at Syon Park, and, in the basement, a national theatre museum. Holland hopes it will be possible to lay a length of track into the Piazza so that London Transport's Museum can run an engine or a tram or two out as open-air bait for tourists. On the east side of the Piazza, and also under the arcade on the north side, cafés are flourishing with tables on the pavements. In the north-east corner on land owned by the Opera House an earlier, temporary garden, called the Italian Garden, opened a place for lunchtime picnics and, during the summer, a whole succession of free entertainments, including the Potzuki Puppet Theatre and sundry bitingly satirical assaults on developers, planners and politicians.

The portico of St Paul's Church, facing on to the piazza, was the scene of that most famous fictional meeting between Eliza Doolittle and Professor Higgins.

More profoundly encouraging in Holland's eyes is the fact that new trades and businesses, such as graphic designers, advertising firms, fashion and specialist shops are beginning to move in to compensate for the great gaps left four years ago. The resident population, which fell below its 1968 level of 3,000 is now, he says, back at that level again. The Opera House plans to extend first westwards, which will give it for the first time adequate backstage facilities and the Piazza a firm northern edge; then southwards, to give it rehearsal space and perhaps a second auditorium, though the planners and the Forum have apparently convinced it and its architects that the colonnades with which it would front the Piazza at this point should house shops and cafés and not, as originally proposed, be backed by blank glass walls.

Opposite the Opera House is Bow Street police station, from which the police are soon to move to give the well patronized magistrates' court more room. The new local police station will probably be in, or on the site of, the old Charing Cross Hospital. North of Long Acre, alongside those "air-conditioned" gardens, the GLC has been building a substantial area of low-rise housing where once the huge, dull neo-classical Odhams newspapers and magazine headquarters stood. In James Street buildings originally earmarked for homes and workshops are now, to CGCA's fury, to be offices; while round the corner in Floral Street other buildings are to become a National Jazz Centre.

Away towards the Strand stands one of Covent Garden's best known and most durable institutions: Moss Bros. It was, says its deputy chairman, Montague Moss, founded by his great-grand-father Moses Moses, and moved to its present site at the corner of Bedford Street and New Row in 1881. Monty Moss joined the firm in 1942, shortly before going into the Army, and is one of the eight members of the family, including one woman, now working there. He points out that Moss Bros sell clothes as well as operating the hire service for which they are best known. He laments that in a "disposable society" people are less prepared to pay for quality, though the firm still, he says, lives up to old Moses's business motto, "Give them good value, sell them good stuff". Moss Bros would have benefited from the original redevelopment plan, which put a road through their present premises and would have allowed them to rebuild elsewhere at the GLC's expense, but in other respects Monty Moss, a member of the Covent Garden Forum, thinks the way in which the area is coming back to life and the buildings are being restored "wonderful" – though the GLC's plans for paving over some roads and making others one-way worry him. "If people can't get here by taxi or car from the Strand, it could ruin our business," he says.

In contrast to Moss Bros, Goods and Chattels in Neal Street is a relatively new business, founded in 1970 by Christina Smith, sometime Terence Conran's secretary. "I went round the world working and sent back little parcels of samples," she recalls. Since 1972 her business has concentrated on imports from China, such as bamboo furniture and basketware. Miss Smith lives in Shelton Street and is a member of both the Forum and the Covent Garden Community Association, which started life in her flat. She is keenly interested in a housing association scheme to provide flats in the top storey of, and in the air space above, the Shelton Street community centre. Among the qualities she likes about her adopted London village, which she came to from Kensington, are the closeness and sociability of the community and the pleasure of just walking

"Have a care: people live here," might sum up the Covent Garden Community Association's plea to the planners. Seen here: pre-school play-group at the CGCA's community centre in Shelton Street.

through its alleys and courts, where it is possible to escape to a surprising extent from traffic. She dislikes rubbish from restaurants and other premises which tramps strew over the pavements in their search for hidden goodies; and also noise from clubs, restaurants and dance-halls. Perhaps, she concedes, in an area with seventeen theatres and something like thirty restaurants, residents ought to be prepared to live with noise; but the Forum and the planners had, she added, worked out an "entertainments corridor", the natural tourist route between the theatres of Aldwych and Drury Lane and those of St Martin's Lane, and now try to concentrate this kind of activity on that corridor.

What Miss Smith and an increasing number of others in the area seek to avert is the "Sohoization" of Covent Garden and the mushrooming of the sleazier kinds of entertainment, which would increase the demand for space and raise rents. She would, she said, like to ensure that Covent Garden is "left alone, that it doesn't become more fashionable than it is becoming". On this point she, Geoffrey Holland and Jim Monahan all seem to agree. Covent Garden needs no sudden boom, just steady, balanced regeneration. They have all observed that any London village which becomes "the place to go" is five years later quite demonstrably the place *not* to go to. Fly-by-night boutiques and other spurious enterprises come, raise rents, and spoil the place for people to live and work in. Covent Garden wants none of that. It wants to be nursed back to health, and then appreciated for its own qualities. With care, and luck, that looks like happening.

24

Hampstead

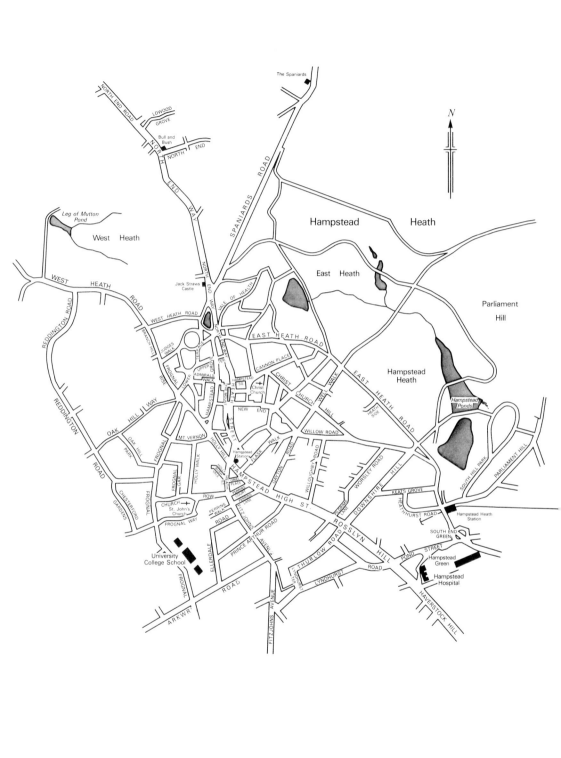

24

Hampstead

Hampstead is not what it was. That is the considered opinion of my wife, who grew up there, picked willowherb on a then bombed site in a then unfashionable road not half a mile from Heath Street, and until recently harboured, I suspect, a deep-down hankering to return. For her the present reality, at least on a Saturday, is too brash, expensive, ostentatious, crowded and vulgar. It makes her, she says, disinclined ever to want to live there should the opportunity arise – a possibility which the general level of house prices in NW3 renders remote. So remote that one would be inclined to dismiss her attitude as sour grapes save that longer-standing residents, still in Hampstead, take a similar view.

I do not. Admittedly "boutiquification" has set in, and useful shops have been forced out; and the people who fill the Saturday streets and restaurants are not all or always as amusing, urbane, exotic and witty as our rose-coloured spectacles show them to have been twenty or thirty years ago. But the basic Hampstead of hills and heath, lanes, alleys, steps, squares and varied, charming, idiosyncratic townscape is still there; and most of those who find it agreeable and sympathetic have themselves something of those qualities. Hampstead is still, in spite of creeping Kings-Roadery, an attractive place.

Its name is arguably the simplest thing about it: *ham* meaning "home"; *stede* meaning "place, site of a building". Put them together and you have "homestead" or alternatively "manor". The Saxon manor of Hampstead first finds mention in a royal charter of the 970s. A century later Domesday refers to it briefly, mentioning a gallows on the heath. Hampstead remained no more than a country village on the northern heights just outside London for seven more centuries. Defoe, however, found it expanding. "On top of a hill, indeed, there is a very pleasant plain, called the Heath, which on the very summit is a plain of about a mile every way: and in good weather 'tis pleasant airing upon it, and some of its streets are extended so far, as that they begin to build, even on the highest part of the hill." The reason for the expansion? Spas were becoming fashionable, and someone "discovered" chalybeate springs at what later became Well Walk. Like Cheltenham and Bath, though rather more convenient to town, Hampstead acquired its pump room and assemblies.

Then came the artists and writers: the Kit-Kat Club (whose members included Vanbrugh, Addison, Steele and Congreve) met at a tavern in Heath Street; and others who came to live or pay visits included Reynolds, George Romney (his studio still stands in Holly Bush Hill), Samuel Johnson, Fanny Burney, John Gay, Keats and Constable, John Masefield, Rabindrath Tagore, Aldous Huxley and Katherine Mansfield and her husband John Middleton Murry. Galsworthy wrote much of *The Forsyte Saga* at a house in Admiral's Walk, and D. H. Lawrence and his German-born wife Frieda lived for a few months during the First World War in the Vale of Health where one night: "We saw the Zeppelin above us, just ahead, amid the gleaming of clouds ... quite small, among a fragile incandescence of clouds. And underneath it were splashes of fire as the shells from earth burst ... It seemed as if the cosmic order

In London, and yet out of sight of town. The sweet rural disorder of Hampstead Heath, cared for by the GLC Parks Department, is perhaps its main attraction.

were gone, as if there had come a new order . . . So it is the end – our world is gone, and we are like dust in the air." Twenty-nine years later, on the eve of the Second World War, a dying Sigmund Freud came from Nazi-overrun Austria to Maresfield Gardens, Hampstead, where his visitors numbered H. G. Wells and Salvador Dali. Dali sketched Freud; Freud thought, "It would be interesting to investigate analytically how he came to create that picture."

But what of Hampstead now? Has it changed for the worse? One long-standing resident who rather thinks it has is Mrs Nan Farquharson, who with her husband Maurice, a former Secretary of the BBC, lives in an attractive Georgian house at Heathside, on the edge of the east heath. Of the shops in Hampstead Village, she says they have changed absolutely and rapidly for the worse. "There are very few good solid shops any more," she laments. "Hampstead has lost its atmosphere, which used to be unique. Now it's just like any other part of London." She dislikes its crowds, its scruffiness, it vandalism and violence, and the great white slab of the new Royal Free Hospital, totally out of scale with the rest of the village and blocking out views from the heath of St Paul's.

How the Farquharsons came to Heathside is worth recording. Nan Farquharson was born in Frognal and when she married "people expected us to take one of those neo-Georgian houses going up at the time in Redington Road." But she wanted an old house, and found one in a corner of her native village she had never previously discovered. An old solicitor of ninety, still going to his office, lived in one 1805 house and kept the other empty, and steadily growing more derelict, because no one would rent it on the six-month tenancy he stipulated. But the Farquharsons persisted and after nine months or so he agreed to sell. Soon afterwards she was hacking away at her small wilderness of a garden when the old lawyer's face appeared grimly over the wall. "Do you want the orchard?" he asked abruptly. "Yes please," she said; and he included it in the price of the house – £2,300. Nowadays Hampstead houses fetch anything from £75,000 to £750,000.

Mrs Farquharson said she still loved the heath, in spite of its untidiness, and added, "I love Hampstead for old times' sake." Her unfavourable view of it today was not, she said, simply founded on nostalgia. "It has changed a great deal in the last ten to fifteen years. It's become cheap, yet in some ways wildly expensive; it's become a tourist trap, with shops run by horrid people who depend on crowds coming from outside."

A different generation's view comes from Mark Pevsner, grandson of Sir Nikolaus. "Hampstead," he says, "is a large collection of roads and passages which don't go in straight lines, houses of different ages, many of them good architecture – but more often it's just the way they fit together, full of nice vistas and surprises. Hampstead is a huge collection of twists and turns." Heredity sometimes clearly transmits perspicuity and a telling turn of phrase.

Mark Pevsner is the son of publisher Dieter Pevsner, who told me there are four Pevsner households, including Sir Nikolaus', all grouped within hailing distance of each other at North End, a hamlet (one can still call it that) that straddles the road to Golders Green on the edge of the heath round the celebrated Old Bull and Bush public house. Dieter Pevsner recalls that he came to England as a small child in 1936, a year after his father had first felt obliged to leave Nazi Germany. Nikolaus Pevsner had a friend and patron in Hampstead Garden Suburb and for that reason found lodgings at North End where he has lived ever since.

The hamlet, which has existed at least since the 1600s, is *of* but in some ways not *in* Hampstead. Things Dieter Pevsner and his wife Florence like about it include the heath; the cutting or gorge through which the road runs between them and Whitestone Pond; the *Hampstead and Highgate Express*, or *Ham and High* ("one of the best local papers in the whole of Britain"); and the way in which the place has individuals who care about it and actually translate that concern into action. Dieter Pevsner cites the abundance of local amenity groups (including a relatively new one, numbering among its activists writer John Hillaby, concerned for the ecological as well as visual well-being of the heath); and individuals such as Ian Norrie, proprietor of the High Hill Bookshop and author of several urbane and lively guides to the area. Their dislikes include "the Royal Free disaster"; the "increasingly Polperro quality" of Hampstead as a conscious tourist attraction; and the "terrible, terrible complacency of some of its assumptions" – for instance, when socially progressive parents planned a treasure hunt for primary school children which, more than ten years ago, assumed that their houses would all have phones.

These days most of them do. For in that period Hampstead has been steadily changing from a socially mixed community to an essentially middle-class one where the council flats in its heartland between Heath Street and High Street remain the one real bastion

Keats' House, Wentworth Place, in what is today called Keats Grove. Here he wrote La Belle Dame Sans Merci, *and his Odes* to Psyche, to a Nightingale, *and* on a Grecian Urn, *among others. Now a museum and public library.*

of wage- as distinct from salary-earners, and vacant two up/two down cottages in the shadow of the gaunt Victorian New End Hospital are snapped up, propped up, tarted up and sold for £60,000 or £70,000 apiece. In this area, too, stands another object of astronomic expenditure: the early-18th-century Burgh House, a handsome Grade I listed building, the property of the borough council, but which has suffered severely from dry rot. As was established by a recent report of the local government ombudsman, Baroness Serota, delay by officials in communicating this fact to other offices and councillors ran to almost a year and amounted to "maladministration". Camden is now spending £195,000 on curing the trouble and renovating the house, but at one stage sought to recoup the money by leasing the house as offices. Hampstead rose in fury, with the *Ham and High* spearheading the counter-attack; for Burgh House, which had served as a community centre, was regarded as Hampstead's own, not Camden's, to do as it liked with. The borough relented to the extent of dropping the offices proposal pending the setting up of a Burgh House Trust, which has raised £50,000 towards the £125,000 needed to take over the building to run it for the community. The whole sorry tale, however, strengthened the distrust of those who believe that, unlike the old Hampstead borough council, Camden fails to look after Hampstead interests, regarding it as "that privileged place up the hill" and automatically discounting its local needs and claims.

Although Hampstead is full of old houses, it has some interesting new ones. Among the most surprising is that of architect Michael Hopkins in Downshire Hill. If you had said to most people: "It is proposed to insert a new, flat-roofed house of steel and glass with 2,500 square feet of floor space into a gap among the Georgian and Victorian houses of this most attractive of Hampstead streets," the instinctive reaction would have been: "Monstrous! It will ruin the street." And yet Hopkins' house, which won the only 1977 RIBA award for London, is in fact quite difficult to find. On a site that slopes down from the road, it presents only the upper of its two storeys to the view of passers-by; and though its front wall is almost entirely glass, it somehow, with the help of the willows that front the site, keeps the rhythm and scale of the Downshire Hill townscape. Another surprise is that it was cheap. Hopkins found to his surprise that he could buy the land from a developer who had acquired it at the height of the property boom and now needed to sell in a hurry; and as for the cost of this elegant "machine for living in", Hopkins could still say in October 1978, "We haven't spent £20,000 yet."

Nor did he have any difficulty with planning permission. The developer from whom he bought had consent for two four-storey houses on the site; the planners were perhaps relieved that this visual "overloading" would not after all take place. While the house was going up (and Hopkins managed the job, doing much of the building himself), he got many puzzled inquiries as to what it would be. He mischievously played along with people's misconceptions. "When they asked me if it was going to be a filling station, I didn't discourage them!". Filling station, car showroom, nursery school – these were just some of the theories people had about it. In the event it emerged as an elegant and flexible house in a part of London where Hopkins never thought he could afford to live, but where among the 18th- and 19th-century buildings stand quite a few notable landmarks of modern design (such as Max Fry's Sun House in Frognal Way). "But does your wife like it to live in?" I asked Hopkins. "Oh, she designed it with me," he replied. "She's an architect, too."

Hampstead has, indeed, a great many architects living in it, a fact that has been known to provoke the jibe that they do their worst in designing hous*ing* for the plebs in inner Camden, then slide quietly up the hill to real hous*es* designed by Georgian master builders. Michael Hopkins is not one against whom that charge can be laid; nor is Erno Goldfinger, who built himself a fine new house on the heath's edge many years ago. But architects may be said to have replaced artists in Hampstead proper where, despite the open-air shows near Whitestone Pond, not many sculptors or painters can now afford to live. By "Hampstead proper", I mean the area bounded to the north-east by North End and the south-east by South End Green, and so not quite taking in Belsize Park, which (though it has Hampstead's old town hall) is a distinct and separate village, nor Swiss Cottage and Finchley Road, which have a totally different character.

Many architects, like others of various professions or none, came to Hampstead in the 1950s or 1960s when its rather grim Victorian terrace houses looked down-at-heel, but were still relatively cheap, and offered them much more space and flexibility than any new house at the same price, certainly in so convenient and agreeable a district. John Tusa, who moved with his wife Ann from Pimlico twelve years ago to an 1870s house in Christchurch Hill, is one of these. He told me that Hampstead is "a very easy place to live in". People are tolerant; they don't bother too much what their neighbours do: "They don't argue about which day you put your washing out. At some time or other most households make an excessive noise at night, but no one does it every night."

Tusa finds it a convenient base for his work as a freelance radio and TV producer. He can get to Broadcasting House, Television Centre or Bush House almost as easily as he used to from Pimlico. He takes pleasure in streets like Flask Walk, the nearness of the heath, the quietness of his own neighbourhood, and the way in which, for instance, his neighbours round the corner in Gayton Road have not only their own amenity group but an annual street festival, with flags, stalls and entertainments. He dislikes "the new Royal Free; the boutiquification of the central shopping area; and a certain kind of Hampstead liberalism" – the kind of sloppy permissiveness which leaves the children of its exponents not knowing where they are or really what is expected of them. His wife, a teacher, came across children who, as a result of this, were "in a very real sense neglected by their parents".

But, adds Tusa, most of Hampstead is not like that; it is a neighbourly, "supportive" place. It has good pubs, some good

Down at the Old Bull and Bush. No one noticeably making eyes, but a convivial enough gathering to catch the spirit of the song.

Hampstead High Street: boutiquification has pushed out many of the "useful" shops, and peace and quiet is a pious hope rather than a realistic expectation.

restaurants, but many more that are no longer good value; and though the middle-class professionals have increasingly displaced the working classes, and are being in turn replaced by wealthy ad men and Japanese, the process is gradual. No ordinary professional can raise a mortgage for a £70,000 family house, he points out, but on the other hand most of those who have houses are not moving out in a hurry. They like the place too much to want to make a quick cash killing. Like many other residents, he worries about what will happen on the empty development site in the High Street where the Blue Star Garage formerly stood. The *Ham and High* commissioned local architect Ted Levy to produce a sketch showing how it could be suitably developed, but nothing has happened except for its temporary use for a Saturday market.

The *Ham and High*'s editor, Gerry Isaaman, is very much a local institution, fighting local causes in his paper (now part of a larger Home Counties group) and exploiting the wealth of local talent and renown for the paper's and the community's good. It once ran an issue skittishly suggesting that Hampstead could declare UDI from the rest of London or Britain and remain viable, with sheep, cattle and crops on the heath and (rather like Vienna after Austria lost its empire) enough professional and technical expertise to serve its own population ten times over.

Gerry Isaaman came to his adopted village and to the paper as a twenty-one-year-old in 1955, when his family moved from Stoke Newington to Hendon, and became editor in 1976. He glories in Hampstead's famous and colourful personalities, past and present:

Joanna Baillie, who drew poets such as Wordsworth and Coleridge to her literary salons at Volta House on Windmill Hill, and John le Carré, who lives in Gayton Crescent. Isaaman is the best of Hampstead guides, not only leading the way to delightful backwaters like Holly Place and Holly Walk (with their tiny, Mediterranean-looking Roman Catholic church, built for refugees from the French Revolution, and colourful rows of cottages), but able to garnish the tour with colourful anecdotes, historical, apocryphal and sometimes racily topical.

Isaaman in a sense embodies the contradictions of Hampstead. He told me he regretted the loss of useful shops, and indeed had fought successfully in the *Ham and High* to keep a cobbler's in Perrin's Court opposite his offices; he is concerned what development may bring on the Blue Star site, regrets that house prices are pushing out the less wealthy, but adds that the incredible tally of estate agents in the village reflects itself in fourteen pages of property advertising for the paper. He is active in the housing association field and acquired his own home through conversion of a building bought relatively cheaply "at a time when housing associations could still work in Hampstead. You could spend your Sunday mornings going round with an architect to find something that would convert well." Now, he says regretfully, housing associations have been priced out of Hampstead. He, like many other residents, sees Hampstead as a place of several layers: the Saturday veneer of tourists and boutiques; the professionals going off to the tube to commute to the West End; chess players at The Prompt Corner and cream-cake eaters at Louis'; the quiet, mid-morning streets behind the high street, with women going shopping, milkmen on their rounds, and cats sitting in the sun – even, he adds, "Saturday solicitors in pink jeans!" Like Mark Pevsner, he loves the tangle of lanes, alleys, steps, yards and squares round Holly Mount and Hollybush Hill. "You could never build that if you designed it from scratch. It would never get planning permission or pass the fire regulations." Yet people live in it and love it – perhaps just because this aspect of Hampstead is unrepeatable.

N

MILL HILL

HIGHGATE

HAMPSTEAD

CAMDEN TOWN

BLOOMSBURY

MARYLEBONE

SOHO

COVENT GARDEN

BEDFORD PARK

CHELSEA

R. Thames

KEW

FULHAM

PUTNEY

CLAPHAM

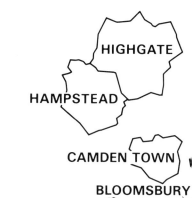